Witness

Spirituality for the World:
Explorations at the Edges of Late Modernity

This open-ended series of books by an internationally recognized theologian looks at important religious and spiritual topics that are being asked not only by those within the worldwide church but also by people of any and even no faith. Each volume seeks to sketch aspects of a spiritual posture needed for navigating transnational dynamics and the sociocultural convulsions that global citizens are consciously experiencing in the late 2020s and 2030s. Theologically informed persons within the global Christian community and religiously interested people convinced about the importance of personal and communally shaped spiritualities for traversing the opportunities and challenges of life in the current age will welcome and benefit from each installment.

Witness: Converting Worlds
Jesus: Mapping Worlds (forthcoming)
Trauma: Repairing Worlds (forthcoming)
Earth: Translating Worlds (forthcoming)

Witness

Converting Worlds

AMOS YONG

CASCADE *Books* • Eugene, Oregon

WITNESS
Converting Worlds

Spirituality for the World: Explorations at the Edges of Late Modernity

Copyright © 2026 Amos Yong. All rights reserved. Except for brief quotations in critical publications or reviews, no part of this book may be reproduced in any manner without prior written permission from the publisher. Write: Permissions, Wipf and Stock Publishers, 199 W. 8th Ave., Suite 3, Eugene, OR 97401.

Cascade Books
An Imprint of Wipf and Stock Publishers
199 W. 8th Ave., Suite 3
Eugene, OR 97401

www.wipfandstock.com

PAPERBACK ISBN: 979-8-3852-5769-0
HARDCOVER ISBN: 979-8-3852-5770-6
EBOOK ISBN: 979-8-3852-5771-3

Cataloguing-in-Publication data:

Names: Yong, Amos, author.

Title: Witness : converting worlds / Amos Yong.

Description: Eugene, OR : Cascade Books, 2026 | Spirituality for the World: Explorations at the Edges of Late Modernity | Includes bibliographical references and index.

Identifiers: ISBN 979-8-3852-5769-0 (paperback) | ISBN 979-8-3852-5770-6 (hardcover) | ISBN 979-8-3852-5771-3 (ebook)

Subjects: LCSH: Evangelistic work.

Classification: BV3792 .Y66 2026 (paperback) | BV3792 (ebook)

VERSION NUMBER 012126

Scripture quotations are from New Revised Standard Version Bible, copyright © 1989 National Council of the Churches of Christ in the United States of America. Used by permission. All rights reserved worldwide.

Contents

Extended Table of Contents | vii
Preface | xi

Introduction: From Mission to Witness, from Evangelism to Conversion | 1

Part I: Christian Witness to/with Others in the 2020s —Apostolic Soundings Then and Now

Chapter 1
Acts and Christian Witness: Then and Now | 7

Chapter 2
Luke and Christian Witness: Then and Now | 31

Part II: Apostolic Evangelism and Conversion in the 2020s —Multi-Transformational Witness Then and Now

Chapter 3
Intellectual Conversion: Apostolic Testimonies Then and Now | 55

Chapter 4
Affective Conversion: Apostolic Passions Then and Now | 78

Chapter 5
Moral Conversion: Apostolic Interactions Then and Now | 104

Chapter 6
Sociopolitical Conversion: Apostolic Engagements Then and Now | 126

Conclusion: Toward a New Evangelization in the Footsteps of the Apostles | 151

Bibliography | 157
Scripture Index | 169

Extended Table of Contents

Ch. 1 – Acts and Christian Witness: Then and Now
    Christian Witness in an Imperial and Pluralistic World: Retrieving Apostolic Perspectives
        The Pax Romana and Caesar's Lordship: Apostolic Discipleship Then and Now
        Mediterranean Cultural-Religious Pluralism: Apostolic Witness Then and Now
    Christian Witness in the Power of the Spirit (Acts 1:8)
        Paradigmatic Expressions (Acts 1:8a) and Martyrological Witness Then and Now
        To/From the Ends of the Earth (Acts 1:8b): Multiethnic/Multidirectional Witness Then and Now
        To the Ends of Time (Acts 1:8c): Witnessing in/for Our Children and Their Children
    From Jerusalem to Judea and Samaria . . . : Apostolic Witness Then and Now
        Many Tongues: Multiple Ethnicities, Cultures, and Economies (Acts 2)
        Many Tongues, Many Practices in the Neighborhood (Acts 3–6) Then and Now
        Liminal Witness to and with "The Other" (Acts 8)
        Christian Witness to, from, and at the Ends of the Earth (Acts 9–28)
    "That Is This": A Fresh Retrieval of Acts' Apostolic Mission amid 2020s-Others

EXTENDED TABLE OF CONTENTS

Ch. 2 – Luke and Christian Witness: Then and Now
    Reading Luke After Acts: Jesus's Witness in an Imperial World
        Preliminaries in Luke's Gospel: The Imperial and "Global" Setting of the Witness Stage
        The Messianic Witness of the Spirit to/Through Many Tongues
    "The Spirit of the Lord Is Upon Me . . . !" Messianic Witness to/with Others Then and Now
        "To Bring Good News to the Poor" (4:18b): Witness with the Poor Then and Now
        "Release to the Captives" (4:18c): Witness with the "Imprisoned" Then and Now
        "Recovery of Sight to the Blind" (4:18d): Witness with the Impaired Other Then and Now
        "To Let the Oppressed Go Free" (4:18e): Witness with Marginalized Others Then and Now
        "To Proclaim the Year of the Lord's Favor" (4:19): The Witness of Jubilee Then and Now
    Messianic Witness and Apostolic Mission Then and Now: Opportunities and Challenges

Ch. 3 – Intellectual Conversion: Apostolic Testimonies Then and Now
    Evangelism and Conversion: Getting Our Bearings
        Evangelism Then and Now
        Conversion Then and Now
        Models and Domains of Conversion
    How Does Intellectual Conversion Occur in the Book of Acts?
        Stephen's Apologetic and Prophetic Witness: Apostolic Intellectual Conversion I
        Peter's "I [Now] Truly Understand . . .": Apostolic Intellectual Conversion II
        Paul's Evolving Witness: Apostolic Intellectual Conversion III
    Christian Evangelism and Intellectual Conversion Today: Reconsidering Spirit-ed Witness Praxis

EXTENDED TABLE OF CONTENTS

Ch. 4 – Affective Conversion: Apostolic Passions Then and Now
　Affectivity, Mission, and Evangelism: Orthopathic Dimensions of Christian Conversion
　　On Emotions, Feelings, and Affections: The Heart or Orthopathic Dimension of Religious Faith
　　Emotional and Affective Dis-ease: The Pathological Brokenness of Human Lives
　　Evangelism and Affective Conversion: Taking Responsibility for Our Emotional Health
　Emotions and Desires in Luke-Acts: Considering Affective Conversion Apostolically
　　Emotions and Affectivity of and in Response to Jesus: Affective Conversion in the Gospel of Luke
　　Overflowing After Pentecost: Affective Conversion in the Acts of the Apostles
　　Eating with Others: Fellowship and Affective Conversion in Luke-Acts
　Christian Evangelism and Affective Conversion Today: Feeling Spirit-ed Witness and Praxis

Ch. 5 – Moral Conversion: Apostolic Interactions Then and Now
　Moral Conversion: Some Missiological, Theoretical, and Normative Perspectives
　　Missiological and Historical Developments
　　Moral Conversion: An Emerging (New-Thomist) Paradigm
　　Toward a Normative Account: Starting with Jesus
　Moral Transformation in Acts: Considering Moral Conversion Apostolically
　　Selling, Distributing, and Having All Things in Common: Apostolic Moral Conversion I
　　The Philippian Jailer: Apostolic Moral Conversion II
　　Moral Character in the Case of Two Centurions: Apostolic Moral Conversion III
　Christian Evangelism and Moral Conversion Today: Transforming Spirit-ed Witness

Ch. 6 – Sociopolitical Conversion: Apostolic Engagements Then and Now
    Sociopolitical Conversion: Taking Evangelistic Responsibility for the Common Good
        The Spirit and the Social: Toward Sociopolitical Conversion
        Luke as Sociopolitical Theologian?
        The Gospel Witness and the Divine Reign: Evangelism Toward Sociopolitical Conversion
    Sociopolitical Transformation in Acts: Considering Sociopolitical Conversion Apostolically
        The Jerusalem Council: Apostolic Sociocultural Interventions
        Pagans in the Public and Political Domains: Apostolic Cultural-Religious Strategies
        Apocalyptic and the Earth: Apostolic Eco-Political Horizons
    Sociopolitical Conversion and Apostolic Evangelism: Extending Spirit-ed Public Witness

Preface

THIS VOLUME IS ENVISIONED as one of the lead installments of a series of shorter books written primarily for a wider audience, including the church broadly understood, titled Spirituality for the World, wherein I consider classic theological doctrines I have not yet substantially engaged and also address more urgent topics of public and ecclesial concern, doing so consistently from out of the spirituality perspective I have been honing over the last almost three decades. *Witness* concerns Christian faith-sharing in the 2020s, even as the subtitle, *Converting Worlds*, refers to the imperative implications and practical (personal and social/ecclesial) applications of the topic, especially for the multi-layered personal complexity of Christian witnessers.

The two chapters in part 1 were developed out of the E. Glenn Hinson Lectures I was invited to give at the Baptist Seminary of Kentucky in Louisville, Kentucky, in March 2023. I am grateful to Dr. John Inscore Essick and his colleagues at the BSK for the invitation, hospitality, and engagement with the overarching theme, then framed as "Christian Witness to/of Others in the 2020s: Apostolic Soundings Then and Now." The four chapters in part 2 were then developed out of the Swallen Mission Lectureship I was invited to give at the Seventh-Day Adventist Theological Seminary and Andrews University in Berrien Springs, Michigan, in June 2023. I appreciate Drs. Wagner Kuhn and Andrew Tompkins for the invitation, hospitality, and interaction around the overarching theme, then titled "Multi-Dimensional Witness and Conversion in the 2020s: Apostolic Evangelism Then and Now." The combined focus of both sets of lectures, now in this book, is the apostolic story as preserved in the Christian New Testament, especially the two books written by St. Luke (the Third Gospel and the Acts of the Apostles), understood especially from the evangelist's hopes that his readers, us included, embrace—convert to, effectively not to mention affectively—the good news of Jesus.

PREFACE

This is my second fundamentally missiological work, that is, addressing the topic of Christian witness and mission in the present time. Like the first, *Mission After Pentecost: The Witness of the Spirit from Genesis to Revelation* (published by Baker Academic), it derives from my coming as professor of theology and mission to Fuller Seminary's (then) School of Intercultural Studies in 2014 (now School of Mission and Theology). If the first attempted to reimagine missiology more broadly, this one looks more specifically at what evangelism and conversion mean today, starting with the lives of missionaries, evangelists, and witnessers. Both volumes, however, operate first and foremost at the level of biblical interpretation, imagination, and retrieval: How might we think about and practice Christian witness in the present age in light of the apostolic mission endeavor? I have deployed this deeply scriptural approach especially since commitments to Christian mission in the present time are carried especially by conservative Protestants of the evangelical, Pentecostal, and Charismatic type, all of whom are biblicistic in their theological approach and accompanying practices. While these pages are written first and foremost for these who I count as my fellow believers, I am hopeful that anyone interested in Christian mission, witness, evangelism, and conversion will find this a helpful and perhaps even provocative invitation to rethink the classical understandings of these matters for new approaches and expressions in our present time.

Thanks to the Fuller Seminary Board of Trustees for a sabbatical in the winter and spring quarters of 2024 that gave me time to bring this manuscript to completion. Additionally, I am grateful to my colleagues and our students in the School of Mission and Theology (SMT)—especially Mary Glenn and Kirsteen Kim—for their feedback on various aspects of this manuscript. SMT PhD student Rachel Jones also sent some helpful observations and questions upon reading the manuscript. I appreciate the efforts of Lizette Saldana Buisa, my graduate assistant, in generating the scripture index. None of these named persons are responsible for errors of fact or elucidation in what follows.

My life partner, Alma, has accompanied me for over forty years (since we met!), and knows the depths of how I have struggled with my own Christian witness over the decades. Yet she continues to believe in me, and in my writing, which is its own form of bearing witness. Her patient love makes possible whatever witness I might be able to provide.

Note: All biblical quotations are from the New Revised Standard Version of the Bible, unless otherwise indicated.

Introduction

From Mission to Witness, from Evangelism to Conversion

THIS BOOK SEEKS TO shift Christian rhetoric and practice from *mission* to *witness*, for the purposes of the church's efforts to serve the world, and from *evangelism* to *conversion*, for the well-being of the church's (would-be and active) evangelists. Let me explain.

First, I have worked over the last decade as a missiologist, meaning as a professor, researcher, and academic in the area of missiology or mission studies. The reality is that Christian *mission* in our contemporary global context is saddled with the legacy of colonialism, racism, Eurocentrism, and, more recently, American imperialism. On the one hand, the rest of the world is less and less inclined to operate according to Western or modernist assumptions about culture, rationality, and also faith. On the other hand, the center of gravity of Christianity has shifted to the so-called global South, and now Christians across Asia, Africa, and Latin America are becoming missionally active in accord with their own cultural perspectives, sensibilities, and commitments.[1] Yet it remains undeniable that Western affluence means that missionary funding will continue to be led especially out of North America and, in that respect, missiological discourse will need to continue to grapple with the hard-earned lessons about the racism, cultural chauvinism, and religious triumphalism of the last few centuries of the colonial mission enterprise. This remains the case since even with missions from everywhere to everywhere[2] and even with what some also

---

1. My first missiological monograph covered these in more detail: *Mission After Pentecost*.

2. See Yeh, *Polycentric Missiology*.

call reverse mission (where those from Asia, Africa, Latin America, South America engage in missional endeavors to western countries and contexts), the leading theories will continue to derive especially from the West even as the major textbooks and publishers will remain for the foreseeable future Western-based.

However, I am writing this book because I believe the church exists to bear witness to the gospel and thus wish to invite us to continue to do so albeit by breaking away from the existing modern mission paradigm. Shifting away from *mission* to *witness*, I suggest, provides an important reorientation, one that enables a fresh biblical reconsideration. To remain on *mission* carries with it the freight of an institutionalized Christendom that is bound up with the machinery of both the modern state (colonial governments or, now, growing nationalisms) and its principalities and powers (their economic mechanisms). To be extracted from these sociopolitical and economic engines would require a renewed spirituality, one that enables gospel witness today to be unencumbered by our cultural prejudices, and thereby to be open to encountering others, and to experiencing the gospel in and through such encounters in revitalizing ways.

Similarly, *evangelism*, while meaning only the proclaiming of the good news of Jesus Christ, has become variously encumbered over the last century. On the one hand, missions and evangelism within the Pentecostal churches I have long been affiliated with and a part of have often indiscriminately targeted those in other churches, contending that church attendance itself does not ensure that persons have been genuinely "born-again." On the other hand, with the increased emphasis on social responsibility, evangelism has then been wedded to other activities, whether food kitchens, temporary shelters, or rehabilitation centers, now, ironically, resulting in accusations that converts are being "bought" by other means. Perhaps most problematically, evangelistic practices, especially those ecclesially organized, have evolved into large events, sometimes held in public auditoriums and called "crusades," and these have then labored under the militaristic connotations of such rhetoric. Critics suggest that more often than not in these contexts, Christian conversions are questionable, perhaps psychologically manipulated if not coerced, to organizations rather than ultimately in relationship to the divine.

And yet, I remain convinced that the gospel is good news that should be shared. The question is: how to be appropriate sharers, or, to put it in the terms of this book, how to be good evangelists by becoming good witness

INTRODUCTION

bearers? The answer, that I will argue in this book, is that our witness will be as authentic as our own conversion is in depth. Put another way, others will convert to the gospel of Jesus Christ to the degree that we as those who evangelize in his name bear witness to our own conversion to him and transformation by his Spirit. More precisely, rather than *mission to*, the emphasis should be on *witness with*, with the good news of Jesus Christ generating a shared and mutual relationality that transfigures "us" and "them." In short, evangelism in a postcolonial era is a two-way affair: a kind of reciprocal partaking and common testimonial through the encounter of evangelists and those being evangelized. Don't get me wrong: I believe in planting new churches, sharing our faith with those who have not heard, and preaching the good news (full disclosure: I am a credentialed minister and actively preach as invited). Yet I think the integrity of Christian witness can be shored up by attending first and foremost to our ongoing conversion as would-be and actual evangelists. As fellow missiologist Michael Stroope urges, our own "pilgrim witness" signifies "our continual conversion to the gospel story."[3]

It is precisely for this reason, then, that the bulk of our energy in the rest of this book is going to be focused on the gospel itself, especially as recounted in the pages of the New Testament. Christian witness and evangelism, and the purpose and goal of Christian conversion, are best and fundamentally understood scripturally. Given that some of the earliest Christian missionary endeavors are narrated in the book of Acts (even earlier New Testament epistles, we might argue, are missionary letters and hence with missiological content, albeit lacking the narrative dimension), we will begin there, and look also at its author's first book: the Gospel of Luke. To be sure, as a lifelong participant in the modern Pentecostal movement, I have long worked on these portions of the Christian Bible, and therefore will speak and write out of what we might call a Pentecostal accent. Yet these Lukan texts are neither copyrighted by modern Pentecostal churches nor owned by them, but belong to the Christian church and to all on the Christian path.

This book thus invites our thinking theologically and missiologically with Luke regarding the important questions of Christian witness in our time. As we shall see Luke articulate, Christians bear witness as those who are sent by the Holy Spirit. On the one hand, Christian witness is therefore

---

3. Stroope, *Transcending Mission*, 202; thanks to Jacob Palma for reminding me of Stroope's proposal.

being sent to, to carry and to lift up the name of Jesus to the world to others. On the other hand, the invitation for us here is to consider how the bearing of Christian witness and the Christian participation in God's mission is not only *to* others but *with* others. We shall see, then, that Christian witness to others is always also Christian witness with others, a mutual witness.

Part 1 of this book sets the more general stage by revisiting the book of Acts and the Gospel of Luke from a missiological perspective. How did Christian witness unfold in the early generations and what are the implications for us today? In close dialogue with the Lukan volumes, including the central role of the Holy Spirit in Jesus's life and mission and then that of his followers, the two chapters of this part form what we might call a Christian theology of Spirit-ed and humble witness to and, most importantly, with others for the twenty-first century. Establishing the broad Pentecost and pneumatic themes in Luke-Acts will both set the stage for different angles on and enable deeper dives into both texts in the second part of this book.

Part 2 then turns to a theology of evangelism and conversion, especially from the perspective of how the first evangelists were converted and transformed by their encounters with others. The argument will be that only a robust Christian theology of conversion for evangelists and witnesses, one that accounts for our transformation not only intellectually but also affectively, morally, and sociopolitically, can empower the kind of evangelism to and with others needed for our present age. Hence, we will read Luke-Acts both evangelistically and from the perspective of conversion, multidimensionally considered, in order to explore what apostolic evangelism and conversion might mean, especially for evangelists and their own ongoing conversion, in the present time. Whereas the first part and initial two chapters of this volume attempts to think through the *what* of Christian witness today in Lukan perspective, this latter and longer set of four chapters looks specifically at the *who* that bears witness. Only those who themselves are converted and always converting can bear adequate and faithful witness to the gospel of the coming divine reign.

Our concluding reflections will step back from the more detailed biblical considerations to reconsider the import of our mutual theses—from *mission to* toward *witness with*, and from *us evangelizing and others converting* to *us converting toward others*—for contemporary missiology. Specifically, we will extrapolate implications for a contemporary theology of evangelism and conversion for a late modern world.

PART I

Christian Witness to/with Others
in the 2020s
Apostolic Soundings Then and Now

Chapter 1

Acts and Christian Witness
Then and Now

WE BEGIN WITH THE second book authored by St. Luke, the book of Acts. Elsewhere I have suggested why it is appropriate to work through this volume first, before turning to Luke's Gospel account of Jesus of Nazareth.[1] Although the latter was the initially written book, the writing of such post-dated the happenings described in the book of Acts, so that it is the unfolding of the apostolic experiences recorded in Acts that provides the historical and experiential backdrop that generates the Gospels, Luke's included. Put another way, without the early apostolic witness narrated in Acts, there would have been no reason to write about Jesus of Nazareth to begin with. Hence, we need to appreciate what the apostolic community and early messianists[2] struggled with and encountered so that we can

---

1. Yong, *Who Is the Holy Spirit*.

2. In the rest of this book, I will use *messianists* mostly as synonymous with the apostolic community of believers in the book of Acts; these would have included Jews, proselytes to Judaism (gentile converts via circumcision according to the law), God-fearers (gentile followers of Jewish views about God but in the process of embracing the legal aspects of the Jewish faith), those called Christians (literally: messiah-people or also, later, gentiles accepted to be in fellowship with Jews albeit alleviated from the need for circumcision, and many other Jewish legal requirements), and those Luke otherwise characterizes as followers of "the Way" (Acts 9:2, 18:25–26, 19:9, 23, 24:14)—all bound together only by various levels of commitment to Jesus as the messiah promised by the ancient Israelite Law, Prophets, and Writings.

then also comprehend better the significance of what is recorded in Luke's Gospel.

This chapter thus first attempts to situate the apostolic world in its imperial and pluralistic context that also enables recognition that some of our contemporary realities were navigated by the messianic community in their own way. The bulk of this chapter's second part then explores Luke's account of the unfolding apostolic witness, *to and with others*, in our reading, both by explicating his central theme—Christian witness is enabled by the Holy Spirit to the ends of the earth—and by tracing out how that theme is organized across the book of Acts' four main parts.

Christian Witness in an Imperial and Pluralistic World: Retrieving Apostolic Perspectives

As we attempt to retrieve these apostolic perspectives, we observe that the apostolic church's mission and experience were similar in many ways to some of the predominant horizons within which we are situated today. As we read from our horizon back to the New Testament—these are the two horizons across which we are navigating throughout this volume—we notice that our own postcolonial and pluralistic world is also in some respects similar to that of the apostolic experience. Let us consider the early apostolic experiences also unfolding in an imperial and pluralistic context.

One caveat before proceeding. The following should not collapse the very real differences between the first-century apostolic world and that of our own twenty-first-century context. Any consideration of similarities has to keep in mind the vastness of two thousand years that separates the former from our time.[3] Yet Christian commitments invite ongoing rereading of their sacred texts, with all the needed care and provisionality that can be mustered, in order to renew faithful discipleship—in the case of this book: Christian witness—for any succeeding age. We hence proceed with some fear and trembling.

---

3. For more on this hermeneutical difference, see my *Hermeneutical Spirit*, and *Learning Theology*, ch. 1; I provide missiological readings of other biblical texts in my *Mission After Pentecost*.

The Pax Romana and Caesar's Lordship: Apostolic Discipleship Then and Now

Think about the fact that the first-century apostolic world was situated against the backdrop of the peace of Rome, the Pax Romana.[4] As we open the book of Acts, one of the first questions that the disciples ask Jesus, at the end of the forty-day time after his resurrection in which he remained with them teaching them about the kingdom or reign of God, connects directly to this theme. At the end of that first "Jesus seminar," so to speak, the disciples queried, "Lord, is this the time when you will restore the kingdom to Israel?" (Acts 1:6b).

I hope we can appreciate this question against the backdrop of the first-century imperial Roman context within which Caesar was understood to be the savior of the empire. The disciples' question, then, is thus not only a religious one, but a political one. The apostolic experience, including its ecclesial and missional dimensions in the first century, hence also unfolded amid a political and politicized landscape. And we can also observe that the whole of the book of Acts takes place within this Pax Romana frame, book-ended by this question of the disciples up front, and the apostles finally arriving at the center of the Roman Empire, which was the city of Rome itself, at the very end. We can thereby see that the story of apostolic mission and witness unfolded across the political arc of the first-century imperial Roman regime.

Our missional witness today is also inextricably intertwined with the political situations and contexts of our world, as complicated, diverse, and pluralistic as it is. My country, the United States of America, is constituted by fifty states, each with its own political ethos, history, climate, and agenda. And of course, as we move to other parts of the world, they will involve different and multiple political realities that the church in every context lives with and has to navigate. Christian witness unfolds within these complex geopolitical contexts. I believe that the apostolic experience can illuminate how the disciples themselves lived into their calling to bear witness to the risen Christ, against the backdrop of imperial Rome.[5]

---

4. This assumption also informs the approach to the final book of the New Testament adopted in my *Revelation*.

5. See also Wenhem, "Purpose of Luke-Acts."

PART I: CHRISTIAN WITNESS TO/WITH OTHERS IN THE 2020S

Mediterranean Cultural-Religious Pluralism: Apostolic Witness Then and Now

We are coming to comprehend the complexity of the first-century Mediterranean world more and more in our time. Part of this comprehension is of this regional milieu as a very pluralistic and dynamic set of inter-mixing religious and cultural realities.[6] The apostolic witness as told across the book of Acts takes place also against this backdrop of a plurality of cultures, languages, and even religious developments. This is also our world today, whether we find ourselves in the middle of the United States or on this country's coasts or around the world. The church today is also called to bear witness in and across a variety of pluralistic contexts. How pluralistic depends on which contexts. Hence, revisiting the apostolic experience in the New Testament gives us fresh opportunity to observe how the earliest followers of Jesus bore witness in the pluralistic milieus within which they found themselves.

As we revisit the book of Acts from these perspectives, we will uncover what can be understood as a messy apostolic middle, in which we find a variety of hybridized approaches that show how these earliest messianists adjusted and shifted their life and message amid various contexts and circumstances. Part of our task is to observe how they bore witness to the living Christ amid particular cultural and political realities within which they found themselves. These observations will provide apostolic perspectives that could be helpful also for us today.

With these background comments at hand, we shall now turn to the New Testament writings. The next two sections in this chapter focus on the various segments of what we might call the table of contents of the book of Acts, which is chapter 1, verse 8, and then explicate on some of the key windows that this road map opens up.

Christian Witness in the Power of the Spirit (Acts 1:8)

Acts 1:8 says: "But you will receive power when the Holy Spirit has come upon you; and you will be my witnesses in Jerusalem, in all Judea and Samaria, and to the ends of the earth." In the next few pages we look at three major themes from this text that frame the apostolic witness recounted in the rest of the book of Acts: martyrological witness, multidirectional

---

6. See Ferguson, *Religions of the Roman Empire*.

witness, and eschatological witness. The discussion sets us up then to follow this verse's geographical references in the next section of this chapter.

Paradigmatic Expressions (Acts 1:8a) and Martyrological Witness Then and Now

This text has been paradigmatic for Christian mission and witness for millennia. Certainly, it is the heart of the modern Pentecostal movement in terms of its associating the reception of what they call baptism of the Holy Spirit with the power to bear witness—verbally and via signs and wonders, miracles, healings, etc.[7]—to the risen Christ. Note also that Acts 1:8 identifies the primary thrust of apostolic witness, historically (then) and subsequently (whenever *now* is), as brought about by the Holy Spirit. The Holy Spirit empowers those on the apostolic way to bear witness in the variety of contexts within which they find themselves. Whereas this verse and these various parts invite us to consider at a high level Christian witness and mission then and also today, its overall thrust also calls us to a witnessing that proceeds out of humility.[8]

On the one hand, then, spiritual and Holy-Spirit-ed *power*, is connected with apostolic mission and witness. Unfortunately, over the centuries including more recently, we have seen the power dimension of this text also become welded with the power of the state, whether the power of the papacy historically, of Christendom in the medieval period, or of the colonial enterprise in the last half millennium. We live, therefore, in the aftermath of the Christian missionary enterprise wedded to these forms of power. Without taking away anything from the sacrificial efforts carrying the name of Christ has been taken to the ends of the earth, in part through his followers embodying and even performing texts like these—under the Holy Spirit's enabling potency, even—it is also irresponsible not to acknowledge that Jesus's name also has been yoked to earthly forms of power, racialized forms of power, political and economic forms of power, ableist forms of power, patriarchal forms of power, the power of European and North American

---

7. These historic themes are reiterated in the recent study of Budiselić, *Uniqueness of the Concept*, esp. ch. 11.

8. The theme of *humility* has been central to missiology over the last generation, e.g., as registered in the title to the volume honoring the work of leading recent missiologist David Bosch: Saayman and Kritzinger, *Mission in Bold Humility*.

civilizations, the powers of whiteness, etc.[9] Entanglement with these forms of power has compromised, if not fatally undermined, Christian capacity to bear ongoing witness to the living Christ in our present age.

On the other hand, Acts 1:8 also invites us to think about the Spirit's empowerment as associated with the full scope of the Greek word translated "witnesses": *martures*. From the root *marturion*, witness here includes testimony to the point of death: martyrdom. Acts 1 includes the ascension of a previously crucified Christ, hence of a risen Christ going to the right hand of the Father. Mission unfolds out of Jesus's sending his crucified-risen-and-ascended spirit to embolden his followers, to bear witness in the form of *marturion*. At least from the Pentecostal tradition that I'm a part of, we welcome the announcement that there is power available through the baptism of the Holy Spirit, but we often do not also highlight the implications of *marturion* as the Spirit's chosen form of witness. This martyrological form of witness actually is much more prevalent even in the book of Acts (not to mention across the Gospel of Luke also) than we have tended to consider.[10] Think about Stephen who was martyred for the sake of the gospel (Acts 7), or about James who was beheaded in Acts 12. Consider also when Paul and his followers were evicted from and beaten outside of Lystra and Derby and left dead (Acts 14). Such a witness is also central to the Apocalypse where the risen Christ is figured in the form of a Lamb slain from the foundation of the world: not just "the Lion of the tribe of Judah" (Rev 5:5), a symbol of power, but the butchered and slaughtered Lamb (e.g., Rev 5:6, 12, 13:8).[11]

Yet note that this final witness borne through death reflects an embodied witness in its life. Only a life that bears scandalous and even offensive witness is one that is put to death. Thus, martyrological witness subordinates the life of the self to the message,[12] that of the coming reign of God manifest in Jesus and now carried in the community of his body, the church,

---

9. Among many acute historical analyses, I recommend Jennings, *Christian Imagination*.

10. Thanks here to the work of Pentecostal biblical scholar Mittelstadt, *Spirit and Suffering*.

11. For more on the slain Lamb imagery in the final book of the Christian canon, see my *Revelation*, 88–91.

12. "Martyrdom is thus an embodied knowledge even unto the extinction of the body, but without any inkling of self-destruction," writes Santos, *End of the Cognitive Empire*, 90, in the context of discussing the knowledge born out of the struggle for survival on the underside of modernity.

as enabled by his Spirit. Yes, there is a verbal dimension to this witness, but such a spoken witness is even more powerful, provocative, and resistant when embodied collectively by the community of witnesses against the sin, unrighteousness, and injustices of the world and those under the sway of the evil one, which in turn generates counter-oppressive measures against the witnesses, even unto death! The Lukan invitation therefore is for us to embody this power of the Spirit in ways that bear witness to the full scope of what is involved along the christic and apostolic pathway, whether that results in health and well-being or in sacrifice and death.

The call, therefore, is for a witnessing out of a humility that moves us away from any kind of triumphalism. There are distinctly Pentecostal forms of triumphalism,[13] but these have emerged out of the wider historical patterns of chauvinism and inflated senses of self-superiority whenever Christian witness has been intertwined with fleeting political, ethnic, racial, economic, cultural, and related forms of earthly power. Acts 1:8a invites us to reimagine Christian witness today from a posture of humility.[14] When we actually move from imagining to performing Christian witness today, yet how many of us would sign up for martyrdom? So, we begin for the moment at this cognitive and imaginative level even as we can consider what it means to live personally and concretely into such a call as we go forward in the rest of this book.

To/From the Ends of the Earth (Acts 1:8b): Multiethnic/ Multidirectional Witness Then and Now

Now we shift to the second clause in Acts 1:8, which extends Christian witness across the known world. "And it will be my witnesses in Jerusalem, in all Judea, and Samaria, and to the ends of the earth." Let's be clear that this is Luke's table of contents for the book of Acts: we see the apostolic witness starting in Jerusalem in Acts 2, involving Judea in Acts 4–6, extending into Samaria in Acts 8, and then encompassing the ends of the earth from Acts 9 and onward. We will return soon to unpack these four movements in more detail. For now, what are some higher level missiological principles signaled by Acts 1:8b?

---

13. Nicely summarized by Couray, *What Has Wittenberg to Do with Azusa?*
14. For more on the virtues of presence, patience, courage, and humility in apostolic evangelism, see Stone, *Evangelism After Christendom*, ch. 10: "Martyrdom and Virtue."

First, this movement from Jerusalem to Judea and Samaria to the ends of the earth invites us to think about Christian witness and mission that shifts from an ethnocentric situatedness or site to multiethnic and transcultural dynamics. Recognize that the Greek *ethnos* in the New Testament and in Acts is often translated as *nations*, for instance, "Now there were devout Jews from every nation [*ethnous*] under heaven living in Jerusalem" (Acts 2:5). The primary representation here is to "the whole house of Israel."[15] Further, there is a wide chasm separating the *ethnos* of the first-century Mediterranean world from the modern nation-state, including the fact that Luke here and in the rest of his book considers Jewishness in a kind of universalizing manner that is its own ethnicity even while being able to include other ethnicities.[16] Yet, it is precisely in and through being graftable (to use Paul's term, e.g., Rom 11:17–24) into such Jewishness via the messiah Pentecost here, and Christian witness more broadly, can be thought of in terms of bridging the gaps between ethnicities, and of occurring at, between, or hybridizing across national boundaries. One might imagine Christian witness as being born out of the meeting of the many ethnicities, nations, peoples, tribes, and languages of the world. This is not to deny the geographical spread of apostolic witness but is to emphasize what has perhaps been neglected in considerations of this verse vis-à-vis Christian missional endeavor: that there is a core relational dimension of the sharing of the faith and that, more often, the ethnic and cultural differences that separate us human creatures are more challenging to navigate before we even attempt to cross national borders.

And we can think about Christian witness and Christian faith also as emerging out of this very dynamic encounter with other ethnicities/nations.[17] This is what I would call a multidirectional meeting. In the first century, we see the movement of Christian witness—from Jerusalem, to Judea, to Samaria, and to the ends of the earth—presumed a Jerusalem centeredness. Yet within this horizon, Acts 2 indicates that there were on the streets of Jerusalem on the Day of Pentecost—which by the first century had become a kind of agricultural feast[18]—both diaspora Jews from

---

15. Dahl, "Nations in the New Testament," 62.

16. Stroup, *Christians Who Became Jews*.

17. In fact, while the peace of Rome granted citizenship across the empire, the *evangel* assumed such formal identification and invited relational reconfiguration, thus "changing God's people from [being] ethnocentric to multiethnic"; see Balch, *Contested Ethnicities and Images*, 247.

18. Soggin, *Israel in the Biblical Period*, 108–9.

every nation under heaven that had returned to reside in the area and other visitors. This does not displace Jerusalem-centrism, but it complicates and dissipates Jerusalem-ethnocentrism, for instance, with Judean Jews enumerated alongside other Jews (Acts 2:9). On the Day of Pentecost, Jerusalem was already a multiethnic reality, including those from Rome (2:10) visiting Jerusalem on that day. So, we do not need to wait until Acts 28 for Roman voices to be incorporated; we hear their accents already resounding in Acts 2. This is a more multidirectional and hybridic witness that the apostolic experience imagines. This book explores the implications for us as we perform Christian witness and evangelism.

To the Ends of Time (Acts 1:8c): Witnessing in/for Our Children and Their Children

There's a third part of Acts 1:8 that doesn't often get highlighted, which I want to lift up for a few moments. And that has to do with the translation of the Greek at the end of this passage that we're familiar with: "You will receive power when the Holy Spirit comes upon you and you will be my witnesses in Jerusalem and all Judea and Samaria, and *to the ends of the earth*" (emphasis mine). The Greek word for *ends* in this passage is *eschatou*, thus connoting the earth's boundaries or edges (also Acts 13:47; cf. Luke 14:9, denoting the last or least space).[19] While it is surely appropriate in this context to understand this geographically in relationship to the ends of the earth, which from a Jerusalem-centered perspective refers to Rome (where the gospel arrives in Acts 28), the semantic range here involves not only the synchronic, geographical distance, but the diachronic and temporal dimension that locates human temporal experience. *Eschatou*, in this latter respect, opens up to the "eschaton," or the ends of the times of the earth,[20] what theological discourse calls eschatology. Two other early passages in the Acts narrative help us to see this.

When those on the streets of Jerusalem asked Peter, "what does this mean?" (Acts 2:12), Luke records Peter drawing creatively from the prophet Joel: "in the last days, I will pour my Spirit upon all flesh . . . before the

---

19. See Westhelle, *Eschatology and Space*, 34.

20. Chapter 7 of Reformed theologian and missiologist Harry R. Boer's *Pentecost and Missions* is titled "The ends of the earth and the end of time," and was one of the first theological interpretations of Acts' missiology in eschatological perspective; our reading builds on Boer's but lift up the temporal and geographical interconnections.

coming of the Lord's great and glorious day. Then everyone who calls on the name of the Lord shall be saved" (2:17, 20–21). The *eschatou tes ges* or "ends of the earth" in Acts 1:8 here connects to the *eschatais hemerais* or "last days" of Acts 2:17, which is the great and glorious day when anyone calling on the Lord's name anywhere and anytime can experience God's salvation, which is the giving of his spirit to all.

That's the front end of Peter's response to the crowd's question. On the back end of Peter's response to the crowd after he preached the Pentecost sermon, the convicted hearers query: "what do we need to do?" (2:37b). "Repent and be baptized every one of you and you will receive the gift of the Holy Spirit," Peter says, "for the promise is for you, for your children, and for all who are far away" (2:38–39). The text here is not about the geographical distance of those who are far away, but the generational distance separating us from our children, grandchildren, great-grandchildren, etc.[21] The witness and gift of the Spirit is available to and from the ends of the earth and also to the ever-receding times of the earth. This eschatological dimension of the gospel thus invites us to live into God's ends or purposes at any present moment and every place.

Every temporal or historical moment that follows what happened on the streets of Jerusalem on the Day of Pentecost can be one that involves the manifestation of the Spirit. This includes the Lukan generation that wrote the book of Acts perhaps as late as the end of the first century. It includes every other generation that has read this text, and has seen that the promise is for them, their children, and their children's children. It's for me, for you, for our children, for our grandchildren, and for those coming after them as well.

The eschatological invitation is for us to embrace God's ends, in whatever our present moment might include. When we consider the promise being for our children, grandchildren, great-grandchildren, and beyond, how might we anticipate Christian mission and its implications for human life in this terrestrial environment? How might Christians bear witness to, from, and for the Earth? What about climate change? Can the Christian gospel enable sustainable inhabitation of our planet, faithful care for our environment, and compelling testimony to the work of the risen Christ by his Spirit across this terrestrial home that we all share? We return in the final chapter to these questions.

---

21. See my essay, "Children and the Spirit."

Hence, there is a transgenerational horizon to Christian witness and Christian mission. Every generation is a new time with new contexts, potentially with new urgencies, involving arguably new invitations to imagine new practices. Every generation is invited to come back to the apostolic witness in light of their questions, and call upon the promise of the Spirit so we can respond faithfully in our times to the different issues that now beckon our attention.

From Jerusalem to Judea and Samaria . . . : Apostolic Witness Then and Now

Now in this section of the chapter, I elaborate on the four sites delineated in the Acts 1:8 table of contents. If we might presume that such a movement from the central apostolic site to the edges of the world would promote any kind of expansionist missiological agenda, we have already in the preceding discussion cautioned against that kind of missiological retrieval even as the following considerations further mitigate against that kind of imperialistic or triumphalistic approach via foregrounding the mutuality of the evangelistic enterprise done *with* others.[22] Throughout, then, we see apostolic witness in various geographically contextual venues, engaging with diverse others, being challenged by these encounters, and transformed in identity and practice.

Many Tongues: Multiple Ethnicities, Cultures, and Economies (Acts 2)

We begin by focusing on Christian witness in Jerusalem, where we see what I call the interdependence of us and others in the global economy, and then, staying with the Jerusalem site, discuss the many witnesses outside and within its spaces. We take off from where Luke initially describes the results of the promised Spirit's arrival in Acts 2:6–11.[23]

---

22. And for other Lukan-specific reasons (overlapping with my own treatment in this chapter) why Acts 1:8 and the ensuing narrative ought not to be read expansionistically, see Kim, "From/To the Ends of the Earth," esp. 46–48.

23. I have been commenting on this text now for over two decades, initially regarding the ethnic and cultural dimensions in my *Spirit Poured Out*, esp. ch. 4.

And at this sound the crowd gathered and was bewildered, because each one heard them speaking in the native language of each. Amazed and astonished, they asked, "Are not all these who are speaking Galileans? And how is it that we hear, each of us, in our own native language? Parthians, Medes, Elamites, and residents of Mesopotamia, Judea and Cappadocia, Pontus and Asia, Phrygia and Pamphylia, Egypt and the parts of Libya belonging to Cyrene, and visitors from Rome, both Jews and proselytes, Cretans and Arabs—in our own languages we hear them speaking about God's deeds of power."

We don't need to decide whether this was a miracle of speech or one of hearing. Rather, the miracle of Pentecost was one of communication that involved not only speaking and hearing but also some comprehension amid the amazement and bewilderment.[24] This was the miracle in which the gospel is witnessed to in ways at least heard by those in their own distinct languages, languages that allowed them to recognize God's deeds of power. The listing here of sixteen locations is a very short version of the list of seventy nations that appears various times in the Hebrew Testament or the Old Testament.[25]

It's not just the brevity of this list that is supposed to be symbolic of that broader list because, again, there is no doubt that for Luke, every nation under heaven living in Jerusalem was represented. This was a representative, not exhaustive, list. But what is represented in this list? A few stand out from a missiological and evangelistic perspective.

Cretans stand out in my mind. We have heard it said in another part of the New Testament, that "Cretans are always liars" (Titus 1:12)! Would Cretan readers or auditors in the first century have forgiven this ethnic stereotype? We might get a sense for how that ethnic stereotype functioned in the first-century world if we considered how other ethnic stereotypes—e.g., regarding blacks, Asian, Hispanics, Norwegians, or whatever else might exist—function in our time. If all Cretans are indeed liars, how would they have been able to bear truthful witness to God's deeds of power? However this is resolved,[26] such a widely known ethnic characterization would have

---

24. See Welker, *God the Spirit*, ch. 5.

25. E.g., Scott, "Luke's Geographical Horizon."

26. Interpreted in its immediate context, one commentator suggests, the author of the Letter to Titus uses this so-called liar paradox "to demonstrate the self-defeating ineffectiveness of making truth-claims which are given the lie by conduct which fails to match them"; see Thiselton, *Thiselton on Hermeneutics*, 222.

meant at least that the discourse of Cretan language and dialects were "difficult to understand" at best.[27] And yet, the miracle of Pentecost consisted at least in part in recognizing the possibility of communicative truthfulness of those from Crete, which thus broke through the stereotypes that existed in the first-century Mediterranean world across ethnic groups, nationalities, cultures, tribes, and languages.[28]

Arabs are also mentioned as present and being heard in their language at Jerusalem on the Day of Pentecost. There is a long history here, reflected in part in St. Paul's contrasts in Galatians (4:21–31) between the Abrahamic peoples from his wife (Sarah, who is not mentioned by name in the letter) and from her servant, Hagar, recognized progenitor to the nomadic Arab tribes through her son Ishmael.[29] The Pentecost event provides a glimpse into the healing possibilities related to these long histories of suspicion (at best) and hostility (at worst). The inclusion of residents from Egypt, perennially enemies of Israel since the times of the deliverance of Israel via the hand of Moses from the clutches of Pharaoh yet foretold by at least one prophet about becoming reconciled to the God of Israel (Isa 19:19–25), is another indication that long-standing national (and ethnic) antagonisms are being overcome in the Pentecost outpouring of the divine spirit on all flesh (even as another Pentecost is now needed, as of the time of final drafting, in light of current hostilities between Israel and Gaza that erupted in October 2023).

But the second part of Acts 2 is just as important: three thousand of those gathered in Jerusalem on that day responded and were baptized, and they began a fledgling apostolic community. Thus, the many peoples of the Mediterranean world, those from every nation under heaven that were gathered, found themselves in a new communal situation in which they needed to adjust and develop an economic means for sustenance. Thus, the many peoples that also derived or hailed from a variety of socialities were now brought together, out of which emerged a form of political economy

---

27. See Linton, "List of Nations in Acts 2," 52.

28. All the more ironically pointed, in Lukan hands, if in fact the saying "In him we live and move and have our being" quoted later at the Areopagus by Paul (Acts 17:28a) is from the Cretan poet or philosopher Epimenides! See also Rothschild, *Paul in Athens*, 67–73.

29. Historical background of multi-tribal Arabia and its fluid "borders" betwixt and between imperial jostling, e.g., between the Pax Assyriana and the Pax Romana up to the time of the New Testament for instance, is detailed in Trimingham, *Christianity Among the Arabs*, ch. 1.

featuring centrally attitudes of generosity and practices of sharing. Acts 2:42–47 reads:

> They devoted themselves to the apostles' teaching and fellowship, to the breaking of bread and prayers. Awe came upon everyone because many wonders and signs were done by the apostles. All who believed were together and had all things in common; they would sell their possessions and goods and distribute the proceeds to all as any had need. Day by day, as they spent much time together at the temple, they broke bread at home and ate their food with glad and generous hearts, praising God and having the goodwill of all the people, and day by day the Lord added to the number of those who were being saved.

So, the Christian witness expanded. The community grew in part because it was porous. There was a back and forth movement in relation to the broader community. There were shifting sites from home to home.

And there was the sharing and having things in common, which crucial meeting of needs was facilitated partly through the mutuality across languages, ethnicities, and cultures.[30] Now we'll see (soon, in Acts 6) this doesn't last in Jerusalem for too long—even if the principles and practices of friendship, mutuality, shared possessions, and hospitality arguably persisted into the early second century[31]—but at least here in Acts 2, such reciprocity was crucial to the early Christian experience.

This passage will occupy us again in chapter 5. At this moment, though, the invitation is to imagine Christian life, witness, and mission with others, without and within. Meaning that the lines between inside and outside, between us and them, need to be permeable. Whatever "boundaries" exist between us insiders and those outside need to be ones that allow for movements of ideas, of beliefs, of practices, and of commitments as well. The gospel creates new collectives, new "we's," through our sharing and receiving with others.

Many Tongues, Many Practices in the Neighborhood (Acts 3–6) Then and Now

As we shift from Christian witness in Jerusalem to Christian witness in Judea, we continue to see opportunities and challenges. This is not surprising,

---

30. I elaborate on this economic aspect of Acts 2 in my *In the Days of Caesar*, §7.3.1.
31. E.g., Montero, *All Things in Common*, esp. chs. 5–7.

as there are many tongues in the Jerusalem neighborhood as there were on the streets of Jerusalem before. We highlight three of these aspects in Acts 3–6.

The first begins with the curing of the lame man at the Beautiful Gate at Solomon's portico (Acts 3:1–10). In this healing, we see one of the referred to signs and wonders accomplished by the apostles.[32] Healings continue to unfold, including many being made whole from the shadow cast by Peter walking along (5:12–15). We included throngs coming in from the countryside and experiencing cures (5:16). But we also see that the early Christian witness, including curing, did not take place in a vacuum. I call this the politics of healing.

Notice, for instance, how Peter and John had resolved to address the lame man on the Sabbath day. After the latter's curing, as the story develops, the two apostles are taken into custody, kept overnight in jail, released on their own recognizance the following day, and warned against doing the things that they were doing that incited the crowds. We understood what part of their testimony was, that they would have to obey the voice of God rather than that of Caesar (4:20). They went back to the apostolic homes, and they began to pray and worship together, drawing from the psalms. Notice this prayer in Acts 4.

> After they were released, they went to their friends and reported what the chief priests and the elders had said to them. When they heard it, they raised their voices together to God and said, "Sovereign Lord, who made the heaven and the earth, the sea, and everything in them, it is you who said by the Holy Spirit through our ancestor David, your servant: 'Why did the Gentiles rage, and the peoples imagine vain things? The kings of the earth took their stand, and the rulers have gathered together against the Lord and against his Messiah' [Ps 2:1–2]. For in this city, in fact, both Herod and Pontius Pilate, with the Gentiles and the peoples of Israel, gathered together against your holy servant Jesus, whom you anointed, to do whatever your hand and your plan had predestined to take place. And now, Lord, look at their threats, and grant to your servants to speak your word with all boldness, while you stretch out your hand to heal, and signs and wonders are performed through the name of your holy servant Jesus." When they had prayed, the place in which they were gathered together was

---

32. See my sermon on this passage in Yong, *Kerygmatic Spirit*, ch. 2.

shaken; and they were all filled with the Holy Spirit and spoke the word of God with boldness. (4:23–31)[33]

Observe, then, that these developments, including incarceration and worship one day after another, were part and parcel of the apostolic experience, and they were not abstracted from the political local situation within which the first messianic followers found themselves. And they realized that they were able to identify even how their Scriptures gave them hopes for persisting in this public space. Theirs was a kind of martyrological witness, effectively, one that involved being willing to be imprisoned in this particular context.

Another window into what's happening in Judea is with the Barnabas and then Ananias and Sapphira stories next to each other, the former at the end of Acts 4 and the latter beginning Acts 5. We read these together because they are two sides of this one coin of how the apostolic experience of sharing and generosity was continued by someone like Barnabas, who sold his lands and brought the proceeds to the apostles and laid it at their feet; but in the case of Ananias and Sapphira, who surreptitiously kept part of the proceeds for themselves, something more like the opposite is reflected. Although we may be familiar with both stories, we may miss the most important features if we read these two narratives separately. Reading them together, however, helps accentuate the contrast. The many tongues in a neighborhood—reflected in that of Barnabas the Cyprian on the one hand and of Ananias and Sapphira as Judean locals on the other—therefore echo a variety of contrary economic decisions.[34]

We know about the complexities of life and how they might be seductive in a variety of contexts. We need to be attentive to these narratives because they illuminate again the challenges of living in complicated socioeconomic and political spaces, encouraging some to share generously but also driving others to be more self-serving and duplicitous. We might think we could do better, although the susceptibilities of human hearts seen in Ananias and Sapphira afflict us all. And, it should also be said, so do the generous and generative postures of Barnabas and others in the apostolic community! Considered together, then, these texts continue to invite us to be discerning, to call upon the Spirit to illuminate our decision-making and enable obedience to the Lordship of Jesus Christ, even in moments of temptation and weakness.

33. Another of my homilies was on this passage, e.g., *Kerygmatic Spirit*, ch. 8.
34. See McCabe, *How to Kill Things*.

Finally, there continued to be internal dynamics within this first-century apostolic context. What we're seeing in the opening chapters of the Acts of the Apostles is a multi-socioeconomically stratified and multiethnic cultural community in the missional neighborhood. Starting from Acts 2 building up to Acts 6, we see a struggle unfolding between Hebrew-speaking and Greek-speaking widows. As conflicts are endemic to any human community, we should not be surprised this happens among this apostolic group, whose journey was being navigated by linguistically, ethnically, and culturally diverse segments constituted by those who are devoutly gathered from many nations under heaven. Their initial speaking in a variety of languages was gradually sorted out, but what was persisting and predominating in this Judean context was Hebrew and Greek. Enough of the Greek and Hebrew to get along, but not enough to address felt inequities or to be fully harmonized. Thus, also, the growing urgent need to be adjudicated by Greek and Hebrew speaking leaders, so first verses of Acts 6 give us a window into struggles regarding this matter at the leadership level, which is additionally politicized and overlain by different cultural values. In short, we see linguistically, culturally, and ethnically refracted windows into first-century patron-client dynamics being tested in this Jerusalem-centered space. Simultaneously, this was a first-century "global" community, which while anachronistically labeled for that time, illuminates in an analogical manner how Jerusalem was both an arrival site for travelers across the known (Mediterranean) world on the one hand and also home to a (Jewish) community dispersed to the ends of the known earth on the other hand.[35]

Acts 2–6 thus illuminates a nascent *ekklesia* renegotiate transnational, transethnic, and transcultural identities locally (in Jerusalem) and, by implication and extension, across the Pax Romana. None of this is simple, almost just like world Christianity today. None of what we're navigating is straightforward; it's all complicated, complex, multi-tiered, multi-cultural, multi-linguistic, multi-political, multi-economic. And the apostolic experience invites us to revisit, to reconsider, to reexamine, and to recalibrate these matters as we think our way forward.

---

35. For further comment on Acts 6, see my *Missiological Spirit*, ch. 6, esp. 133–35, which, for readers wanting more, also follows my comments (132–33) on the Samarian mission in Acts 8, that I discuss further in a moment.

PART I: CHRISTIAN WITNESS TO/WITH OTHERS IN THE 2020S

Liminal Witness to and with "The Other" (Acts 8)

We are now, following the outline given in Acts 1:8, moving onto the third part of Luke's account of the growth of the early church's witness, into Samaria. Our goal here, as throughout this chapter, is to reconsider Christian witness and mission in light of the Lukan telling of the early Christian story. What "others" do we now meet and how do such encounters inform contemporary considerations of Christian missiology? Acts 8 gives us two narratives, one on what happened in Samaria and another on what transpired on the Gaza road.

Luke's transition from Judea to Samaria leaps off Stephen's martyrdom: "And Saul approved of their killing him. That day a severe persecution began against the church in Jerusalem, and all except the apostles were scattered throughout the countryside of Judea and Samaria" (Acts 8:1). Saul's (later, St. Paul) approval of Stephen's murder forms the backdrop of a more substantive persecution then waged against the church in Jerusalem, resulting in apostolic fortification in the city but also the scattering of the deacons and others of the early messianic community from the apostolic center. Perhaps not unexpectedly, it was Hellenists (here fluent in the Greek language and way of life[36]) like Philip, one of the deacons appointed to support the already multiculturally informed community of Greek-speaking widows, who either had sufficient multicultural capacities to venture out beyond Judea or at least did not feel beholden to Jerusalem as a home or haven to remain within the purportedly more secure confines of the apostolic leadership during this trying sequence of events. Multicultural Philip, perhaps and probably also bilingual, was the one who was ready to go to Samaria, not the apostles who, perhaps like most Jews of that era, kept the Samaritans at arm's length. During the first century, Jewish and Samaritan relationships remained strained (John 4:9 tells us, "Jews do not share things in common with Samaritans"). Jews resided in their region and Samaritans in theirs, and they had little to do with each other. This was what made Jesus's parable of the good Samaritan so effective and provocative (Luke 10:30–37). So, it took somebody like Philip, who was already a multicultural and Mediterranean "world traveler," we might say, to be able to navigate the space between Jerusalem and Samaria. Just that one border itself needed a different skill set.

---

36. *Hellenists* in Acts might otherwise be Jewish or gentile believers in the messiah; see Hengel, *Between Jesus and Paul*, 4–11.

Crossing from Judea to Samaria also required a different skill set in part because we can approach the latter from perspectives that illuminate how inhabitants of this region differ from the former not only ethnically but also, effectively, religiously. John's Gospel records the woman at the well in Samaria saying, "Our ancestors worshiped on this mountain, but you say that the place where people must worship is in Jerusalem" (John 4:20), which is suggestive of the divergences marking Jewish and Samaritan theological if not also practical and spiritual commitments. Philip was the first to "break new ground," to so speak, in Samaritan territory, engaging with these ethnic and religious others on their soil, and perhaps at least in that respect on their terms.[37] Thus, the gospel came to Samaria via signs and wonders, as the Lukan account unveils. And then, Peter and John were to come and follow up on that conversation.

In the second half of Acts 8, apostolic ministry and witness advanced from Samaria into the Gaza road with the Ethiopian eunuch. I call the Ethiopian eunuch the multiply stigmatized other: stigmatized by the color of his skins, because of his place of origin (location), due to his elitist position working on behalf of a high-ranking government official in charge of the emperor's treasury (this is both the social/class and economic dimensions of his being rejected by the masses), and simply because of his physical impairment: being a eunuch. According to the Old Testament, eunuchs were not allowed into the Holy of Holies or to participate in certain priestly duties, so mention of his status as a eunuch was stigmatizing from that perspective.

And yet, here we have Christian witness unfolding in Samaria, against the ethically authorized group and against this multiply and otherwise stigmatized individual. Acts 8's account thus represents so many of the stigmas and the otherizations of the first-century Mediterranean world. The text therefore invites us to reconsider how our own cultural situatedness, location, and the related political, economic, or other dimensions of our lives lead us to otherize a variety of other groups based upon our own definitions and biases.

When we see what happened with the apostolic sojourn into Samaria and then alongside the Ethiopian eunuch on the Gaza road, I think also about witness to and with others on the other side of history, especially those on the ethnic margins of history, on the darker-skin underside of

---

37. I discuss first-century Jewish-Samaritan relationships in terms of religious differentiation in my *Spirit Poured Out*, 240–44.

history, so to speak. Samaritans and Ethiopian eunuchs were thereby also on the political underside of history and on the socioeconomic undercurrents of history. And, eunuchs, like all persons with disabilities, as we now use this term to categorize those with certain impairing conditions, derive also from the other side of what we might call "ableist" history, the accounts told by those of us with temporarily able-bodies.[38]

Christian Witness to, from, and at the Ends of the Earth (Acts 9–28)

And finally, the fourth part of the Acts of the Apostles is Christian witness to, from, and at *the ends of the earth*, which begins formally in Acts 9–10 and extends to the final chapter 28, with the arrival of the gospel to Rome, the furthest reaches of the empire considered from the Jerusalem perspective.[39] We will not be covering all of this material in detail here, of course (part 2 of this book revisits various sections from a variety of angles). Our focus instead will be on the major themes of our approach: Christian witness to and with others in a pluralistic imperial world. What deserves commentary when read through these bifocal lenses?

If the Ethiopian eunuch (engaged on the Gaza road and hence still within the Judean realm) was not "other" enough, the movement of the gospel outward to the rest of the earth begins with the gentile—denoted as *ethne*, signifying derivation from the non-Jewish ethnic world (Acts 10:44b)—Cornelius, and culminates, en route to Rome in Acts 28, with the indigenous natives—denoted as *barbaroi* in Greek (28:2–3)—on the island of Malta where Paul was shipwrecked. And there are many others in the intervening chapters, from the proconsul of Paphos (13:7) to Lydia the immigrant at Philippi (16:14–15), from the Ephesian city clerk (19:35) to Mnason the Cyprian immigrant to Caesarea (21:16), or from the triad of governmental heads Paul addresses (Felix, Festus, and Agrippa) to Julius the centurion (27:1). Most of the readers of these words will be gentiles, by definition, of non-Jewish derivation. But from a Jerusalem-centered Jewish perspective, we are all ethnic others to the nth degree, some more welcome to Jewish communities, others less so.

---

38. See also my discussions of ableism and of the Ethiopian eunuch in Yong, *Bible, Disability, and the Church*, 8–12 and 68–69, respectively.

39. See Walaskay, *"And So We Came to Rome."*

It doesn't matter whether we're Caucasian, African, Latinx, or whatever, as gentiles we are impure. That was the point about the Cornelius episode. Peter had to get the vision of the unclean animals lowered three times and be told to eat three times. And he, the pious Jewish follower of the Jewish messiah, was the one who finally came to recognize, "God has shown me that I should not call anyone profane or unclean" (10:28b). While we will return for a deeper analysis of this passage in chapter 3, the point here is that it doesn't matter where you and I are located ethnically. Each of our own groups have our ethnic others that historically we have had nothing to do with. Acts 10 invites us beyond those pre-authorizations. The Maltese "barbarians" were those who saved the life of the Jewish disciple of Jesus cast up on their shores after fourteen days at a stormy sea and shipwrecked without hope, without means, without resources. And these same "barbarians" were those who embraced and hosted Paul and Luke and their traveling compatriots, effectively also, then, welcomed the deity that they represented.[40] In other words, those called to bear witness to the gospel to the ends of their world were now invited to mission in humility, to bear witness by receiving the gifts of the indigenous others.

And notice that Paul is not recorded as saying anything, indeed there is no explicit mention of his evangelizing the Maltese Islanders. The only thing we are told that Paul does is he prays for Publius who got sick, resulting in the latter's healing. Yet we know how the church in Malta dates itself back to this unplanned encounter. A church is initiated not because the missionaries were particularly eloquent communicators, as far as Luke was concerned, but because they were hungry, vulnerable, and in desperate need of the gifts of the "barbarians." So Christian witness now unfolds with and through the other's actions in this particular context.[41]

Christian witness to, from, and at the ends of the earth invites us to identify with all of the ethnic others who the apostles interacted with. How did these mostly Jewish messengers, Paul particularly, come to partner with others, like the Hellenists before and now including Silas, Timothy (a multiethnic person—multiracial to use current nomenclature due to having a Greek father and Jewish mother), Apollos, Priscilla and Aquila, etc., in their efforts? How was initial contact initiated or established, how were shoulders rubbed, how did collaboration come about?

---

40. See also Jipp, *Divine Visitations*.

41. I unpack further Acts 28:1–10 on the Maltese episode in my *Missiological Spirit*, 126–28.

We find many of these dynamics at Antioch, which emerges as an alternative site of Christian witnessing initiatives starting in Acts 11. Luke tells us that it's in Antioch that they were first called Christians (11:16). And we also know that it's in Antioch that there was a multiethnic/national and multicultural—at least from Cyprus (Barnabas) and Cyrene, if not also from Niger and other parts of the Mediterranean world (13:1)[42]—school of prophets and teachers that commissioned Paul and Barnabas on what is now known as Paul's first missionary journey to go even further westward (away from Jerusalem) that led to a second and a third missional endeavor wherein, finally, the messianic witness arrives in Rome at the ends of the earth. Read from this on the way to the ends of the earth, Jerusalem was never centered after all. Things may have begun there, but the narrative is an ongoing decentering of this Jewish capital that invites us to consider its marginality less vis-à-vis imperial Rome and the coming divine reign. To be sure, from a Rome-centered point of view, Jerusalem was a marginalized site. From the early Christian apostolic experience perspective, Rome may have been at the ends of the earth geographically, but as the entirety of the earth was the Lord's footstool (7:49), every site was an equal-opportunity space for the manifestation of the divine spirit.

Where the center is and where the margins are depend, for finite human creatures, on where we're situated and located. But pentecostally put, where we're situated and located could become a center even if marginalized from other perspectives; or, wherever Christian witnesses find themselves full of the divine spirit are sites for making known the mighty works of God. In this particular case, the "Christians" of Jerusalem may have had existential priority and even have nurtured the diaconal leaders that ended up taking the gospel to Antioch (11:19), but the messianic group in this Syrian city began to exercise missional leadership quickly, not only in sending Paul and others out but also in supporting sister ecclesial communities in times of need, e.g., ecclesial communities in Judea suffering the effects of famine (11:29). Perhaps articulable otherwise: If the Judean famine enervated the believers there and contributed to the decline of Jerusalem's authority as an apostolic site, these developments also allowed for the emergence of congregations like that at Antioch. And then of course, the Antiochian site waxed and waned over time.[43] History admonishes us

---

42. For more on Antioch as a crossroads for the Pax Romana, see Bridge, "Christians and Jews in Antioch," 208–14.

43. I discuss the Antiochene church as a waxing and waning site for early Christian

to hold our centeredness humbly, as part of Christian faith and Christian discipleship, to recognize that our centeredness oftentimes is undergirded by our own forms of circumstantial power and access to resources that we then attempt to galvanize politically for our own benefits. That's what history is, but inevitably, kingdoms and empires come and go. How do we hold the kingdoms of this world and its powers lightly even as we fix our sights on the divine reign that beckons us, and focus on the city that calls us beyond ourselves and relativizes our earthly potencies for the sake of the good news?

"That Is This": A Fresh Retrieval of Acts' Apostolic Mission amid 2020s-Others

As we arrive at the end of this chapter, consider, again, how this Acts narrative, which we've gone through very quickly at a high level of generality, challenges and confronts us with the difficult questions of our third millennium time. We continue to grapple with missional questions, political questions, questions about nationalism (and Christian nationalism more specifically), questions of climate change, questions of the inequities of history and society, questions about the multiplicity, plurality, and diversity of cultures, etc. On the one hand, the gospel relativizes all of these "realities," but on the other hand, we have more often than we care to admit interpreted the gospel in ways that have allowed us to perpetuate the status quo, not least when they have benefited us interpreters. To be sure, the gospel touches all of life, and there is neither any space nor any time that is left unaffected by the good news of Jesus and the coming divine reign. Yet, this leads not to the triumphalism of any imperial missionization but to a witness out of the many tongues of the multitudes, speaking truth to power and yet not mobilizing for a political revolution.

Can we reengage these difficult matters today, and if so, how can we do so honestly across the many differences stretching from the first-century apostolic experience to our own efforts in very different spaces and times? Part 2 of this book will circle around and spiral into the Acts of the Apostles, which for the Pentecostal church of my upbringing contained all of the answers to the most difficult questions of life, but which also can speak, for Christians across the church ecumenical, to the global issues and questions of our day and time. Will we continue to stay with the apostolic record and

---

theological education in my "Not Many of You Should Become Teachers . . ."

be resourced in our contemporary efforts? If so, we might first need to be converted to and transformed by this same text, including its prequel, the Gospel of Luke, to which we now turn.

Chapter 2

Luke and Christian Witness
Then and Now

THIS CHAPTER FOCUSES ON Luke's theology of Christian witness as reflected in his first book, the gospel account of Jesus's life, ministry, and teachings. As in the preceding, ours is less an exegetical approach (as I am not a biblical scholar) but a theological and missiological reading driven at least in part by our contemporary concerns. We will first set up the Third Gospel in relation to the discussion in the previous chapter, in particular situating the apostolic world in its imperial and pluralistic context that also enables recognition that some of our contemporary issues and realities were navigated by the messianic community in their own way. Then, in the substantive second part of this chapter, we will follow Luke's outline of the gospel account provided in chapter 4, verses 18–19, similar to how Acts 1:8 provided the template for the sequel. The concluding section, transitioning to part 2 of this volume, highlights how Luke's account of the unfolding apostolic witness, to and with others, in our reading, is accomplished by the two books explicating his central theme: that Christian witness is enabled by the Holy Spirit to the ends of the earth precisely in and through witness bearers encountering and adjusting to others along the missional pathway.

Reading Luke After Acts: Jesus's Witness in an Imperial World

The first sentence of the book of Acts summarizes the prior book: "In the first book, Theophilus, I wrote about all that Jesus did and taught from the beginning until the day when he was taken up to heaven . . ." (Acts 1:1–2a). The reference here is to the earlier work also addressed to Theophilus (Luke 1:3). If written in that order, it would make sense to read them in the same sequence, and biblical readers who read regularly from cover to cover will encounter the Gospel of Luke first before the book of Acts. And yet, it is precisely what happened with the early apostolic community, told in the book of Acts, that prompted various persons in different parts of the church to write what we call the Gospels. As we saw, the apostolic witness born throughout the book of Acts is about Jesus, so the Acts events generated the writing of the Jesus story to begin with. It is the apostolic experience in Acts which leads this medical doctor, Luke, to write his Jesus story first, and then the book of Acts second. From that perspective, we ought not to be surprised to observe themes seen in the sequel and in the prequel.

Preliminaries in Luke's Gospel: The Imperial and "Global" Setting of the Witness Stage

When Luke sat down to write the gospel of Jesus, he had already experienced the advance of that gospel, via Paul's incarcerated sojourn, to Rome at the ends of the earth. At some point (scholars believe perhaps in the ninth decade of the first century if not later), Luke "decided, after investigating everything carefully from the very first, to write an orderly account" so that his readers, beginning with Theophilus, who he names, "may know the truth concerning the things about which you have been instructed" (Luke 1:3–4). His careful investigation included consultation with eyewitnesses and also consideration of a number of other pre-existing accounts, maybe Mark's Gospel, and also other sources (1:1–2). Yet he did not merely repeat what he had heard or read but crafted his own distinct narrative, one featuring and anticipating the multiethnic, multicultural, ends-of-the-earth reality that the Jesus movement had become.

The known world that Jesus was delivered into was unified in the sense that it was under the auspices of the Roman Empire. Luke himself so sets the Jesus story squarely within this context, not only "in those days a decree went out from Emperor Augustus that all the world should be registered" (Luke 2:1), but also, to be as clear as possible: "In the fifteenth year of the reign of Emperor Tiberius, when Pontius Pilate was governor of Judea, and Herod was ruler of Galilee, and his brother Philip ruler of the region of Ituraea and Trachonitis, and Lysanias ruler of Abilene" (3:1). Not for no reason, some have assumed Luke's massive (by the standards of his time) literary output was devoted to "legitimizing the Jesus movement in the midst of empire."[1] We do not have to go that far (not that we shouldn't) to appreciate that what Luke has to tell us about Jesus's life and teachings can be understood as a critique of the social and political powers of his day,[2] and in that sense is relevant for our own efforts in a time of global market capitalist hegemony, among other imperial forces.

Luke in this respect also believed the Jesus story was meaningful beyond Israel, for the fullness of his known (Roman) world. Thus, Simeon's song while holding the infant Jesus in his arms draws variously from the prophet Isaiah in recognizing the significance of the child not only for Israel but for the gentiles: "Master, now you are dismissing your servant in peace, according to your word; for my eyes have seen your salvation, which you have prepared in the presence of all peoples, a light for revelation to the Gentiles and for glory to your people Israel" (2:29–32).[3] Comparable words are reported by Luke as proclaimed by John the Baptist, in this case the author explicitly acknowledging as drawn from the prophet Isaiah, "The voice of one crying out in the wilderness: 'Prepare the way of the Lord, make his paths straight. Every valley shall be filled, and every mountain and hill shall be made low, and the crooked shall be made straight, and the rough ways made smooth; and all flesh shall see the salvation of God'" (3:4–6; cf. Isa 40:3–5). Jesus, the glory of and for Israel, is nevertheless for all peoples, indeed, for "all flesh" as also indicated in Acts (2:17).

At the very end of Luke's Gospel, the risen Jesus in his pre-ascension moments reminds the disciples about his mission in similar terms, albeit now anticipating the follow-up book: "Thus it is written, that the Messiah is to suffer and to rise from the dead on the third day, and that repentance and forgiveness of sins is to be proclaimed in his name to all nations, beginning

---

1. Which is the title of ch. 13 of Conway and Carr, *Contemporary Introduction to the Bible*.

2. See Painter, "Gospel of Luke and the Roman Empire."

3. Isaianic allusions here include 40:5, 42:6, 49:6, and 52:10 (although not in this order in Simeon's song); for more on Luke's use of Isaiah, see Beers, *Followers of Jesus*.

from Jerusalem" (Luke 24:46–47). Precisely because the Jesus story has been one for all peoples, so also the disciples are then told: "You are witnesses of these things. And see, I am sending upon you what my Father promised; so stay here in the city until you have been clothed with power from on high" (24:48–49), so they also can herald the gospel in Jerusalem, through Judea, through Samaria, to the ends of the earth.

Against this backdrop, we can zero in on how Luke himself maps the Jesus story, which happens in the fourth chapter, verses 14 through 21. Just like Acts 1:8 gives us a table of contents or a road map for the Acts narrative, this passage plays a similar role, not so much in terms of the sequential segments of the Gospel of Luke, as much in terms of the themes elaborated.[4] Whereas the follow-up book lifts up the geographical and ethnic/national horizon of where the gospel goes, this one accentuates the various groups and categories of people for whom Jesus comes with the good news.

The Messianic Witness of the Spirit to/Through Many Tongues

The relevant passage follows Jesus's baptism in water by John and his overcoming the temptations of the devil in the wilderness by the power of the Holy Spirit (4:1), and reads thus:

> Then Jesus, filled with the power of the Spirit, returned to Galilee, and a report about him spread through all the surrounding country. He began to teach in their synagogues and was praised by everyone. When he came to Nazareth, where he had been brought up, he went to the synagogue on the sabbath day, as was his custom. He stood up to read, and the scroll of the prophet Isaiah was given to him. He unrolled the scroll and found the place where it was written: "The Spirit of the Lord is upon me, because he has anointed me to bring good news to the poor. He has sent me to proclaim release to the captives and recovery of sight to the blind, to let the oppressed go free, to proclaim the year of the Lord's favor." And he rolled up the scroll, gave it back to the attendant, and sat down. The eyes of all in the synagogue were fixed on him. Then he began to say to them, "Today this scripture has been fulfilled in your hearing." (4:14–21; cf. Isa 61:1)

---

4. See Prior, *Jesus the Liberator*.

We first look at the background behind this text and then turn to the foreground.[5]

In the background, the reference to the prophet Isaiah derives from the sixty-first chapter. The messianic servant is prominent throughout Isaiah 40–66.[6] By the time we get to this passage in Isaiah 61, where Jesus is reading from the scroll, we have already had numerous announcements of both the messianic role and witness. While there is a great deal of scholarly conversation about who the messiah is (an individual or Israel or both?), which we need not resolve, part of the point is that the servant's witness is borne to the nations. The familiar texts have already been echoed in Simeon's and John's words, e.g.:

- "Here is my servant, whom I uphold, my chosen, in whom my soul delights; I have put my spirit upon him; he will bring forth justice to the nations" (Isa 42:1);
- "I am the Lord, I have called you in righteousness, I have taken you by the hand and kept you; I have given you as a covenant to the people, a light to the nations" (42:6);
- "Let all the nations gather together, and let the peoples assemble. Who among them declared this, and foretold to us the former things? Let them bring their witnesses to justify them, and let them hear and say, 'It is true'" (43:9);
- "It is too light a thing that you should be my servant to raise up the tribes of Jacob and to restore the survivors of Israel; I will give you as a light to the nations, that my salvation may reach to the end of the earth" (49:6).

These, along with the other Isaianic references to the nations in these texts, are all brought forward by Jesus as recorded by Luke.

The same Spirit then who anointed the disciples in the book of Acts is the one who anoints the messiah in the Gospel. The Pentecost motif thus not only works forward from Acts 2 to the end of that book, but is set up by the gift of the Spirit to Jesus, effectively as the anointing that makes Jesus the messiah (literally: the anointed one). The outpouring of the Spirit at Pentecost continues what was begun at the synagogue in Nazareth since,

---

5. For homiletical considerations, see also Yong, *Kerygmatic Spirit*, ch. 13.

6. I discuss these Isaianic chapters in light of the divine spirit's work in my *Mission After Pentecost*, 120–30.

as Jesus himself said: "Today this scripture has been fulfilled in your hearing" (Luke 4:21). Or, put otherwise, the gift of the Spirit to Jesus, and the subsequent outpouring on his disciples, is the fulfillment of the prophetic promise regarding the messianic anointing that bears witness to the nations. The messiah in the Gospel of Luke and the messiah's people in the book of Acts bear witness to the nations and to the ends of the earth by the power of the Spirit.

So, as Jesus heralds good news through the empowering of the Spirit, the disciples follow in his footsteps by the same Spirit. Yet, Jesus obeys the Spirit's promptings to witness to the reign of God not just generally to all the nations but also to specific groups of people and persons. More specifically, we not only see the reign of God announced, heralded, proclaimed, and manifest in the life of Jesus in his relationships that he has with the many others who he meets, but we also hear echoes of the gospel witnessed in their lives and voices.[7] If in Acts, the church's witness is to and with others, so also, I suggest, we shall see that in the Gospel of Luke. Who then does Jesus minister to and interact with?

"The Spirit of the Lord Is Upon Me . . . !" Messianic Witness to/with Others Then and Now

In the preceding chapter, we have heard some of the many voices in the book of Acts. How do we recognize these voices in Luke's Gospel? Just as Acts 1:8 mapped the first-century apostolic mission, in the rest of this chapter I want to use Luke 4:18 also as a window into the Gospel of Luke. This is not because the first three chapters of the book lack missiological content, but more because in this text, there is a kind of thematic map—not the chronological or sequential one provided by Acts 1:8—to help us anticipate the rest of the Jesus narrative. In particular, we will see how Jesus witnesses in his relationships to and interactions with others. What Jesus declared as fulfilling Scripture on the first day of his public ministry thus becomes the proper framework for our reading of the rest of the Gospel of Luke. What did the Spirit anoint Jesus to do? What message did the Spirit inspire? Who are the recipients of Jesus's witness and what witness do they bear in turn? What are the implications for our own witness today? We take each clause in order.

---

7. See Nadella, *Dialogue Not Dogma*, 49–64.

"To Bring Good News to the Poor" (4:18b): Witness with the Poor Then and Now

The Spirit of the Lord "has anointed me to bring good news to the poor" (4:18b). Who are *the poor*? Many of us might anticipate this is a very complicated category in the Gospel of Luke. But it is also very uncomplicated from another perspective: as a contrast with wealth. Readers familiar with the Third Gospel will recall there is a great deal of mention about wealth and poverty therein, more than in the other Gospel accounts.[8] From this perspective, there's a binary between poverty and wealth, the poor and the affluent. But such a binary account impedes recognition that both categories are much richer (pun intended) than when simply contrasted; there is a multi-dimensionality certainly to what *the poor* refers to.

The poor are surely, but not only, the economically or monetarily impoverished. There are whole person dimensions of poverty including material, physical, and spiritual aspects. Comparing and contrasting Jesus's beatitudes from Luke's Sermon on the Plain with Matthew's Sermon on the Mount provides one window into these matters. In the former, Jesus is recorded as saying, "Blessed are you who are poor, for yours is the kingdom of God. Blessed are you who are hungry now, for you will be filled" (Luke 6:20b–21); while in the latter, the First Gospel's version is thus: "Blessed are the poor in spirit, for theirs is the kingdom of heaven . . . . Blessed are those who hunger and thirst for righteousness, for they will be filled" (Matt 5:3, 6). We need resolve neither the issue of priority nor of sources to observe that Matthean beatitude leaves a lot more room to define poor in other than material ways. But the Lukan message, read alongside Matthew's, very clearly zeroes in on the poor in imminent historic and concrete socioeconomic dimensions. While this does not exclude the spiritual realm, as we'll see momentarily, the starting point is actually impoverished persons, those who are poor financially and materially.

In that respect, Luke invites us to embrace a preferential option for the poor in this fundamental sense. Even if we have heard this in liberation theology and may be suspicious of going in this direction,[9] I am inviting us to think about this in a Lukan way. Jesus here foregrounds the preaching of the gospel to the poor. This is surely an uncomfortable stance for

---

8. A sampling of the secondary scholarly literature includes Pilgrim, *Good News to the Poor*; Hensman, *Agenda for the Poor*; Phillips, *Reading Issues of Wealth*; Takatemjen, *Banquet Is Ready*; and Metzger, *Consumption and Wealth*.

9. E.g., Bahmann, *Preference for the Poor*.

those of us who may be more affluent in various respects. And there is certainly much to be uncomfortable about, not least in the sense that Luke himself portrays these as contrasting categories. There is a rich ruler who has to make certain kinds of choices (Luke 18:18–23), even as there are other characters in the Gospel of Luke with whom readers are invited to empathize and even embrace and be in solidarity with, like Lazarus who was "covered with sores, who longed to satisfy his hunger with what fell from the rich man's table; even the dogs would come and lick his sores" (16:21b–22), or the widow who labored against an unjust system (18:1–3). Jesus insisted that, following the scriptural vision, he had come to preach to the poor, to beggars like Lazarus, or struggling widows, and he told stories about them for our sakes.

In another context and as recorded by another evangelist, Jesus said out loud what we all recognize: "For you always have the poor with you" (Mark 14:7). That is our history, part of the human journey. If the promise of the gift of the Spirit is to our children and to our children's children, as we saw in Acts (2:39), then the Spirit-anointed messianic proclamation is for them especially if and when impoverished. Such Spirit-empowered witness extends over the long arc of history, even eschatologically. The latter horizon is clearly limned in the parable of the great dinner, told on one such occasion. Jesus's initial point was those with the capacity to be dinner hosts should "invite the poor, the crippled, the lame, and the blind," and even if these would be unable to repay or extend a similar bid, such would be rewarded eschatologically (Luke 14:13b–14). In response, one of the listeners said, "Blessed is anyone who will eat bread in the kingdom of God!" (14:15), perhaps seeking to be alleviated from such gracious acts (on this side of the eschaton).[10] Jesus's response was to speak of the Father's eschatological banquet summons, and this was in turn rejected by preoccupied persons and then made available to the same groups of "the poor, the crippled, the blind, and the lame" (14:21b). While noting that these categories of persons overlap with those described in Luke 4:18 (not to mention also repeated in 7:22), in this case, and at the great eschatological banquet, the invitation remains extended to the poor. It's almost as if there will never be a time, even eschatologically, when the poor will be no more. At the least, those present at the eschatological banquet will recognizably

---

10. For more on this passage, see Gosbell, *"Poor, the Crippled, the Blind, and the Lame,"* ch. 5.

contrast—phenomenologically, phenotypically, kinesthetically, and otherwise!—with the socially elite who may be used to being invited to or frequenting posh dinners.[11]

Those less wealthy may rejoice in this message of good news for the poor. Yet, even those in poverty may not like to be reminded that they are who Jesus addresses. And, surely, those with some means would be happier to ignore this aspect of the gospel message and focus on other parts perceived as less indicting. Alternatively, we might give a bit to the local rescue mission or to missionaries abroad in order to quell our guilt. Or we may simply rejoice that the center of gravity of Christianity has shifted from the wealthier north or Euro-American west to the developing global South where many have converted to Christ among the poor, even as we hope that this conversion will lead to socioeconomic uplift for them and their children. But is there a way for us to be more in solidarity with the poor than we are? This requires that we not only learn from stories about the poor but that we convert in light of their witnesses (about which more in part 2 of this book).

"Release to the Captives" (4:18c): Witness with the "Imprisoned" Then and Now

The Spirit of the Lord has anointed Jesus (and us) "to proclaim release to the captives." What kinds or forms of captivity are being referred to? The most obvious may be the incarcerated or, relatedly, prisoners of war, and while these may not be excluded (on which more in a moment), what kinds of confinement or constraint are observable in the rest of the Gospel of Luke? Let me suggest Lukan depictions of the demonized and mentally ill give us alternative perspectives on the kind of release Jesus might have had in mind.

One fairly non-debatable aspect of release from captivity evident throughout the Gospel account is what we might call deliverance from unclean spirits.[12] Jesus exorcises these evil spirits tormenting individuals

---

11. Elsewhere I have argued that eschatological human bodies will retain the marks of their impairments albeit in redeemed, but even there no less recognizable, form; see Yong, *Bible, Disability, and the Church*, ch. 5.

12. An earlier, and still reliable, account is provided by Garrett, *Demise of the Devil*; the literature on exorcisms in Luke and the Gospels is extensive, with Twelftree, *Jesus the Exorcist*, continuing to provide orientation.

throughout the Gospel. There is the man with an unclean spirit in Capernaum (4:31–37) and the convulsing young boy (9:37–43) even as on occasion it is suggested that there was widespread deliverance of those so captivated (6:18, 7:21). So, those who are spiritually in servitude in terms of being demonized are emancipated from their anguish.

There is another related category, that of the psychosomatically tormented, or to put in contemporary parlance, the mentally ill other. We know now that our modern diagnoses of mental illness overlap phenomenologically at least with what is preserved in ancient textual descriptions of what people were enduring.[13] Luke's version of the demonized man in the region of Gerasenes secluded by the Sea of Galilee (8:26–39) provides indicators of some of the mental disorders he was saddled with: multiple self-identification, being hounded by internal voices, social isolation, if not solitary confinement,[14] in part due to inability to interact appropriately with others or interface with social expectations, etc., so much so that after Jesus's exorcism, when "people came out to see what had happened . . . they found the man from whom the demons had gone sitting at the feet of Jesus, clothed and *in his right mind*" (8:35, my italics). Demonic affliction and mental dis-ease need not be mutually exclusive, even if we need to be extra cautious not to impose the former on those with symptoms of the latter in our own assessments and diagnoses.[15] The point here is that release of the captives that the Spirit-inspired messiah accomplishes applies also to those afflicted by mental conditions and spiritual circumstances.

Last but not least vis-à-vis what release from captivity might entail in Jesus's ministry is the woman "with a spirit that had crippled her for eighteen years" (13:11b). Luke reiterates that "she was bent over and was quite unable to stand up straight" (13:11c), thus elaborating on the form of subjugation that stretched across the entire (almost two decade) period of her malady. That her crippling was caused by the satan (*ho satanas*) is clear even as it was also evident that her almost two-decade-long "bondage" (also 13:16) had become internalized into a self-enclosed, including spiritual, mindset. Intriguingly, Jesus addresses the latter set of manifestations—"Woman, you are set free from your ailment" (13:12b)—and this results

---

13. See Girgis, *On Satan, Demons, and Psychiatry*, ch. 8, for one such reading of Luke 8:26–39.

14. E.g., Menéndez-Antuña, "Of Social Death and Solitary Confinement."

15. E.g., a psychoanalytical reading of the parallel pericope in Mark 5:1–20 as the Gerasene's journey toward restoration of personal dignity; see Leslie, *Jesus and Logotherapy*, ch. 10.

also in an exorcism (rather than expelling the satan in order to make the woman whole).

The most obvious understanding of captivity would be those in forced confinement. I will return later in this chapter to discuss those enslaved, but here briefly address the imprisoned. To be sure, there are important differences between those rightly versus wrongly incarcerated, although even the former group need both rehabilitation and reconciliation as part of their process of obtaining parole. Whereas there is scant mention of those in custody in the Gospel of Luke, there are multiple such references in the book of Acts, almost always referring to the unjust detention of the apostles, whether it is Peter and John for curing the lame man (Acts 4:1–3), Peter at the hands of King Herod (12:1–4), Paul and Silas in Philippi (16:22–24), or Paul held by various authorities, including under house confinement (in the last quarter of the Acts narrative). The last instance is the only one that does not involve a release, although Luke is explicit in stating that while Paul remained under custody, he was free to do what he had been called to do: "proclaiming the kingdom of God and teaching about the Lord Jesus Christ with all boldness and *without hindrance*" (28:31, my italics).[16]

The captives in these accounts are all beset by various constraints. The majority discussed in Luke were of the spiritual sort, yet even those distresses included both mental and physical expressions so that spiritual internment is often accompanied by psychosomatic ailments and vice-versa. The point is not to demonize mental illness or those suffering from chronic and crippling conditions but to appreciate Jesus's ministry of release from captivity. Similarly, we might dismiss the incarcerated as deserving of their arrest and confinement. Yet, in other places, Jesus says that he is to be found with prisoners (Matt 25:31–46). The messianic ministry Not only involves release of the captives but also invites us to consider being in solidarity with them. How might we participate in Jesus's ministry and mission of releasing captives otherwise than by familiarizing ourselves and even being in solidarity with their captivity?

---

16. Paul is, even when "in chains," always a missionary and evangelist. See the most extended study of Paul the prisoner to date, Rapske's *Books of Acts in Its First Century Setting*, 432–34. For a more succinct discussion of Paul the chained evangelist, see the appendix to Cassidy, *Paul in Chains*, 211–34: "Paul as a Chained Prisoner in Acts."

"Recovery of Sight to the Blind" (4:18d): Witness with the Impaired Other Then and Now

The Spirit of the Lord has anointed Jesus and us to bring recovery of sight to the blind. I believe this category of the blind can be expanded in a variety of ways to impairments more generally. How does Luke detail this recovery of sight for the blind, and how might this illuminate understandings regarding sickness, chronic debilitation (a glimpse of which we have already observed in the bent over woman), and impairment and disability?

On the one hand, if good news for the poor is to be taken at least literally, then recovery of sight to the blind should mean restoration or reversal (for the first time) of visual impairment. This is seen in Luke's account of the opening of the eyes of the beggar on the road to Jericho (18:35–43). Earlier, in response to John the Baptist's question about whether Jesus was indeed the messiah, the response given provides some of the rationale for understanding the blind as representative of the broader group of persons who are at least physically impaired, whether with regard to mobility or sensorily in terms of hearing: "Go and tell John what you have seen and heard: the blind receive their sight, the lame walk, the lepers are cleansed, the deaf hear, the dead are raised, the poor have good news brought to them" (7:22). Above, we also saw that the blind are set alongside the crippled and the lame (14:14, 21). The latter category of persons would have included the paralytic who Jesus not only cured but also declared to be forgiven of his sins (5:17–26) and the man with the withered right hand that was restored (6:6–11). So literally, eyes are being opened, but other impairing conditions are also being addressed and cured.

Blindness and other kinds of disabling impairments are extended conditions, and thus overlap with illnesses, diseases, and other chronic illnesses that are similarly impeding. An example of the latter is the woman who had been hemorrhaging for a dozen years (8:43–48), while the former would have included the ill servant or slave of the centurion at Capernaum (7:1–10). Early on in Jesus's public ministry, when he visited Simon's home and rebuked the high fever of his mother-in-law (4:38–39), Luke follows up this report with a broader brush summary: "As the sun was setting, all those who had any who were sick with various kinds of diseases brought them to him; and he laid his hands on each of them and cured them" (4:40). Later, in commissioning his disciples to emulate his ministry, Jesus instructs: "Whenever you enter a town and its people welcome you, eat what is set before you; cure the sick who are there, and say to them, 'The kingdom of God has come near to you'" (10:8–9). Whether it is physical/sensory impairments, bodily sickness, or psychosomatic illnesses or disorders, the messianic anointing includes alleviation of the symptoms, ailments, and even disabling conditions,[17] not only for those so afflicted but also for those who desire to bear witness in and to his name.

To be sure, impairing conditions are ameliorated, although not always by cures. Zacchaeus, of short stature, was accepted by Jesus without getting any taller. As we will have occasion to engage with the Zacchaeus's story variously in what follows, suffice to say for the moment that Jesus touches and transforms his life by going to his house, not curing his shortness of stature.[18] The social model of disability and impairment today invites us to consider how addressing societal prejudices, which are often internalized by people with disabilities, and ensuring availability of and access to accommodations goes a long way to integrating people with impairments into society in ways that enable flourishing. The wholeness experienced here may be even more important than bodily cures, indicating that the opening of blind eyes involves alleviating visual impairment and also enabling the thriving of visually impaired people through friendship, koinonia, and mutuality of missional service in the world.[19]

To be sure, we have to be very careful with imposing our own contemporary understandings simplistically on first-century accounts, yet any attempt to live faithfully into Jesus's mission and witness today invites us to do the hard work of rereading these familiar texts in light of our own experiences. The messianic anointing to open the eyes of the blind and to touch bodies that are disabled, impaired, ill, or disordered in any way remains centrally important even in the twenty-first century. The reality is both that people continue to come to faith in Christ because of some experience of healing or curing, whether themselves or a loved one, family member, or close friend, and that even for those in late modern societies, access to healthcare remains a high priority. To be sure, access to health care remains a very complicated, if not highly politicized, matter. Yet the fact that there are historical, economic, social, gendered, and other factors behind why some groups of folks have greater access to health care and

---

17. See Fox, *Disability and the Way of Jesus*.

18. See Parsons, *Body and Character*, ch. 5.

19. See also my *Bible, Disability and the Church*, ch. 3, for more on the curing-healing distinction in the Gospels.

others less so does not minimize its urgency. Instead, this highlights just how missiologically charged messianic witness was in its time, and therefore is also still today.[20] Luke's narrative opens the door to reconsidering the historic conditions, systemic politics, and structural socioeconomic realities that create the conditions of suffering into which the gospel is both heralded and embodied. Solidarity with "the blind," and all this represents as we have briefly unpacked above, is a prerequisite to grasping their needs and enabling effective witness in our late modern world.

"To Let the Oppressed Go Free" (4:18e): Witness with Marginalized Others Then and Now

Penultimately in terms of Jesus's mission, the messianic anointing liberates those who are oppressed. Whereas the preceding deliverance is from those in captivity (whether because of imprisonment or under the grip of evil spirits), here the reference is those broken, bruised, shattered, and crushed by life's circumstances, so it is implied. Our contemporary understandings of being socioeconomically marginalized connect to some of what Jesus is referring to here.

Take, for instance, the widow of Nain that Jesus and his followers encounter on the outskirts of that small town. Various notations in Luke's description alert us to the ever-deepening oppression and devaluation of this woman's experience: the fact that her husband has passed leaving her widowed; now she was being left economically bereft, with the death of her only son, who would have taken care of his mother otherwise; and thereby also without political representation, which we are reminded about since the encounter between Jesus and the woman takes place at "the gate of the town" where the elders (in this patriarchal society) would have met regularly to make decisions impacting the fate of the town's inhabitants (7:12a). Here is a woman literally whose only socioeconomic safety net was being buried. The good news in this case is not only the resuscitation of life afforded the young man but renewed hope for his mother. Luke explicitly adds that when the young man commenced speaking, exercising his voice and bearing witness to the power of the messianic Spirit, "Jesus gave him to his mother" (7:15b).[21] The thoroughly discounted existence at which the

---

20. E.g., Cattermole, "Global Health."

21. Hearkening to how after raising the son of the widow of Zarephath from the dead, Elijah "gave him to his mother" (1 Kgs 17:23); see Price, *Widow Traditions*, 85–91.

widow was staring evaporates as her son is raised from the dead, thereby enacting her own rescue and deliverance.

We have already noted, above, Jesus's calling attention to lepers being cleansed (7:22), which did follow one instance of his cleansing such a person (5:12–15). Here is another group of persons beleaguered by conventions designed to protect communities from what was believed to be contagious and infectious. Later in the same Gospel, Jesus encounters ten lepers, multiply marginalized, first and foremost because of their condition, but second, in a liminal village space between Jerusalem and Galilee on one side and Samaria on the other (17:11), so that they would have been, effectively, unwelcomed in either and hence, even when they approached Jesus, are explicitly said to have maintained their distance (17:12b). While leprosy as a diseased condition could have been included above in our discussion of bodily impairments and sicknesses, the resulting social conventions added an additional layer of ostracism on these lives.

Similarly, the story of Zacchaeus might also have fit in the preceding discussion particularly if we foregrounded the physiognomic dwarfism implicated by his being "short in stature" (19:3b).[22] Yet, there are further complicating factors including his being a tax collector, and thus working on behalf of the oppressors of the Jews rather than serving his own community, even if such a profession might have been all he could have attained given the stigmatization he suffered because of his shortness. If there is one set of parallels, that of ostracization because of bodily forms and shapes, that binds Zacchaeus to the lepers in the Jesus story, another set of parallels, that of discrimination related to socioreligious taboos, binds them both together with the woman "who was a sinner" who "brought an alabaster jar of ointment" to wash the feet of Jesus with her hair (7:37–38). In the last case, Jesus allows his feet to be washed by the woman; with at least the first leper he encounters, Jesus touches the infected one (5:13a); in regard to Zacchaeus, Jesus agrees to be a guest in his home (19:5–7).

Note also, though, how Jesus liberates the oppressed in these circumstances. The lepers have their diseases cured and are instructed to get priestly certificates of health to allow for communal reintegration. While Zacchaeus's witness to and promise of fourfold restitution for any fraudulent collection should not be minimized (more on this in the next chapter), unlike others with impaired bodily conditions his shortness is not adjusted; instead, like with the woman with the alabaster jar, Jesus proclaiming that

---

22. Or "vertically challenged"; Green, "Cognitive Narratological Approach," 109.

"today salvation has come to this house, because he too is a son of Abraham" (19:9) has force precisely because Jesus had already entered the home of a sinner, intentionally breaking social convention against the heard complaints of those observing his behavior (19:7). With regard to the woman with the jar of ointment, Jesus welcomes her presence and embraces her touch as gestures of *agapeic* love; and while he declares in the process that her sins are forgiven, he suggests that she realized this was so even before his pronouncement, which motivated her actions: "'Therefore, I tell you, her sins, which were many, have been forgiven; hence she has shown great love. But the one to whom little is forgiven, loves little.' Then he said to her, 'Your sins are forgiven'" (7:47–48).[23]

Later in this book we will return to the woman's and Zacchaeus's conversions to interrogate further different aspects of these narratives, in particular what they imply for our own affective and moral transformation, respectively. For the moment, however, I want to focus more on the "you" Jesus addresses in the presence of the woman with the alabaster ointment, which is not she but Simon the Pharisee, the host of the dinner at which table Jesus was reclining. Right before saying those words, Jesus effectively unmasked the Pharisee's self-righteousness, saying to him: "I entered your house; you gave me no water for my feet, but she has bathed my feet with her tears and dried them with her hair. You gave me no kiss, but from the time I came in she has not stopped kissing my feet. You did not anoint my head with oil, but she has anointed my feet with ointment" (7:44b–46). Yes, the woman's remorse was evident in the way she approached Jesus, but now her actions were bearing witness to the gospel, in stark contrast to the Pharisee's smug sanctimoniousness. More to the point, if the sinner woman felt she could take the risk of approaching Jesus given what she had observed about the way he had welcomed others like her, it was an even larger gamble to do so in the house of a Pharisee. Without taking away anything from her prior sinful choices and way of life, we also do not know the circumstances that led her down that path. We do know, however, that it was precisely attitudes like Simon's, and his colleagues, that excluded and rejected the woman with the jar because of what she was known for! Jesus's point to Simon, derived from this woman's active witness, is that he also, as a deeply religious person and also religious leader, needed to come to a new perspective. Jesus therefore explicitly directs Simon, "Do you see

---

23. See Christiansen, "Sinner According to Words of the Law."

this woman?" (7:44a).[24] More pointedly: Consider the woman's embodied testimony and consider adopting her point of view and acting like her![25] Simon is as much, if not more, in need of change and transformation as the woman witnessed to.

The reality of the oppressed persists because there are oppressors, conscious or not. The former know, feel, and are on the receiving end of the gaze of the latter, with the full weight of societal assumptions and expectations communicated in those stares and whispers. That leery eyeing itself is in as much need of redemption as those who are under its view. Release from oppression requires addressing the gaze, as Jesus did in addressing Simon. Zacchaeus, on the one hand an oppressive tax collector, also, on the other hand is oppressed in part because of how he acted but also in part because his stature drew society's ogle: "So he ran ahead and climbed a sycamore tree" (19:4a) provides a viewpoint consistent with those of gawkers and gapers watching him go.[26] Freeing the oppressed, thus, includes a societal dimension, one that addresses, undermines, and overturns society's biases, prejudices, and chauvinism.

No wonder the evangel resonates with those who find themselves on the underside of history. And for any one of us, being unrecognized or ignored can be experienced across multiple dimensions, registers, or tiers and levels. As a Chinese Malaysian immigrant to the US, I've had to come to awareness of my own internalized understanding of being a perpetual foreigner in North American society, never being white enough to belong, so to speak.[27] I have had to grapple with my own efforts to assimilate into the dominant culture's expectations, to live in certain ways in order to be received, approved, and recognized, and then I have perpetuated these expectations on other Asian Americans, including my children, who, because I'm married to a Mexican American woman, are now multiply marginalized and have multiracial and multiethnic perspectives to teach me about my interiorization of white normativism.[28] Jesus came to release those

---

24. See also Reid, "Do You See This Woman?"

25. Within the broader context of Luke's narrative (7:18–35), the woman was like those who received John's witness, and through John, Jesus's message, in contrast to Simon; see Gowler, *Host, Guest, Enemy*, 220.

26. Which I unpack in Yong, "Zacchaeus: Short and Un-Seen"; see also my *Kerygmatic Spirit*, ch. 5.

27. Which I discuss in the concluding chapter to a book I co-edited: "Mission After Colonialism and Whiteness."

28. See the published dissertation of my son, Aizaiah G. Yong, *Multiracial*

disregarded for their non-conformity to dominant cultural norms then, and invites us to participate in this deliverance for all today, including the majority cultures that are the status quo.

"To Proclaim the Year of the Lord's Favor" (4:19): The Witness of Jubilee Then and Now

Finally, the messianic Spirit anoints Jesus's and our proclamation of the year of the Lord's favor. That day, Jesus insisted, this message was being fulfilled, and the year Jubilee was being actualized.[29] The reference is to the year of sabbatical renewal and communal restoration described in the book of the Law, the Torah, which not only provides for a sabbath for the land every seventh year but also returns land to their prior owners every fiftieth year (Lev 25).[30] The land is regularly renewed even as family debt is canceled and debtors get a fresh start each generation. We know, of course, that the Jubilee provisions were never enacted throughout Israel's history, and that the Babylonian exile was imposed for as long as it was, seventy years, in relationship to the number of Jubilees that had not been observed (see 2 Chr 36:20–21; cf. Jer 25:11, 29:10).[31] Thus, the Isaianic prophecy anticipated that the messianic arrival would also accomplish this Jubilee year and promise, which Jesus retrieves as part of his own understanding of what he has been charged to herald and bring about.[32]

The bringing forward the year of Jubilee means that the forgiveness of sins and of debts are interrelated in the Spirit-propelled messianic reign.[33] In instructing the disciples about how to pray, for instance, Jesus invited invoking: "forgive us our sins, for we ourselves forgive everyone indebted to us" (Luke 11:4). In addressing Simon before the woman with the jar, Jesus began by referring to "two debtors; one owed five hundred denarii, and the other fifty. When they could not pay, he canceled the debts for both of them. Now which of them will love him more?" (7:41–42). The woman loved Jesus more than Simon as she knew she was much greater indebted and forgiven. Forgiveness in Luke thereby operates at least at two levels:

Cosmotheandrism.

29. See Ringe, *Jesus, Liberation, and the Biblical Jubilee.*
30. Soggin, *Israel in the Biblical Period*, ch. 15.
31. See Jonker, "Exile as Sabbath Rest."
32. Gurtner, "Luke's Isaianic Jubilee," 123–46.
33. See Tan, *Jubilee Gospel.*

that of the transgressions we all have committed against one another and before God, and that of the indebtedness pertinent to the poor, the loans extended by creditors, the rich, to needy people that are further impoverishing. Not unexpectedly, then, the outpouring of the messianic Spirit on the disciples at Pentecost enacted at least initial steps toward fulfillment of the Jubilee principle, not directly related to the land but directly connected to the needs of the poor and indebted: "All who believed were together and had all things in common; they would sell their possessions and goods and distribute the proceeds to all, as any had need" (Acts 2:44–45). The apostolic community recognized the implications of Jesus's messianic ministry, whereby the year of the Lord's favor linked interpersonal health with social reconciliation and community flourishing.[34]

But the communism of the apostolic group did not last long, in part because, as we saw, factions arose arguing about rights and portions. As we human beings in history accumulate things, material and otherwise, including social capital and political power, forgiving debts and sharing with others less fortunate than us is more and more difficult. If it is challenging to erase seven years' worth of indebtedness, it is impossible to do so after a half century! In today's terms: I have paid off my student loans, so why should I allow someone else's student loans to be written off? Or, neither I, nor my parents, nor my grandparents owned slaves, so neither are we racists nor should the descendants of slaves today be recompensed for what happened to their ancestors from four or more generations ago! The year of Jubilee provisions are no less palatable today than they were for the Israelites of old and during the first century. This presses though the prior point: that the forgiveness of our sins is itself impossible, except via the messianic spirit. If we have domesticated our understanding of forgiving sins, perhaps we can once again appreciate its radicality when we reconsider the relationship between our sins and our debts.

The evangel turns the world upside down—as was said of the apostolic message and way of life (Acts 17:6)—because it upends the calculus of where you and I have hurt one another, have sinned against one another, and have incurred obligations to each other that cannot be easily repaid. The evangel overturns our socioeconomic conventions and agreements—of debtors and creditors for instance—in a similar way. It invites us to reimagine our socioeconomic relationship after every seven years. Luke, as we know, talked about the gospel of reversal, where the first shall be

---

34. See my essay, "Jubilee, Liberation, and Pentecost."

last and the last first.[35] What kind of world is this? It is appropriate here to retrieve also Mary's Magnificat from the infancy portion of the Gospel, the voice of a lowly servant girl, part of which anticipates the world turned right-side-up:

> the Mighty One has done great things for me, and holy is his name. His mercy is for those who fear him from generation to generation. He has shown strength with his arm; he has scattered the proud in the thoughts of their hearts. He has brought down the powerful from their thrones, and lifted up the lowly; he has filled the hungry with good things, and sent the rich away empty. (Luke 1:49b–53)

The lowly, the sidelined, the outcast, those lacking access to resources: the Lord has heard their cries and sent his Spirit to raise up and anoint liberators to meet them where they are at and bring about righteousness and deliverance from their oppressors. The powerful and the rich have always had options, until the messianic outpouring; now, the lowly and hungry are neither impotent nor lacking. Do we just rejoice with Mary and others on the underside of history like her? Or, if we are among those with more capital, resources, and access, are we anxious if the world is a zero-sum game so that the uplift of the underclass negatively impacts those of us privileged to be closer to the imperial or socioeconomic center?

Messianic Witness and Apostolic Mission Then and Now: Opportunities and Challenges

The gospel is a challenge for discipleship especially for us first world inhabitants who have been neither invited to consider the forgiveness of debts every seven years nor confronted with returning to the dispossessed land that ancestors had somehow, however legally, obtained. Many readers of this book live in our suburban bubbles, unconfronted with the busyness of what happens in our major metropolises, where those from many nations, cultures, ethnicities, races, and languages speak in bewildering terms about things that we have never experienced and can only dimly, if at all, comprehend. If we think we are going to bear effective witness to the ends of the earth, much less beyond the enclave where we are sequestered, we need to come back out into our streets, and be exposed to the many tongues the

---

35. See York, *Last Shall Be First*, ch. 11.

Spirit speaks through the many voices. And exposure to the many tongues invites attending to them, being instructed by them, experiencing transformation through their witnesses.

Readers might protest that any contemporary missiology should be *fully* biblical, meaning that even if the consideration of Luke provided so far were to be accepted, there are other Gospels, not to mention a broader New Testament witness, that should inform our theology of mission. While not disagreeing with this broader point, which was exactly part of the purpose behind some of my earlier work,[36] such an argument cannot license either a minimization nor dismissal of the Lukan missiological witness. More to the point, Luke's Gospel (and the book of Acts) also provide important perspectives on the rest of Scripture, including about what it means to participate in the good news of God in Jesus Christ. From this perspective, then, can we also reimagine what evangelism looks like, including what it might be for those on the receiving end of our evangelistic efforts? How else might the preceding christological and messianic considerations inform our own articulation of an apostolic theology of evangelism? Here are a few summary points in anticipation of the second part of this work.

First, the outpouring of the Holy Spirit on Jesus and the disciples invites us to embark upon a multidimensional and holistic witness that sees, hears, and works with racial, ethnic, gendered, political, religious, cultural, and linguistic others of our world.[37] Second, witnessing to and evangelizing others invites our abiding, even living, with others; this involves not just a deeper humility that embraces such invitations but the risk of hybridity, or embarking on a journey of transformation together.[38] Third, the lines between "us" and "other" will be blurred, if not overcome, whether it's church planning, evangelism, NGOs, development organizations, or any other mission/witness initiative; the alterity of others will become ours in our own way, and our commitments will become that of others in their own way, so that we will be different together. Last but not least then, evangelism in apostolic perspective invites our ongoing repentance, our ongoing reception of the Spirit that's promised to us and our children and our children's children, our ongoing transformation and our ongoing conversion to and with others. Conversion, apostolically speaking, begins with evangelists,

---

36. E.g., my *Mission After Pentecost*, and *Missiological Spirit*, both provide biblical and theological considerations.

37. See Kgatle, "Missiology as Social Justice."

38. Note Barreto, "Crafting Colonial Identities."

which is us called by the power of the Spirit to bear transformed witness to the living messiah. The next part of this volume presses into greater detail regarding such a reimagined theology of evangelism and conversion.

PART II

Apostolic Evangelism and Conversion in the 2020s
Multi-Transformational Witness Then and Now

Chapter 3

Intellectual Conversion
Apostolic Testimonies Then and Now

THIS PART OF THE book focuses on evangelism and conversion. In traditional missiology, these two notions are fairly straightforwardly understood: believers evangelize and the evangelized convert under the powerful sway of the gospel. Put otherwise, evangelism leads to conversion: disciples of Jesus, missionaries, and evangelists address unbelievers, those who have never heard the gospel, or those not yet committed to Jesus, and expect the Holy Spirit to turn the latter around, enable their repentance and movement in the opposite direction from where they were previously headed.[1]

As we have seen so far in part 1 above, however, the lines between evangelists and those being evangelized are not as easily demarcated, and there is as much need for the former to be converted in relationship to and even by the latter as the other way around. This chapter's first part explores the relationship between evangelism and conversion in greater depth, explicating in what follows multiple domains of the latter: intellectual, effective, moral, and sociopolitical. Part 2 focuses on the dimension of conversion we are probably most familiar with, the intellectual, and does so following especially our hermeneutical approach, which means focusing on the apostolic record. The chapter concludes by returning to contemporary missional praxis: What are the implications of apostolic intellectual conversion for Christian witness in the present time?

---

1. E.g., Wells, *God the Evangelist*.

Our hopes here and in the rest of this book are to engage those who wish to respond to God's call to engage in missiological witness and evangelism, and who desire that the hearts of others will be in that process turned to the divine. How then to "do the work of the evangelist," as Timothy was instructed (2 Tim 4:5)? How then to be conduits of the conversion that we believe God wishes to accomplish through our evangelistic activities? Adequately considering these questions requires that we take a look at the nature of conversion and then ask also how that informs the work of evangelists, including the activity of evangelism. Given our theological motivation, our exploration will involve the normative dimension of how we ought to consider conversion, including intellectual conversion in this chapter, and then how conversion is to be experienced, not only by others but, most importantly, by us. Given these normative obligations, as Protestants we rely first and foremost on scriptural excavation, and in light of our Pentecostal-Charismatic inclinations, with priority given to the apostolic narrative. Thus, Luke-Acts serves as our canonical center. How do the narratives of Jesus's life and teaching and the apostolic embodiment of such illuminate these various aspects of conversion in order to better transform our evangelistic, missional, and witnessing commitments today?

Evangelism and Conversion: Getting Our Bearings

We begin by looking more closely at evangelism in relationship to conversion. The latter will then be explored not only phenomenologically but also theologically, including explication of its multiple dimensions. This section then transitions by opening up the nature of intellectual conversion.

Evangelism Then and Now

Contemporary Christian understandings of evangelism are probably most informed by widely renowned exemplars like Billy Graham. Protestants of all sorts, including of the evangelical, Pentecostal, or Charismatic sort, probably have familiarity with revivals, crusades, street preachers, door-to-door witnessing initiatives, and perhaps have deployed evangelistic tracts in their efforts. Contemporary theologies of evangelism are increasingly holistic, viewing proclamation as intertwined with engaging social concerns, thus comprehending church planting and development are mutually reinforcing.[2]

William Abraham is a Wesleyan theologian who has written a classic text on a theology of evangelism that emphasizes the roles of proclamation, of the process of Christian initiation, and of the Catechism in shaping evangelism and evangelists.[3] The *telos* or purpose of evangelism is the forming of disciples oriented toward the coming divine reign. Priscilla Pope-Levison has more recently explicated on models of evangelism.[4] There's personal evangelism, small group evangelism, visitation evangelism, liturgical evangelism (how we might structure our worship times as spaces of outreach to the community), church planting evangelism, church growth evangelism, prophetic social or integral evangelism, revivalist evangelism, and new media evangelism.[5] Many of us, even those who may not consider ourselves evangelists per se, have engaged in one or more of these forms of sharing our faith.

The question I want to invite us to reimagine again is what might the apostles have to say about mission and, more concretely, evangelism? How does the New Testament depict apostolic evangelism? More narrowly, how would Jesus evangelize, is a related question we might ask?

Luke-Acts provides some orientation, including the appearances of two key verbs and their cognates: *kerusso* (to preach or proclaim) and *euangelizo* (to evangelize or to announce the good news). The former appears sixteen times divided equally across these two books, while the latter appears with similar frequency in the first volume but thrice more in the second Lukan book. *Euangelizo*, includes its object, good news, so that the activity of evangelization is always of the gospel. In all cases this is assumed, although occasionally it is added, that the apostolic evangelists went about "proclaiming the word" (Acts 8:4), or that they "proclaimed the word of God" (13:5; cf. 15:35-36 and 17:13). With regard to *kerusso*, there are different subjects and objects including John the Baptist proclaiming "repentance for the forgiveness of sins" (Luke 3:3; cf. Acts 13:38), the man who had been delivered from evil spirits exclaiming "how much Jesus had done

---

2. E.g., Coalter and Cruz, *How Shall We Witness?*; Bonk et al., *Speaking About What We Have Seen and Heard*; Dowsett et al., *Evangelism and Diakonia*; and Knight, *Evangelism Renewed*.

3. See Abraham, *Logic of Evangelism*; see also Abraham, *Art of Evangelism*.

4. Pope-Levison, *Models of Evangelism*.

5. Women have led the way in developing more holistic approaches to evangelistic practice, including but not limited to Warner, *Saving Women*.

for him" (Luke 8:39), the disciples heralding the divine reign and healing (9:2; cf. Acts 20:25, 28:31), Philip preaching the messiah to the Samaritans (Acts 8:5), Saul lifting up Jesus in the synagogues (9:20), and even the Jews proclaiming Moses (15:21). There seem to be no limits on what messages can be pronounced or who can preach.[6]

This last point deserves further comment for our purposes: there are various evangelistic agents in Luke-Acts. It has already been noted that even the Jews are evangelists, of Moses's law, it is clear (Acts 15:21). Besides the preaching of the key protagonists in the second volume—both Peter and Paul—and the famous prophesying daughters (21:9) of Philip the evangelist (8:5), the good news or gospel is declared by angels (Luke 2:10, or Gabriel in 1:19), John the Baptist (3:3, 18; cf. Acts 13:24), "some men of Cyprus and Cyrene" at Antioch (Acts 11:20), Barnabas (13:5, 32, 38; 14:7, 15, 21), and even Luke himself (among whoever else may have been Paul's traveling companions: 16:10). Luke also tells about "a slave-girl who had a spirit of divination and brought her owners a great deal of money by fortune-telling. While she followed Paul and us, she would cry out, 'These men are slaves of the Most High God, who proclaim to you a way of salvation'" (16:16–17). This spiritually oppressed girl evangelizes by calling attention to the apostolic evangelists. None of this should be surprising given the outpouring of the Spirit on all flesh (2:17), including male and female servants (2:18).

Does Luke record also who are converted in these accounts? Priests like Zechariah and shepherds "keeping watch over their flock by night" (Luke 2:8b) for starters, and among the entirety of the people of Israel whom John the Baptist confronted (Acts 13:24), at least tax collectors and soldiers responded (3:12, 14). Conversions in response to the apostolic message included Samaritans like Simon Magus, to be sure, some Greeks (Acts 11:20–21), Gentiles in Antioch Pisidia "destined for eternal life" (13:48), and a large number of residents of Derbe (14:20b–21). Stepping back out to the broader canvas of Luke-Acts, Fernando Méndes-Moratalla has identified a conversion loop, usually traceable to or set in motion by conflicted experiences.[7] Such dissonance leads to a kind of awakening and then involves a repentance from sin, including the receiving and giving of forgiveness, that opens up into a new relationship or fellowship with others.

---

6. This and the next paragraph have been adapted from my article, "Apostolic Evangelism," esp. 154–55.

7. Méndes-Moratalla, *Paradigm of Conversion in Luke*.

There is usually a climatic pronouncement of this turning, a new orientation to Jesus. Yet it is not only a reconciliation to and with God but also in relationship to fellow humans, especially in the new people of God, the church. Joel Green puts it this way: "for the narrator of Luke-Acts conversion is the transference of one's orienting allegiances which (1) gives rise to and is confirmed in practices appropriate to those new allegiances, (2) opens the way to ongoing, sometimes profound transformations in one's theological and moral imagination, and (3) necessarily locates and immerses one in the multi-ethnic community of God's people."[8]

Conversion Then and Now

I want to briefly review what else the New Testament says about conversion. One study of the conversion of the New Testament more recently has lifted up seven major themes beginning with God's graciousness: conversion is divinely initiated and in that sense is related to God's mysteriously prevenient work.[9] Then, unsurprisingly, conversion is centered in Jesus Christ, orienting us toward the coming divine reign he proclaimed. Third, conversion involves a behavioral response, some kind of turning from the sin, darkness, and death that once predominated, and ushering us into the presence of grace, light, and life. Such life turning inevitably leads, fourth, to a relational newness with others, and this in turn results in new understandings of ourselves. Fifth: This new relationality inevitably includes a full person transformation. Extending from there, sixth, families might be involved in such transformational wholeness, not least in the church, the body of Christ, that reconfigures all initiated members, afresh through baptism and the Lord's supper or Eucharist. And finally, as a result of all that, conversion also prompts fresh witness from those who are converted. A converted life is thus one that unfolds gradually and bears continually deepened witness to that ongoing transformation.

Over the last two millennia, then, we have observed a number of historic paradigms for the understanding and practice of Christian conversion.[10] In the post-apostolic period, the early church fathers established a catechumenate wherein those new to the faith would oftentimes embark on a multi-year process of instruction culminating in sacramental entrance

8. Green, "To Turn from Darkness into Light," 104.
9. Witherup, *Conversion in the New Testament*.
10. Kling, *History of Christian Conversion*.

into the sacramental life of the church with renunciation of the devil and then baptism and Eucharist, thereby signaling attainment of full participation as members in the body of Christ. Christian conversion in this patristic period was thus a dynamic process that stretched out over time. Beginning during this same period but then extending into the medieval centuries, monastic communities developed conversion and initiation catechisms attending also to matters related to sanctification, lifelong discipleship, and formation in the apostolic way.[11] Conversion was an ongoing process of orientation to the divine, not only but most clearly enunciated in Eastern traditions as culminating in *theosis*, becoming "participants of the divine nature" (2 Pet 1:4b). Right, being made into the image and likeness of God in Christ by the Spirit.

During the Reformation, the emphasis was placed on conversion being received by grace through faith with the minimization of works. Roman Catholic reactions were carried by their missionaries, extending the patristic and monastic models of evangelism in ways that invited indigenous peoples across Latin America, Africa, and Asia into a process of cultural formation as part of full conversion to Christ.[12] The great revivals more recently in the last few centuries across the Anglo-American world exchanged the behavioristic rituals of converted agents for affective expressions of converted souls.[13] The penitential experience forged by revivalist fervor and enthusiastic encounter with God has shaped our understanding of conversion most deeply making essential remorseful repentance followed by the fruits of such: a way of life reflecting the assumptions of former sinners now saved by grace. This more evangelical tradition was deepened by Pentecostal revivalism, only now divine graciousness is experienced as Spirited encounter with the living Christ as our savior, healer, Spirit-baptizer, sanctifier, and coming king. With almost every paradigm, there is at least one, often multiple moments (stages for some[14]), of powerful spiritual experience in which deeper levels of conversion and transformation happen.

11. See also Smith, *Transforming Conversion*, chs. 3–4.

12. Modern colonial missions, Catholic and Protestant, evangelical and Pentecostal, have all been tinged, if not singed, by cultural pride that assumes conversion to Christ ought to follow the forms and expressions of the culture of the evangelizing missionaries, usually European and white North American; an early description of this assumption is in Hartt, *Toward a Theology of Evangelism*, ch. 8.

13. See Hindmarsh, *Evangelical Conversion Narrative*.

14. Milton, *Shalom, the Spirit and Pentecostal Conversion*, ch. 4.

INTELLECTUAL CONVERSION

Models and Domains of Conversion

More recent analyses of conversion have produced some major theoretical models. Walter Conn's work, although over three decades ago now, has become a classic in the literature on conversion, which in general terms he unfolds as including moral, cognitive, and affective dimensions.[15] Here was a Protestant theologian who developed a tri-dimensional understanding of conversion, albeit then also extending moral conversion in the direction of Christian conversion specifically. Preceding him were Roman Catholics like Karl Rahner and Bernard Lonergan whose works inspired what we might call a new-Thomist paradigm, including much of what developed during the Second Vatican Council. I myself have been most informed by a charismatic Jesuit theologian, the late Donald Gelpi (1934–2011), who updated the new-Thomist thinking about conversion for the twenty-first century.[16]

Gelpi presents us five normative domains of conversion, each being a distinctly identifiable realm of human experience: intellectual, affective, moral, sociopolitical, and religious.[17] Each one of these converts or each one of these domains are dynamically interrelated, rather fluid, and mutually informative. At any moment of our lives, or at different periods of our sojourn, conversion in one or other domain may come to the fore while others recede to the back. Often, conversion is facilitated across two or more dimensions collaboratively. Given the nature of how we might continue to be transformed across these various axes, conversion is never, on this side of the eschaton, finally finished.

Most importantly, for Gelpi, conversion in any of these domains involves adjustments we make from prior (what we might call) conventional or previously established frames of reference toward new frames of reference that inspire us to take responsibility in new ways. Taking responsibility includes being accountable for and accountable to. Take religious conversion, for instance, which involves reorienting ourselves ultimately (as Christians by and to Jesus), so that prior to such, we exist as driven by penultimate concerns. Upon being converted by Jesus religiously (not just

---

15. Conn, *Christian Conversion*, esp. ch. 4.

16. My initial foray into Gelpi's *oeuvre* is detailed in my article, "In Search of Foundations."

17. Gelpi, *Conversion Experience*, esp. "Exercise 2," with RCIA standing for the Catholic Church's Rite of Christian Initiation for Adults process; also, Gelpi, *Charism and Sacrament*, is less phenomenological and more singularly theological.

intellectually, etc.) or converting to Jesus religiously, in light of who Jesus is and what he invites of us, we begin to think about the world in different ways, and be accountable to members of his body, the Church, for how we exist ultimately in the world. This taking of responsibility thus illuminates why each domain of conversion is informed in part by other domains: to take religious responsibility for our lives will involve intellectual, affective, moral, and sociopolitical transformations. We will say more about how conversion includes taking responsibility as we go forward.

Gelpi treats religious conversion separately in part because his theological account identifies such, as a Christian, in terms of being transformed into the image of Jesus.[18] This involves conversion along the other four registers even as Christian conversion in turn informs our intellectual, affective, moral, and sociopolitical transformations. In the rest of this book, I focus only on these latter four domains for the opposite reason to why Gelpi sets religious conversion apart: because I will be discussing all of these layers of conversion in light of our ultimate conversion as disciples of and witnesses to Jesus. Each of this part's four chapters will consider further, with Gelpi, normative aspects of conversion in these realms of experience.

For Protestants for whom new-Thomism may be a leap too far too quickly, James Fowler's well-established stages of faith may be helpful. Fowler's model orients us temporally across the lifespan. Stage one is an intuitive faith pertinent for most young children, wherein their beliefs are projected according to what they receive from their caregivers. Stage two is literalistic understanding of faith myths or stories held mostly by elementary school aged children. Stage three is more synthetic faith held in late adolescence into young adulthood, often aligned with authoritative belief systems mediated personally or institutionally. Stage four's individualized and reflective faith happens if those who encounter dissonance press on to make better sense of and then own what they eventuate with. Stage five's conjunctive faith is often jolted by life's crises—whether that of mid-life or otherwise—resulting in a more multidimensional understanding. The final sixth stage of universalizing faith applies only to some who press further onward in their journey and come to appreciate how the journeys of others differ and yet their faith positions or postures are or at least may be no less valid.[19] Fowler unfolds these stages of faith mostly from a developmental and sociopsychological point of view, which means at least that the stages

---

18. Thus, Gelpi's three-volume christology is called *Firstborn of Many*.
19. Fowler, *Stages of Faith*.

are not mutually exclusive even as elements of prior stages both inform and even constitute significant aspects of later stages.

From a phenomenological perspective, Fowler's developmental and temporal stages complement Gelpi's experiential domains and dimensions. Both locate conversion at the level of the individual but not apart from their relational environments. Movements ebb and flow, waxing and waning, both developmentally in and through stages and experientially within and between domains. There is a dynamism that drives conversion in faith, catalyzed by the circumstances of life's journey.

If the goal of evangelism is conversion, how does the preceding conversion inform our evangelistic activities? A short answer would be that our evangelization should invite intellectual, affective, moral, and sociopolitical conversion, all as part of the religious conversion we are aiming for. Fair enough. In fact, we may even see these various dimensions of conversion in the apostolic *locus classicus* in Acts 2. Upon hearing Peter's sermon explaining what was transpiring on the streets of Jerusalem, the gathered crowd asked, "What should we do?" (Acts 2:37b). Peter's response was: "Repent, and be baptized every one of you in the name of Jesus Christ so that your sins may be forgiven; and you will receive the gift of the Holy Spirit" (2:38). First, repentance involves a change of mind, the cognitive and intellectual aspect. Then, baptism is an action, thereby requiring affirmation of the will, the moral aspect. Third, forgiveness of sins touches upon the various ways in which sin taints our lives and hearts, the affective aspect. Finally, receiving the gift of the Spirit leads promptly to mutual sharing with one another, the sociopolitical aspect.

Are we reading into Luke Gelpian categories? Perhaps. On the other hand, in this and the rest of the chapters of this book, I want to pose three sets of questions for us. First, how does the apostolic narrative illuminate these various domains of conversion, if noticeable at all? Second, what are the implications of these conversion narratives for evangelists themselves and for the evangelistic undertaking, the work of evangelism? Finally, as evangelists, can we do anything to encourage or facilitate these many aspects of conversion if expressed in the apostolic witness?[20]

---

20. Here and in the rest of this part of our book, then, we will be re-reading of Luke-Acts in light of the Gelpian framework; however, the approach and results here are consistent with the more exegetical engagement, even if also in dialogue with cognitive science perspectives by Green, *Conversion in Luke-Acts*.

PART II: APOSTOLIC EVANGELISM AND CONVERSION IN THE 2020S

How Does Intellectual Conversion Occur in the Book of Acts?

In the rest of this chapter, we will be diving into the theme of intellectual conversion. What is involved in intellectual conversion? How does Luke describe intellectual conversion?

For starters, considering conversion intellectually or cognitively on its own terms to begin with (we know we can't segregate this from the other domains forever, but for now only), this involves the exchange of information. Intellectual conversion cannot be bought, for instance (moral conversion might be, we shall see later). In other words, intellectual conversion can only be persuaded, based on the strength of the information provided. The use of persuasion, then, necessarily involves rationality, truthfulness, humility in engagement, and sensitivity to cross-cultural factors, etc.[21] We should not, therefore, deploy physical, psychological, social, or other means to "encourage" people to change their minds.

But the issue remains: How do we know what we know? This is the epistemic question. How might we take responsibility for how we know what we know? When we consider this matter, we realize we often find ourselves changing our mind not necessarily because we were looking to do so, but because things have happened to us that lead us to see things differently. Does intellectual conversion take place in the apostolic witness in this way? Does the apostolic story reveal how people change their minds and take new responsibility for their beliefs? Over the next few pages, we will explore three intellectual conversions in the book of Acts: Stephen's, Peter's, and Paul's.

Stephen's Apologetic and Prophetic Witness: Apostolic Intellectual Conversion I

We begin with St. Stephen, the first martyred witness in the apostolic community. What evidence do we have about Stephen's intellectual journey, including how that informs not just what he believes but what he does? Luke records a lengthy speech of Stephen's that, I suggest, provides traces of his intellectual transformations in his roles, from that of a deacon to an apologist and also a prophet.[22]

21. Thiessen, *Ethics of Evangelism*.
22. While not distinguishing Stephen's roles in the way I am doing, the discussion

We meet Stephen first in the dispute regarding "the daily distribution of food" between Hellenist and Hebraic widows (Acts 6:1b) when he, along with six other Hellenists—obviously because of their Greek names—were introduced as being able to provide resolution for the community. This group of individuals was also described as being "full of the Spirit and of wisdom" (6:3a). Of Stephen, it is reiterated as one "full of faith and the Holy Spirit" (6:5a). The apostles commissioned this group of deacons with the laying on of hands specifically "to wait on tables," so that the Twelve should not "neglect the word of God" (6:2b), and the diaconal-apostolic collaboration seemed to work smoothly: "The word of God continued to spread; the number of the disciples increased greatly in Jerusalem, and a great many of the priests became obedient to the faith" (6:7). In this role, Stephen at least worked in some kind of oversight capacity in the daily distribution of food, not quite in the role of apostle, prophet, evangelist, or pastor-teacher (see Eph 4:11), "serving tables" with the women of the community.

Yet as the narrative unfolds, Stephen begins to do the work of an evangelist, it is arguable. At the least, he begins to engage "some of those who belonged to the synagogue of the Freedmen (as it was called), Cyrenians, Alexandrians, and others of those from Cilicia and Asia, [that] stood up and argued with" him (Acts 6:9). If the early messianic community was comprised of those from every nation under heaven, as we have seen, the earliest opposition to that community also seemed to quickly expand from the local Jewish leaders (who we saw being antagonistic to Peter and John's healing of the lame man at the Beautiful Gate) to include other factions from across the Jewish diaspora of that time, including also Hellenized Jews, once but no longer (having obtained release) slaves variously across the Roman Empire.[23] Such Freedmen, however, exposed as they were to how Jewish beliefs and practices in diasporic contexts were being watered down as such inevitably happens from any number of perspectives, were zealous for preserving "the customs that Moses handed on to us," including what transpired in Jerusalem and, ritually, in its temple (6:14). As a Hellenist messianist, on the other hand, whatever else Stephen had been doing, he had also been given or at least had taken advantage of the apostolic platform, and on that stage had appeared to have been advocating otherwise.

---

of Kilgallen, *Stephen Speech*, helpfully lays out how, in Luke's hands, Stephen's speech or sermon functions synthetically, both with regard to the cumulation of his ideas and with regard to how it brings the initial hostilities between messianists and the Jewish leaders to an initial culmination, which thereby invites the kind of reading we are embarking on.

23. See Olson, "Freedmen, Synagogue of the," 855.

In contrast to the Freedmen who, in their newfound liberty, sought to revitalize the Mosaic practices, Stephen, in his newfound identity in Christ, sought instead the reappropriation of the Mosaic law, indeed, what amounted to an interpretation too far beyond what the Freedmen could allow or follow. What did Stephen come to believe and then argue for, in the presence of, initially, and then directly against, eventually, the Freedmen? We can identify some of Stephen's evolving beliefs in the monologue Luke ascribes to him in Acts 7. For instance, if the Freedmen were focused on "this place" (6:14), meaning in Jerusalem as the center of Jewish religiosity, Stephen comes to conceives of a much more diverse and multicultural, if you will, etiology of Jewish messianism, one launched out of Abraham's Mesopotamia and mediated via the Chaldeans and those in Haran initially (7:2, 4), and then developed further through the "resident alien" (7:6) experiences of his progeny in various places, not least in Egypt, indeed, in and through "all the wisdom of the Egyptians" (7:22, 29).[24] More to the point, if the Freedmen were insistent on the authority of the law of Moses, Stephen comes to see that Moses "received living oracles [*logia zōnta* or words of life] to give to us" (7:38b). Thus, Stephen locks in on Moses's own anticipation that "God will raise up a prophet for you from your own people as he raised me up" (7:37; see Deut 18:15, 18).

Last but not least (for our purposes), if the Freedmen were focused on the centrality of the temple in Jerusalem for faithful Jewish practice, Stephen had come to see that the messianic era opened up the possibilities of where the divine presence could be encountered. Yes, "it was Solomon who built a house for him. Yet the Most High does not dwell in houses made with human hands"; rather, coming to new understandings and applications of what was written in the prophets, Stephen insists with regard to where worship is allowable: "Heaven is my throne, and the earth is my footstool. What kind of house will you build for me, says the Lord, or what is the place of my rest? Did not my hand make all these things?" (Acts 7:47–50; see Isa 66:1–2). Along each of these trajectories, Stephen comes to new perspectives on Mosaic faithfulness in a messianic age, one that envisions "an alternative configuration of power, an alternative politics,"[25] and engages the Freedmen thus.

---

24. Put otherwise, a diasporic audience and thereby also of messianists is anticipated by a selective retrieval of the patriarchs as those "who themselves journeyed outside the land God has promised"; see Whitenton, "Rewriting Abraham and Joseph," 162.

25. Dinkler, "Politics of Stephen's Storytelling," 63.

INTELLECTUAL CONVERSION

But Stephen the deacon turned apologist does not stay at an academic level, not content with merely redescribing or reinterpreting the law in conversation or debate with the Freedmen. As the argument unfolded over time—the sermonic form of what Stephen said simply summarized the content of his interactions with the Freedmen rather than denoting that they happened all at once, on the occasion of one homily—Stephen undergoes a final, fatal (in hindsight) transformation of convictions, one that moves him from mere apologetics to prophesying.[26] At some point in his evangelistic and apologetic ministry, Stephen addresses the Freedmen confrontationally and accusationally:

> You stiff-necked people, uncircumcised in heart and ears, you are forever opposing the Holy Spirit, just as your ancestors used to do. Which of the prophets did your ancestors not persecute? They killed those who foretold the coming of the Righteous One, and now you have become his betrayers and murderers. You are the ones that received the law as ordained by angels, and yet you have not kept it. (Acts 7:51–53)

The Freedmen are enraged; the result is Stephen's stoning and martyrdom.[27]

Stephen began as a deacon, waiting on tables, but developed theologically and then also vocationally. As a Hellenist, Stephen may have come back to Jerusalem for the Pentecost Feast but encountered the living Christ, and grew in the apostolic teaching. He may have begun intellectually (and religiously) in a place very similar to the Freedmen, a least with regard to the centrality of the temple in Jewish life and practice, but he came to understand, over time, that the God of Abraham was also the God of all persons, no matter the nation or ethnicity of derivation, no matter where the location, no matter the class (widows or Freedmen), and no matter the language (Greek, or Hebrew, or perhaps other tongues). These transformed beliefs galvanized, irresistibly so, his apologetic and then prophetic efforts. With regard to the earlier apostolic question, "Whether it is right in God's sight to listen to you [those opposing the gospel's proclamation] rather than to God" (4:19), Stephen, like Peter and John before him, landed on the former. The ongoing transformation of his beliefs could not exempt him from prophetic witness, as costly as that was for him personally.

---

26. For more on Stephen's prophetic message, see Clark, *Parallel Lives*, ch. 8.
27. See also Yong, *Kerygmatic Spirit*, ch. 14.

Peter's "I [Now] Truly Understand . . .": Apostolic Intellectual Conversion II

Whereas in the case of Stephen we extrapolated particularly from what is presented as his final sermon precipitating his murder to follow the arc of his intellectual conversion, in the case of Peter, we will zero in on his encounter with Cornelius the centurion, and on the deepening of his thinking in the wake of that episode.[28] If Stephen's intellectual transformation is presumed in our account to have unfolded over some time, Peter's happened much more incisively, but with unfolding implications and applications. Luke's records provide at least three sets of descriptive windows into Peter's acknowledgment of his own ongoing intellectual conversion, particularly in relation to the implications of how they impacted his actions and relationships.

The first such self-realization occurs with Peter's arrival at the house of Cornelius the gentile, when Luke explicitly records that Peter "went in," entering the home to find "that many had assembled" (10:27). Perhaps Luke also recognized this momentous step since it is followed by Peter's apology: "You yourselves know that it is unlawful for a Jew to associate with or to visit a Gentile; but God has shown me that I should not call anyone profane or unclean" (Acts 10:28). "Gentile" in this case is the Greek *allophylō*, which the Septuagint uses to denote specifically philistine barbarism (cf. 1 Sam 17:36–37, 31:9, 2 Sam 1:20, 3:18), thus also with negative connotations regarding his foreigner and alien status.[29] Upon receiving Cornelius's explanation for the invitation, that he and his household were ready "to listen to all that the Lord has commanded [Peter] to say" (10:33b), Peter began his message with a further confession: "I truly understand that God shows no partiality, but in every nation anyone who fears him and does what is right is acceptable to him" (10:34–35). "I truly understand" is in the middle present voice in the original Greek and thus can also be translated, "I now realize . . ." (New International Version), although what is suggested is not just present awareness, but that which also takes hold of the self, or that

---

28. There is widespread acknowledgment regarding and discussion of Peter and Cornelius both converting—e.g., Parsons, *Luke*, 156–84, is a section titled "The Conversion of Peter, Cornelius, and Others," although he does qualify application of the notion of conversion to Peter vis-à-vis his coming "to a new point of view" (157)—although I am distinguishing their respects in this book, here focused on Peter's intellectual conversion and, in ch. 5 below, on Cornelius's moral conversion.

29. See Balch, *Contested Ethnicities and Images*, 243.

which is grasped by or owned by the self, e.g., "I now come to cognitively comprehend and also to own in my being . . . ." Whereas prior to his visions about killing and consuming creatures Jewish law considered unclean, after receiving these thrice, Peter was opened up to responding positively to the invitation of Cornelius and his men. His meeting with Cornelius exposed his own ethnocentrism under the light of divine inclusivism, not restricted to the Jews but open to "every nation" or every ethnicity.

What did such divine acceptance entail? Peter's recounting of the visit to Cornelius provides further elaboration on this matter while also serving as a second window into his ongoing intellectual journey. Upon returning to Jerusalem, there were questions, including: "Why did you go to uncircumcised men [gentiles] and eat with them?" (11:3). Note that this is the first mention of Peter having eaten with Cornelius, which is itself consistent with what we saw earlier: Jesus's eating in the presence of the sinner woman and Zacchaeus, for instance. Peter then tells of his visions, and then of how the Spirit alerted him to their meaning, which was to minimize his hesitation about accepting the summons since there was no "distinction between them and us" (11:12a).

More important, he recalls not only that the "six brothers" Cornelius sent extended the invitation but also that upon meeting Cornelius, the latter communicated he wanted to meet with Peter because he was led to believe that Peter "will give you a message by which you and your entire household will be saved" (11:14). Notice that in Luke's initial account of the meeting between Cornelius and Peter, the former's summary of the events leading up to the meeting concludes only that "now all of us are here in the presence of God to listen to all that the Lord has commanded you to say" (10:33b). There is no mention of salvation. But now, in Peter's recounting, Cornelius's soteriological expectations were more explicitly delineated: that he and his whole household would be saved (11:14).[30] If in the earlier moment Peter made explicit his realization that gave him permission to cross the threshold into Cornelius's home, in this recollective moment, Peter makes unequivocal that the results of that encounter were anticipated, but now reflected back into Cornelius's own words, effectively providing a dual witness—Cornelius's and his—to what the Jerusalem community had come to see as well, certainly in light of the baptisms received and performed (10:47–48).

---

30. I gained this insight from Shellberg, *Cleansed Lepers, Cleansed Hearts*, ch. 5, esp. 153–54.

Yet Peter's intellectual conversion is tested. Opening this third window requires a bit more background. In one of his letters, Paul recounts that at one point, "when Cephas [Peter] came to Antioch, I opposed him to his face, because he stood self-condemned; for until certain people came from James, he used to eat with the Gentiles. But after they came, he drew back and kept himself separate for fear of the circumcision faction. And the other Jews joined him in this hypocrisy, so that even Barnabas was led astray by their hypocrisy" (Gal 2:11–13). While there is no definitive way to date this in relation to the Acts account, taking Paul's word for what transpired locates these events after the Jerusalem Council.[31] There are other plausible scenarios, however, including earlier in the first year or two of the emergence of the Antiochene mission to prominence. After recounting Peter's testimony at Jerusalem of what happened in Caesarea—one or two points of which we have mentioned in the preceding paragraph—Luke then turns to discuss the emergence of Antioch as a leading messianic center, where "the disciples were first called 'Christians'" (Acts 11:26b). In this brief sketch, Luke says that the Antioch mission, so to speak, was initially focused on "no one except Jews" (11:19b), but then missionary reinforcements from Cyprus and Cyrene arrived and it was they who began to witness to Hellenists (11:20). Therefore, as word that Hellenists along with Jews were responding to the gospel reached the church in Jerusalem, Barnabas was sent first (some prophets following later) to Antioch (11:22b, 27a) who in turn brought Saul (before he was named Paul) also, and "for an entire year they [the two] met with the church and taught a great many people" (11:26a).

The scene was now set, if we imagine Peter's arrival to Antioch sometime within those twelve months, initially settling in to eat with gentiles until another faction hewing closely to James's leadership arrived, at which time Peter reverted to maintaining the purity laws and eating only with the Jews.[32] We do not know Peter's side of this story, even as, be reminded,

31. That Paul's argument with Peter at Antioch happened after the Jerusalem Council in Acts 15 assumes the latter is referred to in Gal 2:1–10, as urged in painstaking detail by Dunn, "Incident at Antioch (Gal 2:11–18)."

32. This is a hypothetical reconstruction; if we accept a broader hypothesis that Luke's second book is motivated in part (perhaps larger than lesser) by the goal of rehabilitating Paul's apostleship toward the end of the first century—e.g., Phillips, *Paul, His Letters, and Acts*, 195–97—then this more overarching Lukan purpose goes a long way toward both explaining the silence about the apostolic confrontation and providing warrants for our consideration, which point is sustained regardless of where/when we locate the Antiochene dispute.

we are reading these developments into this sequence of Luke's narrative. On the other hand, we see Peter only once more in the book of Acts, at the Jerusalem Council, where Paul and Barnabas were defending their decision not only to bear witness to Hellenists and gentiles but also that these new messianist converts did not need to be circumcised or keep the details of the law exactly like Jews, against the insistences of the Pharisees and related groups (15:1, 5). It is in this context that Peter chimes in, asserting authority gained from his experience with Cornelius first (15:7)—now recounted (by Luke) a third time—before saying of the divine acceptance of gentiles:

> God, who knows the human heart, testified to them by giving them the Holy Spirit, just as he did to us; and in cleansing their hearts by faith he has made no distinction between them and us. Now therefore why are you putting God to the test by placing on the neck of the disciples a yoke that neither our ancestors nor we have been able to bear? On the contrary, we believe that we will be saved through the grace of the Lord Jesus, just as they will. (15:8–11)

Here, Peter goes beyond recognizing the salvation of the gentiles to insist that this ought not to be accomplished by the additional yoke of either circumcision in particular nor other aspects of the law. One might detect echoes here of segregated eating, for instance within the earlier narrative sequence, a practice understandably associated with the circumcision he had begun to overcome in his original meeting with Cornelius (again, 11:3), but had, according to Paul, waffled on for a time. In this conciliar space, however, Peter comes to a definitive public stance of what he had known but struggled with: if Jewish and gentiles hearts are all purified by faith through the gift of the Holy Spirit, then Jewish purity laws, including those dictating eating protocols, should not separate those from divergent tribes, peoples, or nations (ethnicities).

Peter comes to understand perhaps one truth—that God shows no partiality to Jews or gentiles—but with ever deepening facets of its veracity. Transformation of his beliefs led in turn to transformation of his practices, from entering the homes of gentiles to baptizing them to eating with them, even in the presence of fellow Jews, perhaps thus also inviting a deeper mutuality among Jews and gentiles that find themselves in common spaces. Clarity is gained over time—arguably, Peter's religious conversion to Jesus also happens in stages, e.g., at his initial calling by Jesus, after his denial of Jesus during the passion week, here in what we have presented, etc.—brought about by the (sometimes forced) applications of new understandings to new practices and ways of being in the world.

Paul's Evolving Witness: Apostolic Intellectual Conversion III

Luke's account of Paul's religious conversion will provide us with the frame for considering his intellectual transformation.[33] We will explore how conversion by and to Jesus resulted in adjustments of his philosophical, theological, and vocational understanding. Whereas with Stephen we traced the intellectual evolution of a vocational sojourn and with Peter we unpacked different layers of a significant cognitive insight, with Paul we will explore various realms of his intellectual conversion.

Philosophically, we begin with Luke's depiction of Saul—the transition to Paul happens en route on the first missionary journey (Acts 13:9), and we will follow Luke's usage—being confronted by a heavenly light on his way to Damascus. Having fallen to the ground, he "heard a voice saying to him, 'Saul, Saul, why do you persecute me?' He asked, 'Who are you, Lord?' The reply came, 'I am Jesus, whom you are persecuting'" (9:4b–5). As a Pharisee who was, as recounted in later testimonials, "educated strictly according to our ancestral law [and] belonged to the strictest sect of our religion" (22:3b, 26:5), the possibility of eschatological resurrection was one that he adhered to, unlike other Jewish groups like Sadducees (23:8). Yet the Damascus road encounter troubled what was up to then only a theoretical commitment, however well-informed and authorized (under leading and respected teachers like Gamaliel, no less; 5:34, 22:2a). Whereas before he had "sought to do many things against the name of Jesus of Nazareth" (26:9), opposing what he considered a misguided and dangerous legacy, Paul now had to reckon existentially and relationally with that person, whose identity was confirmed soon after by Ananias, a disciple in Damascus, as "the Lord Jesus" (9:17). Jesus was alive! Resurrection from the dead was thus no longer only an idea; instead, this was embodied in Jesus who had knocked him down to the ground.

Theologically, then, realization that the resurrection had already begun to occur with Jesus fundamentally transformed Paul's worldview and shaped his subsequent message. The Lord had also told Ananias to inform Saul: "he is an instrument whom I have chosen to bring my name before

---

33. For a succinct overview of Luke's account of Paul, see Rosenblatt, *Paul the Accused*.

INTELLECTUAL CONVERSION

Gentiles and kings and before the people of Israel" (9:15).[34] All of his intellectual beliefs had to be recalibrated now, and his witness as preserved in the book of Acts thereafter reflects the emergence to centrality of Jesus's resurrection. From an evangelistic standpoint, this is the crux of the difficulty regarding the gospel message, that one who was crucified is no longer dead. In his first recorded sermon in a synagogue in Antioch of Pisidia (13:16–41), for instance, to a predominantly but not only Hellenized Jewish community, over one-fourth of a long message was focused on Jesus having been raised from the dead (13:30–37), linking to the scriptural promises, including those suggestive of life after death (13:33–35; cf. Pss 2:7, 16:10, and Isa 55:3).[35] Then, having established the continuity of Paul's message with the apostolic (Petrine, so far in Acts) tradition, when bearing the gospel to pagan audiences later, for instance at Athens (17:16–34), even when engaging them on terms more natural to their own philosophical and poetic traditions (17:22–29),[36] this apostle to the gentiles continually invokes "Jesus and the resurrection" (17:18b), whose coming judgments of the world God "has given assurance to all by raising him from the dead" (17:31b). Paul further intones testimonially in various legal and regal contexts:

- before authorities and especially Jewish religious leaders: "I am on trial concerning the hope of the resurrection of the dead" (23:6);

- before governor Felix and his other accusers: "I have a hope in God—a hope that they themselves also accept—that there will be a resurrection of both the righteous and the unrighteous . . . . It is about the resurrection of the dead that I am on trial before you today" (24:15, 21);

- before King Agrippa and his audience: "Why is it thought incredible by any of you that God raises the dead?" (26:8).

---

34. Macnamara, *My Chosen Instrument*, argues that God's message to Ananias regarding Saul in Acts 9:15–16 provides a narrative arc for Luke's account of Paul's ministry and mission, at least through the Jerusalem Council in terms of his own analysis, although, as will be noted in the rest of this section, fulfillment of this divine calling continues to be documented in the later part of the book of Acts, not least Paul's witness before kings in Acts 24–26.

35. And if the message of salvation and christological kerygma is unfolded over Acts 14:26–37—e.g., Zhang, *Paul Among Jews*, 136–47—then over 70 percent of these verses are devoted to the death and resurrection of Jesus.

36. Here and elsewhere in Acts, Paul "works within the religious logic of the Gentiles"; see Jipp, *Reading Acts*, 99.

Even his captors recognized that Paul was being held because of "certain points of disagreement with him . . . about a certain Jesus, who had died, but whom Paul asserted to be alive" (25:19). Not for no reason, Paul's own writings confirm that this conviction lay at the core of his efforts: "If there is no resurrection of the dead, then Christ has not been raised; and if Christ has not been raised, then our proclamation has been in vain and your faith has been in vain" (1 Cor 15:13–14). Jesus's being alive was not only of personal relevance but was of central theological and evangelical (evangelistic) import.[37]

Vocationally, however, there is another layer to Paul the evangelist and preacher: he was also called, as the Lord told Ananias to communicate: "I myself will show him how much he must suffer for the sake of my name" (9:16). It is worth noting that Saul was on his way to Damascus to mobilize the authorities there against "any who belonged to the Way" (9:2). Believing that coming down hard on the likes of Stephen was essential (7:58), he began to target other messianists, "ravaging the church by entering house after house; dragging off both men and women, he committed them to prison" (8:3). In his own words (at least as recorded by Luke), "I persecuted this Way up to the point of death . . . . By punishing them often in all the synagogues I tried to force them to blaspheme; and since I was so furiously enraged at them, I pursued them even to foreign cities" (22:4a, 26:11). Here was a deeply convicted person, with an expansive agenda driven by his ideological commitments. Now, the persecutor was called to a path of suffering and being persecuted precisely because of the name that he had burnished in his oppression of others. Thus was the depth of his intellectual transformation, to the degree that he risked being conspired against (9:23–24) and, for his newfound views, hazarded stoning (14:19), imprisonment (16:22–24), and riots (19:30–31), among other perils (cf. 2 Cor 11:23–29). Paul's embrace of this vocation of suffering is one way in which he takes responsibility for his beliefs about the resurrected Jesus.

Taking responsibility for his newly discovered understanding meant rethinking himself from the ground up, something he did over a three-year span in the deserts of Arabia (Gal 1:17–18). Paul's conversion to Jesus is nurtured by deepening intellectual transformation,[38] as we see in his

---

37. Witness to Jesus's resurrection is central to apostolic mission in Acts, introduced early as a criterion for Matthias's appointment to replace Judas, for instance (Acts 1:22b); see also Green, "Witnesses of His Resurrection"; and Marguerat, "Resurrection and Its Witnesses."

38. From our modernist perspective about religious conversion being from one faith

sojourn. There is a clear sense that his "I die every day!" (1 Cor 15:31) is not only about the suffering he had endured and continued to persevere through for the sake of the living Christ, but involved an ongoing commitment, a continual renewal of fortitude and consideration.

Christian Evangelism and Intellectual Conversion Today: Reconsidering Spirit-ed Witness Praxis

How might we summarize the foregoing? What important takeaways about intellectual conversion emerge from our considerations of Stephen, Peter, and Paul above? Much can be said, yet consider the following.

First, *conversion to Christ is witnessed to by evangelists who are also on an intellectual journey.* Even before focusing on those we are intent on evangelizing, it is helpful to recognize our own path. Apostolically speaking, this is most clearly seen in Stephen and Peter, whose comprehension widened and deepened, so that, along the way, they bore differentiated witnesses to the gospel. Evangelism involves the transformation of those evangelized, yes; yet it involves also the ongoing renovation of evangelists, including their understanding. This assumes that our minds are never fully made up, and that there are always new perspectives, vistas, and understandings. Such a realization also invites us to be open to being curious, to welcome wonderment, and even to embrace and stay with cognitive dissonance, at least long enough to being open to exploring pathways of inquiry into that confusion.

Second, *adequate Christian witness involves ongoing conversion at least to the experience of others.* This is most clearly evidenced in Peter: he had to come to experience Cornelius and other gentiles from a perspective other than offered vis-à-vis his own Jewish presuppositions. With regard to Stephen and Paul, as Hellenized (diaspora) persons, they were already inculturated in the Greco-Roman milieu, although their messianic encounter led to a reimagination of the tenets of their faith and a fresh recommunication of them. And ongoing interactions, including for instance fellowshipping and eating together, as Peter struggled with, also have implications for what and how we know others different from ourselves. All too often, we

---

to another, Paul never ceases to remain a Jew, so his Christian conversion is first intellectual and then second personal, to Jesus; see Stendahl, *Paul Among Jews and Gentiles*, 7–23, who urges that what we have with the apostle to the gentiles is a calling, not a conversion.

are simply ready to criticize others, to provide apologetic responses, or to change the subject.

Third, *doing so, then, leads "us" to reject the invitations of others.* Peter's struggle was real, leading to a withdrawal and to Paul's rebuke. To be sure, xenophobia is not something that afflicts only first-century messianists or contemporary Christians; all human beings gravitate to their tribe or group or people and are wary of others. Perhaps that is why Christians are *martures*/witnesses: there is suffering involved since the journey from wherever our Jerusalem is to the ends of the earth will bring us into contact with very different others who will challenge our assumptions and our way of life. We are not comfortable with being vulnerable to the differences of others, and therefore shore up our own lives and immunize them from exposure.

What then are some contemporary missiological implications of the foregoing consideration of apostolic intellectual conversion? How might Spirit-inspired and empowered Christian witness and evangelism today be informed by the intellectual conversion we see in the apostolic record? For those of us who would be missionaries and evangelists, let me raise the following questions at this stage of our own journey.

First, *are we committed to the lifelong renewing of our minds following the Spirit of Jesus who leads us into all truth to/from the ends of the earth?* Ongoing learning requires commitment. Acts 28 ends on an open note, leaving the rest of the story to be told by messianists in each successive age. "Jesus Christ is the same yesterday and today and for ever" (Heb 13:8), and yet Christian understanding of him remains mediated "in a mirror, dimly" (1 Cor 13:12a); that, "what we will be has not yet been revealed. What we do know is this: when he is revealed, we will be like him, for we will see him as he is" (1 John 3:2). Thus, the call to "be transformed by the renewing of your minds" (Rom 12:2) remains a prerequisite for Christian discipleship generally, and Christian witness more specifically.

Second, *is it OK that, often, the conversion of our minds is facilitated through our encounter with and experiences of others?* And what if these others are the ones we believe we are called to evangelize? Should we not expect, as a general rule of thumb, that in our encounter with those that we are evangelizing, our own minds will be changed? Those evangelized can bear witness to the depth or extent of their own transformation, but we are responsible for our testimonies, the degrees to which the Spirit has empowered and changed us on the apostolic pathway, in and through our evangelizing efforts. If we approach others in the humility of the gospel, our own horizons will be extended, our minds will be expanded, our own ways of being in the world will be enriched and transformed.

Finally, for now, *are we willing to listen and open our hearts to and learn from those we are called to evangelize?* This question rightly connects our openness to intellectual conversion and transformation to the affective level of our gut. How open we are to others intellectually is related to how open we are relationally and personally, and this is no longer an abstract question of our minds but one that operates at the level of our loves and fears. Intellectual conversion, it turns out, is not merely theoretical: it requires a deeper level exploration of how we consider ourselves in relationship to these others to whom God may be calling us to evangelize.

Chapter 4

Affective Conversion
Apostolic Passions Then and Now

WE NOW TURN TO affective conversion. What exactly do the *affections* refer to and how might we understand and define them? Jonathan Edwards's *Religious Affections*,[1] almost an instant classic since its appearance in the mid-eighteenth century amid the revivals in New England where he was a pastoral leader, clarified that our affections were discernible in their bodily effects like zealousness, happiness, confidence, and animatedness, which might be especially convincing due to their greater intensity, fluency, and fervency. Yet, for Edwards, these were insufficient to confirm that they were truly of God. Instead, gracious and holy affections consisted of deep remorse for sins, authentic humility, faithful convictions, and imitations of Jesus's own temper. Our affections, preliminarily stated, then, are the feelings, emotions, and sentiments that operate first and foremost in and through our bodies.

If in the preceding chapter our focus was on intellectual conversion and being reoriented toward right-thinking or *orthopistis* (literally: right faith or belief or doctrine), then here we explore affective conversion and being repositioned toward right-feeling or *orthopathos*. The chapter's first section surveys conversion in greater depth at the level of human affectivity, and the second studies affective conversion in Luke-Acts. The final

---

1. There are many editions of Edwards's *Religious Affections* available, with the definitive scholarly annotated version edited by Smith, *Works of Jonathan Edwards*, vol. 2: *Religious Affections*.

section concludes by returning to contemporary missional praxis: What are the implications of apostolic affective conversion for Christian witness and evangelism in the present time?

As has already been indicated, we are abstracting affective conversion as part of religious conversion operating alongside, so far, intellectual conversion. In the next chapter, we will then take up moral conversion and how this transforms us behaviorally toward right-action (*orthopraxis*). Yet intellectual, affective, and moral conversion work together toward religious conversion. At moments, one or the other might be more on the surface, or conversion in one domain may be delayed, sometimes inexplicably so. Yet conversion is never complete either in any of these arenas, nor even if we were to put them all together, except that there are always deeper levels of transformation that can be attained, or experienced, both separately and, by extension, together. What are the implications for evangelism, especially for us today who sense a vocational call as evangelists?

Affectivity, Mission, and Evangelism: Orthopathic Dimensions of Christian Conversion

Contemporary neuroscience clearly shows that there's a lot going on within our bodies that informs our cognition and thinking. In fact, what finally arrives to mental consciousness is only a fraction of what our nervous system processes, and oftentimes, our actions are dictated by our instincts, habits, and feelings first and foremost, and only secondarily do we then consider warrants or justifications for what we have done. And even when we attempt to "explain ourselves," we often struggle to actually name what has been transpiring within us. In other words, human feeling, emotion, and affectivity are just as, if not more important, as—certainly more foundational, so to speak, than—human intellect and cognition.[2] In the following, we will explore this affective level of human experience in more depth, attempt to comprehend when and how it is disordered and dis-eased, and then understand better how to take responsibility for our affectivity and emotional health. This discussion sets us up to appreciate deeper affective conversion in the apostolic record (this chapter's second section) and, from there, be more open to the divine salvation, redemption, and transformation of our affections in Christ by the Spirit.

---

2. Neuroscientists like Antonio Damasio have been making this case for the last three decades; a summary and more recent statement is Damasio's *Feeling and Knowing*.

On Emotions, Feelings, and Affections: The Heart or Orthopathic Dimension of Religious Faith

Most of us are familiar with orthodoxy as that which relates, technically, to right worship: *ortho* meaning "right" and *doxa* meaning "worship." Orthodoxy has also become synonymous, over time, with right belief or right doctrine, although *orthopistis*—right faith—has also served this purpose. In the next few pages, our focus will be on the feeling or pathic dimension of our lives before God.[3] What does it mean for our feelings and emotions to be rightly ordered—orthopathically—toward the divine?

John Wesley called this the heart dimension of Christian faith. Wesley's own initiation into Christian faith came through his famous account of having a "heartwarming" encounter with God at Aldersgate Street. While Wesleyan and other scholars have long debated about the significance of Wesley's Aldersgate experience,[4] no doubt that for him, this was a psychophysiological experience that was all at once an awareness of sin, realization of needed inner transformation (with outward effects), and reassurance of faith felt in terms of peace, joy, and love. In short, whether tied in with initial religious conversion or in relationship to the experiences of sanctification about which Wesley's own theology (and that of the Wesleyan tradition after him) has focused, emotional affect was central. Thus, Wesleyanism has been known as a "religion of the heart," whereby what happens at the level of feeling, emotions, and affections is lifted up.[5]

A parallel to Wesley on this side of the Atlantic, although preceding him by a few decades, is the already mentioned Jonathan Edwards. Edwards wrote *Religious Affections* to provide guidance to his New Englander parishioners about how to both understand and embrace the revivals they were experiencing. The revivals were producing a wide range of physical manifestations, some new and novel, others long observed in similar contexts and circumstances. Edwards felt it was important to correctly interpret and therefore support this new and surprising work of the Holy Spirit, particularly in terms of how it impacted human bodies, feelings, emotions, and psyches. Not all feelings and emotions, even in the heat of religious services and even revivals, so to speak, are of the Holy Spirit; some are

---

3. For how orthodoxy or right worship is informed by *orthopistis* (right belief), *orthopathos* (right feeling), and *orthopraxis* (right practice), see Björkander, *Worship, Ritual, and Pentecostal Spirituality-as-Theology*.

4. E.g., Olson, *Wesley and Aldersgate*.

5. See also Clapper, "*Orthokardia*: John Wesley's Grammar."

mere bodily—arguably fleshly, in the negative Pauline sense—expressions; other psychophysical manifestations might indeed by catalyzed by the Holy Spirit's movements in the congregation and community. Thus did he pen his book, to provide guidance on when such affectivities were truly gracious and holy, as opposed to being merely of human kinesthetic response.[6]

While our definitions are meant heuristically and not meant to be definitive, most important for our purposes so far is that emotion calls attention to the biophysical dimensions of what we are and how we are constituted. Our fears, anger, joys, loves, etc., are fundamentally rooted in our bodily instincts, for starters, even as they might be cultivated, consciously or not, into more lasting emotional feelings and sensations. In the latter respects, our emotions might extend into moods or into states or dispositions that endure over time, even across extended durations. Feelings might be fleeting but moods can persist over minutes, hours, days, or weeks. Our affections are those of perduring moods that provide directionality to our lives, undergirding our hopes, motivating our desires, reinforcing our loves. Our emotions feed our feelings, which are integrated into our affections, and these move us forward integratively and harmoniously in our lives.[7] When we wake up every morning not because we have to or because we're thinking about what needs to be done, but because we are eager to get to the things that are meaningful and significant for us, then we are being galvanized affectively, not only (if at all) cognitively. We love, hope for, and work toward these desires that animate our affect rather than those that are only convincing to our intellect.

Attending to this biophysical and feeling level of our lives, then, locks in on what is driving us underneath what we consciously think about or are able to articulate to ourselves and others. No wonder when Jesus was asked what was the most important commandment, it was that which was registered affectively: to *love* God and neighbor, and if that were not sufficient, *to love* in a certain way, with all our hearts, all of who and what we are! Disciples and followers of Jesus are hence defined most foundationally orthopathically, at the affective level: by who and what and how they love. This should also then apply to evangelists, right? What is the character of the feelings and the desires and hopes and aspirations that ought to move a

---

6. For more on Edwardsean affections, especially in dialogue with Pentecostal theologians, see the chapters in part 1 of Studebaker and Yong, *Pentecostal Theology and Jonathan Edwards*.

7. See Siegel, *Developing Mind*, 233.

disciple of Jesus as opposed to someone who's not a disciple of Jesus? What's the character of the emotions and feelings that should motivate Christian evangelists?

Emotional and Affective Dis-ease: The Pathological Brokenness of Human Lives

What stunts emotional and affective growth, including growth toward maturity? When is it that our emotions don't function as well? As we know, emotions like anger and fear alert us to developments in our environments, signaling danger on the horizon. But there could be forms of anger, fear, and anxiousness that extend beyond where they should and that's when our emotions might become dis-eased, and our accompanying activity also become disoriented. If wrong thinking might be when we draw preliminary, mis-/under-informed, or erroneous conclusions, wrong feeling is when our instincts are inappropriately triggered (we feel joy rather than fear or vice-versa), when our emotions are inappropriately manifest (we laugh when we should be crying, or vice-versa), when our affections are misplaced (we desire only self-gratification for instance rather than longing also for the common good). Emotional regulation adjusts our feelings so they are more rather than less appropriately expressed in any context. Key to such emotional regulation is the management of life's stresses,[8] in particular having the emotional maturity and intelligence to express relevant emotions in relationship to specific circumstances. It is not whether we ought to be emotional—e.g., to love God with all of our hearts, using Lukan phraseology—but how we ought to respond emotionally.

If *pathology* names the modern science of causes and effects of diseases, then our theological *orthopathos* identifies when our feelings are rightly oriented toward God, and *heteropathos* when they are wrongly directed away from the divine, perhaps dominated by life's circumstances and stressors in ways that express unhelpful rather than helpful emotions in particular situations. Human brokenness can thus also be understood pathologically, for instance, prolonged sadness leading to anxiousness that overwhelms and, in that respect, our emotions and feelings can undermine our capacity to function. Our emotions can both overwork and under-achieve, in the former case, be overly extended, and in the latter case, be muted or minimized. In either direction, our emotions result in

---

8. Kidman, *Staying Sane in the Fast Lane*, ch. 1.

bodily dis-ease, including the inability to appropriately respond in various circumstances, not only for ourselves, but also in relationship to others. We will over- or under-react, not necessarily in comprehensible ways.

Our emotional dis-ease could also be denied or spiritualized. The former is prevalent when we overlook our brokenness, the latter more often as an excuse to preserve the status quo. If the emotional regulation of our bodies allows us to live within the appropriate boundaries and constraints and parameters of what it means to be human, then when under-regulated or mis-regulated, our emotions will inhibit self-functioning and social intercourse. We fall into extremes, become overly judgmental (of ourselves, usually, although also of others in our lives), mis-communicative (and are misunderstood), or self-justifying of our feelings or behaviors (even at the theological level).

I am neither certified to diagnose our neuroses or psychoses nor is this book intended to operate at that level of affective analysis. So, when considering our coming to awareness of our addictions, for instance, we are operating not so much at the level related to drug, alcohol, or smoking consumption (although getting those under control is helpful) but at that which drives our consumerism and workaholism in global system of late modern capitalism. Reformed Charismatic philosopher James K. A. Smith has written about how our loves drive our habits, mostly in unhealthy directions in today's world.[9] Our "decisions" in such a world energized by desires—for fame, money, power, things, etc.!—are malformed since they are guided toward idolatrous ends. And these are all the more potent since they are not recognized as such, but presumed to be appropriate and normal (which they are when assessed according to the conventions of late modern capitalism!). If we love the things of this world rather than the God that created this world, then our affections are distorted, our feelings misshapen, and our emotions curved in on ourselves,[10] rather than opened up to the Holy Spirit.

Affective and emotional health therefore could come from, if you will, hearing the word of the Lord and being delivered by it. We may recall that Jonathan Edwards, mentioned above, was also famous for preaching a sermon about sinners in the hands of an angry God.[11] Sermons of this sort

---

9. Smith, *You Are What You Love*.

10. Here speaking hamartiologically (regarding the Christian doctrine of sin), e.g., Jenson, *Gravity of Sin*.

11. Edwards, "Sinners in the Hands of an Angry God."

were designed to admonish and warn listeners to turn to God. Even if this form of homily is less preached today than before, Scripture is full of these kinds of emotionally loaded warnings. For example, the book of Revelation contains many such threats,[12] and our own Gospel of Luke includes: "I tell you, my friends, do not fear those who kill the body, and after that can do nothing more. But I will warn you whom to fear: fear him who, after he has killed, has authority to cast into hell. Yes, I tell you, fear him!" (Luke 12:4–5). We will therefore make our way through parts of the New Testament on the lookout for emotionally laden words such as fear, joy, and love, to see what the biblical narratives communicate at this gut level about not only the human heart but also human health. If our health, effectively our salvation, depends on appropriate diagnosis of our bodies and our feelings, how might Scripture inform the reorientation of our emotions and desires?

Evangelism and Affective Conversion: Taking Responsibility for Our Emotional Health

What are pathways of affective conversion? Gelpi, our framing guide, suggests that affective dis-ease spirals from being initially suppressed, to habitual suppression, to periodic irruption (when triggered by stressful circumstances), and finally to dysfunction (needing therapy or other bio- or psycho-medical interventions).[13] The last-named level is outside of our areas of expertise. Taking responsibility for our affectivity, according to Gelpi, often arrives through some kind of crisis experience, but always emerges through realization that one is affectively disordered. The path of responsibility-taking involves reintegrating emotions and feeling, re-channeling emotional forces, and nurturing emotional expressions that foster aesthetic and existential well-being.

First steps, then, include realization that our emotional lives are not merely there or, as conventional "wisdom" might suggest, unavoidably manifest in this or that way only. Instead, there is understanding that we can be different, that we can acknowledge, live with, and express our feelings responsibly. Christianly and theologically, second, we could, even should, pause to call upon God and upon all the resources that God might provide toward a pathway of healing for ourselves. Third, then, is being open to, if not also seeking out help for, and being supported through our

---

12. Which I discuss in my *Revelation*, 240–41.
13. Gelpi, *Conversion Experience*, 34–37.

journey of affective conversion and emotional growth. Each of these are challenging steps, although for different reasons. We don't like to concede our having fallen short, and we often are un-inclined to divulge our need of assistance from others, including God.

Yet emotional health is essential not only for us as individuals but also for our relationships. Not only do un-regulated or mis-regulated emotions impact our ability to interact with and relate to others, but affect regulation and effective coping can emerge from out of caregiving and -receiving relationships.[14] There are ever-widening circles of relationships here, beginning with those closest to us, including our family members and significant others, and moving outward from there. Emotional regulation and health therefore involve both internal and external dimensions.[15] How do we then approach conversion affectively?

Concretely, we begin to address emotional dis-ease in and through our bodies, behaviors, or thought-patterns, mostly unnoticed by us. Internally, we attend to our bodies and their reactivity and sociability. Some of these internal mechanisms that modulate our emotions may come to consciousness after the fact, for instance when we notice that we are breathing less heavily than we were moments ago. Speaking of breathing, this is one form of intentional intervention: telling ourselves to breathe, more gradually, in and out, to moderate the emotional charge in that moment. We can make a good deal of headway on affective regulation via the classic spiritual disciplines including but not limited to meditation, contemplation, prayer, and related forms of embodied devotional practice. These practices will enable recognition of what is going on in our bodies in relation to ourselves. More holistic strategies including the developing of sustainable rhythms of daily life, eating healthily, taking Sabbath regularly, and cultivating other practices enable us to be the best that we can amid the stresses of our lives.[16] Such a holistic approach then also builds on how we care for ourselves to how we care for others and how we receive such care from others. How do we respond to one another, cooperate with one another, reciprocate with one another, allow each other access to our lives and access the lives of others, and so on? Affective conversion at this relational and interpersonal level therefore includes a kind of resocialization, re-acclimating our bodies

---

14. Bradley, *Affect Regulation*, 105–7.

15. See Siegel, *Developing Mind*, 268–69.

16. E.g., Scazzero, *Emotionally Healthy Spirituality*; on the dietary and nutritional dimensions, see also Dillon, *Emotional Health*, chs. 9–10.

to be not only aligned with our hearts but also reoriented in relationship to others.

Orthopathy thereby involves aesthetic and moral norms, the former related to our self-integration vis-à-vis our environment and the latter related to our interactions with other creatures (especially but not only human). Emotional regulation, thus, invites consideration of both aesthetic and moral norms that best support us to be fully who we are in relationship with our significant others, our children, our families, and those in the body of Christ, and beyond that, with our neighbors, coworkers, and others we share the world with. Right feelings—orthopathy—are not merely about emotion at the subjective level of our experience, but how they reorder who we are in relation to our world and others in it.[17]

And as Christians, these aesthetic and moral norms are also finally theological ones that help us to love God and our neighbor (as ourselves). Our dis-eased affections can be healed when touched divinely, which in turn moves us toward wholeness and rightness initially before God and, through a (lifelong) process of conversion, to others. Our hearts, hopes, desires, and loves will no longer simply dictate who we are and how we act, but the Spirit will enable us to take greater and greater responsibility for these feelings and re-dispose them toward the divine. Of course, ultimately, our full healing and salvation is eschatological, yet theologically speaking, this is not only other-worldly but begins (even if it does not finish) in the here and now with the first affective transformation.

Emotions and Desires in Luke-Acts: Considering Affective Conversion Apostolically

The preceding lays out the broader theological framework for affective conversion. In the rest of this chapter, like in the preceding, we look through a few windows of Luke-Acts to explore aspects of conversion in the apostolic narratives. We start with Jesus in Luke's Gospel, then turn to the apostles in the book of Acts, before focusing on a common theme of eating with others found across the two volumes. Throughout, we consider affective conversion apostolically in order to appreciate its implications for our own conversion today and for our evangelistic vocation in tandem.

---

17. See also Parkinson, *Heart to Heart*, ch. 5, "Regulating Emotions," which is mostly focused on interpersonal aspects of our modulating our affective intensities.

Emotions and Affectivity of and in Response to Jesus: Affective Conversion in the Gospel of Luke

Assessments on Jesus's emotional life have lagged far behind that of Paul,[18] in large part because of the literature that came out by the late nineteenth and into the early twentieth century that looked at Paul as the father of Christian neuroses. Everybody wanted to study Paul's psychology, even as that study led slowly into studies of emotions. In the last few decades, there has been a greater and greater consideration, including attentiveness by New Testament scholars, to the Gospels and particularly to Jesus's psychological and emotional life.

Along the way we have begun to identify and catalog the range of emotions across the New Testament and, more relevant for our purposes, the life of Jesus particularly as manifest in Luke's Gospel.[19] Jesus's expressed emotions run the full gamut from amazement, compassion, love, joy, and hope on the one side to jealousy, fear, sorrow, distress, and anger on the other, all of which need to be understood in the first central Mediterranean context. In this regard, Luke's Gospel, including his depictions of Jesus's emotions and then of the apostles, written in all probability by a Hellenistic Jew, needs to be read against the backdrop of the Hellenistic world.

Scott Spencer has given us a contextually rich synchronic rather than diachronic perspective on Jesus's emotions.[20] He highlights Jesus's regrets, broken-heartedness, anger, anguish, and disgustedness or contemptuousness, and compares these with Jesus's joy and love. Most relevant for us, Spencer observes how Jesus grows and evolves in love, not only in scenes where he comes to unexpected awareness and appreciation of relevant new relational knowledge—as in his being amazed by what he learns about the centurion at Capernaum (Luke 7:1–10)—but especially in how other Gospels also relate him growing in love for his followers (e.g., his Beloved Disciple in John 13–20). As in all aspects of his human life, we can see the expansion of Jesus's own horizon of love in a humble fashion.

Inspired by Spencer's emotional hermeneutic applied to the Gospels, how might we reimagine Jesus's own ongoing emotional maturation from his teachings? While reading across the Third Gospel does not necessarily

---

18. Going back the last century, including an interim report a generation ago now: Callan, *Psychological Perspectives*.

19. See Voorwinde, *Jesus' Emotions in the Gospels*, ch. 3.

20. Spencer, *Passions of the Christ*.

allow us to trace Jesus's own psychological development, chiefly since scholars have not come to any consensus about either the historicity or chronological reliability of Luke's account, yet I suggest that the gospel arc invites considerations about how Jesus's own understandings may have gained in depth and clarity. Starting with the earlier—in terms of when it appears in Luke's text—Sermon on the Plain, then, we see Jesus teaching about love principally:

> Love your enemies, do good to those who hate you . . . . If you love those who love you, what credit is that to you? For even sinners love those who love them. If you do good to those who do good to you, what credit is that to you? For even sinners do the same. If you lend to those from whom you hope to receive, what credit is that to you? Even sinners lend to sinners, to receive as much again. But love your enemies, do good, and lend, expecting nothing in return. Your reward will be great, and you will be children of the Most High; for he is kind to the ungrateful and the wicked. (Luke 6:27, 32–35)

All of this is right and good. Amen, we will say in response to Jesus—then and now! Yet so loving our enemies remains challenging, then and today, even as we recognize how sinful we remain in that it continues to be easier now to love our friends and creditors.[21]

Jesus's later teaching about love, after he has sufficiently trained up his disciples and begun to commission their own ministry in the region, provides a window into a deeper level of understanding. At a moment devoted to celebrating the disciples' ministerial efforts, a lawyer asks about how eternal life might be inherited and, while Jesus's interaction elicits from the former recognition that the law's guidance foregrounds the greatest commandments of loving God and neighbor, the follow-up conversation is what is relevant for our purposes. The lawyer, in seeking self-justification, inquires with Jesus, "who is my neighbor?" (10:29b), and in further response, Jesus talks about the Good Samaritan:

> "A man was going down from Jerusalem to Jericho, and fell into the hands of robbers, who stripped him, beat him, and went away, leaving him half dead. Now by chance a priest was going down that road; and when he saw him, he passed by on the other side. So

---

21. Thus, there is surely both a cognitive and volitional dimension to love of enemies, yet all of this combines to identify the impossibility of such love except that it emanates, finally, from the heart, the center of one's entire being; see Elliott, *Faithful Feelings*, 145–47.

likewise a Levite, when he came to the place and saw him, passed by on the other side. But a Samaritan while traveling came near him; and when he saw him, he was moved with pity. He went to him and bandaged his wounds, having poured oil and wine on them. Then he put him on his own animal, brought him to an inn, and took care of him. The next day he took out two denarii, gave them to the innkeeper, and said, 'Take care of him; and when I come back, I will repay you whatever more you spend.' Which of these three, do you think, was a neighbor to the man who fell into the hands of the robbers?" [The lawyer] said, "The one who showed him mercy." Jesus said to him, "Go and do likewise." (10:30–37)

Three sets of comments are apropos at this juncture. First, the parable answers the question about what it means to love God and neighbor in relationship to eternal life. Love, and affectivity, are thereby central to these matters of ultimate concern. Second, however, note that the priest and the Levite both "passed by on the other side" (vv. 31–32). While this may have been because being of the priestly class impeded their approaching a defiling corpse-like body,[22] their intentional avoidance of this person in need is reinforced emotionally by disgust, fear, anxiety, or any other related feelings that repelled rather than drew them in. In contrast, and here third, the Samaritan who would have had additional reasons not to approach the Jewish man—here presumed in light of this story being part of a discussion between Jesus and the Jewish lawyer and in light of the long-standing sense of these communities being felt enemies of each other[23]—was yet able to overcome whatever emotional revulsions he may have had and, beyond that, find it in his heart to respond; "he was moved with pity" is what drew him in (10:33b),[24] and this affective response was recognized by the lawyer, who acknowledged at the end that the Samaritan exemplified loving his neighbor as "the one who showed him mercy" (10:37). Loving neighbor and God is no mere intellectual enterprise, but is affectively embodied.

Part of the point being made here, however, is that in this instance, Jesus comes to see the need not just for reasserting more abstract propositions

---

22. See Green, *Gospel of Luke*, 430–31.
23. See Donahue, "Who Is My Enemy?"
24. "[L]iterally 'moved in the guts,' the same Greek word used of Jesus when he raises the widow's son in 7:11–17," which we saw in ch. 2, and as we are reminded by Miller, "Good Sinners and Exemplary Heretics," 465; note the subtitle of Miller's article anticipates our hermeneutical turn in chapter 6 to the social and political dimensions of conversion.

such as were provided in his Sermon on the Plain but to root teachings on the love commandment in parabolic form. Telling a story about human love allows for empathetic identification in ways that propositional declarations do not. A normative commandment rests suspended over time and history, while a parable sets listeners (and readers) out on a journey, one that they can then also perhaps choose to continue on with. Is this a matter of Jesus coming into deeper insight about love or achieving greater clarity that teachings about love should be storied, with the latter allowing for greater appreciation, reception, and enaction? Even if only the latter point were to be granted, such would be a significant acknowledgment of Jesus's maturation in these communicative and principled matters.

Before turning to the apostles and the book of Acts, however, I want to return to a figure we have already seen in the second chapter of this book: the woman who anointed Jesus's feet with an alabaster jar of ointment. Here is someone who exemplifies taking responsibility for her emotional self-understanding in the presence of Jesus. We start at the end of the account, when Jesus says to her directly: "Your sins are forgiven" (7:48). We already commented previously that the woman already perceived she was accepted, if not also forgiven, by Jesus, and this was both demonstrated by her actions, including her "crashing the party" (so to speak) of Pharisees, and recognized explicitly by Jesus in his explanation to Simon: "her sins, which were many, have been forgiven; hence she has shown great love" (7:47b).[25]

Let's stay in this realm of self-awareness for a few more moments. This woman "who was a sinner" (7:37b) recognizes that even her many sins (explicated by Jesus, no less!) were not insurmountable barriers inhibiting Jesus's acknowledgment, welcome and acceptance. Recognition of her own sinfulness, no doubt, involved degrees of guilt, shame, self-condemnation, and felt-traumatization, each of which are affective, embodied, and social experiences, not even secondarily intellectual and personal ones. Remorse and grief would have been involved in her even contemplating approaching Jesus in this context, even as the capacity to receive the forgiveness of sins involves, beyond the exchange of intellectual information, a deeper level

---

25. Although the Greek grammar allows also for love to be the condition, rather than the result, of forgiveness, the overall Lukan narrative favors our own latter reading; see Szkredka, *Sinners and Sinfulness in Luke*, 145–50. Note it is also the case that Jesus's explicitly forgiving the woman's sins was as much if not more for the other Pharisees and guests at the dinner as Luke ends the story by reporting immediately: "But those who were at the table with him began to say among themselves, 'Who is this who even forgives sins?' And he said to the woman, 'Your faith has saved you; go in peace'" (7:49–50).

of affective honesty about who we have known ourselves to be and that we can know ourselves differently. Then courage would have been needed to overcome all of the hesitations, doubts, and anxieties about following Jesus into the private dinner event in a hostile environment (for a sinful person in the presence of religious leaders in the community). This would have particularly been the case if some parts of her own senses of shame, guilt, and traumatization derived from interpersonal or other personally and even hurtful or morally injurious interactions with the religious leadership of that community, or at the least from having had to navigate the systems and structures—indeed, the principalities and powers—that would have been represented by the Pharisaic members palpably populating the room. Yet sensing deeply enough feelings of not only self-acceptance but renewed self-worth moved her to not only risk her actions but also opened up to a torrent of emotional tears and weeping. The narrative thus presumes and depicts various moments, spiraling around each other no doubt, of affective conversion: remorse, self-acceptance, and courageous vulnerability before others.

And this woman takes responsibility, incrementally and step by step, as it were, for her emotional and personal health. If before her self-identity was defined at least in part by her own sinful choices and behaviors and in part by the marginalizing and condemning gaze of others, her encounters with Jesus leading up to this moment invited her to know deeply that she was accepted and loved despite what she had done, not just because others were ignorant of such. What is manifest is a fully affective and embodied knowing that is interpersonal expressed: following Jesus;[26] picking up an alabaster jar; bringing that into an alien social space; kneeling and crouching behind Jesus; bathing his feet with her tears; wiping them with her hair; "excessive" and "copious" kissing[27] and anointing his feet with the ointment; and showing "great love" (7:47b) out of her own experience of being loved, etc. Simon, by contrast, feels little and remains primarily at the cognitive register: "If this man were a prophet, he would have known . . ." (7:39b); no remorse, no emotional self-awareness, no love! One is unable to take responsibility for what one does not feel.

26. While Luke is silent about when the woman initially encountered Jesus, that does not mean she met him only right before this event; as the scene here resembles the earlier episode of Jesus healing the paralytic and forgiving his sins (5:17–26), the woman may have first glimpsed Jesus's love in that sequence of events. For retrieval of the former story in this dinner context, see Johnson, *Gospel of Luke*, 129.

27. Spencer, "Woman's Touch," 88–89.

PART II: APOSTOLIC EVANGELISM AND CONVERSION IN THE 2020S

Overflowing After Pentecost: Affective Conversion in the Acts of the Apostles

We now look at the book of Acts. We begin with the overflowing of affectivity in the apostolic experience, and then press further into descriptions of joy across the book. Space constraints inhibit exploration of other emotions in the early apostolic community even as our assessment considers apostolic affections, and apostolic joy and rejoicing more specifically, in light of conversion and what can be gleaned from Luke's account about taking responsibility for our emotional health and lives.

Why not begin with the signal apostolic event that commenced in the Upper Room on the day of Pentecost:

> And suddenly from heaven there came a sound like the rush of a violent wind, and it filled the entire house where they were sitting. Divided tongues, as of fire, appeared among them, and a tongue rested on each of them. All of them were filled with the Holy Spirit and began to speak in other languages, as the Spirit gave them ability. (Acts 2:2–4a)

What is described here reflects the fully embodied experiences of those so gathered. Observe the kinesthetic dimensions of the Pentecost outpouring: hearing the "sound like the rush of a violent wind"; feeling the wind as "it filled the entire house where they were sitting"; seeing the appearing of the divided tongues; sensing and perceiving those tongues resting on them; speaking from out of the center of their bodies—e.g., the belly, heart or innermost being as *koilías* is translated in John 7:38–39 where Jesus is recorded as speaking about the manifestation of the coming gift of the Spirit—as sensed to be inspired by the violent wind, etc.[28] No doubt there is a cognitive dimension involving speech understood at least by listeners outside the Room in the streets of Jerusalem. Yet what is happening cannot be reduced to an intellectual experience.

Embodied experience connotes what unfolds at the affective register. After at least another week or so together in the Upper Room, socioemotional bonds had been forged. What is felt by each is, in a sense, felt by them all, cumulatively: affectively, any private experience was not possible. Instead, since sounds are heard not only through our eardrums but in our bodies, the violent rushing wind can only be described as filling the

---

28. This section summarizes what I develop elsewhere at greater length about the kinesthetics of Pentecost; see my *Hermeneutical Spirit*, ch. 2.

entirety of their embodied space, literally moving their bodies in its arriving impact. The Spirit thus surrounds and resounds, effectively: permeates our space, our bodies, our movements, so that we burst forth in tongues, as if we have been filled inside, even while we are fully enveloped, almost but not quite suffocated.[29] The Spirit blows, rests, touches, overwhelms, almost irresistibly inspires. This is not a cognitive exercise but a full-bodied and saturated experience of the living divine wind.

It should not be surprising then, that joy emerges as an indicator of the Spirit's presence and activity across the book of Acts. Although current psychological research tends to consider joy in relation to happiness, itself understood as a basic type or category of emotion, joy has also long been considered a primary passion of the human psyche.[30] And while Luke does present joy and rejoicing as a result of the Spirit's converting work, they can also be understood as part and parcel of what happens in conversion. And when we distinguish between communal or congregational and personal accounts of joy, we can further observe how such affective conversions catalyze taking of responsibility.[31]

At the communal level, Luke seems more clear that joy is both an effect and an affect of the Spirit's converting work. Philip's evangelistic ministry in Samaria is accompanied by exorcisms, healings, and other signs and wonders, so that, as Luke sums it up, "there was great joy in that city" (Acts 8:8). Then, at Antioch of Pisidia, although Paul and Barnabas struggled mightily to get a hearing in the synagogue, they found a receptivity among gentiles and so although driven by some Jews out of the city to Iconium, Luke records them going on their way "filled with joy and with the Holy Spirit" (13:52). Later, on their way to the Jerusalem Council, as Paul and Barnabas "passed through both Phoenicia and Samaria, they reported the conversion of the Gentiles, and brought great joy to all the believers" (15:3b), and then, when they arrived back at the church in Antioch after

---

29. For more on the sounds of Pentecost, see my article, "Proclamation and the Third Article."

30. There are plenty of contemporary typologies of human emotions in none of which (that I am aware of) joy is absent. Even René Descartes, in his efforts to explore how the passions of the human psyche that moved human bodies could be related to human minds—recall the Cartesian effort to bridge the mind-body dualism/chasm—discusses the central role of joy, among other emotions; see the discussion in part 2 of Descartes's "Passions of the Soul."

31. Story, *Joyous Encounters*, ch. 7, which at almost 150 pages that is almost half of the book, is focused on Acts.

the Council with the report of what had been decided about the inclusion of gentiles among the messianic body, Luke is clear to report that, "when its members read it, they rejoiced at the exhortation" (15:31). Each of these cases, not surprisingly, reflects the joy and rejoicing related to the advance of the gospel beyond Jerusalem and Judea, beginning with the Samarians and then extending to gentiles.[32]

Luke also describes other more specific groups and individuals rejoicing or being filled with joy. The disciples, after having been jailed overnight for healing the lame man at the Beautiful Gate, explaining themselves more to the Jewish leadership council, and flogged as a further warning, on departure, Luke records that "they rejoiced that they were considered worthy to suffer dishonor for the sake of the name" (5:41b); the disciples thereafter persist boldly in their witness. Next, after hearing about the messiah from Philip and being baptized in water, upon the latter being snatched away, Luke tells us that the Ethiopian eunuch "went on his way rejoicing" (8:39b); Ethiopian church tradition tells us that this officer of the court of Candace the (then) queen returned to his homeland and his witness led to the founding of the Christian community there. A second "overjoyed" (12:14) individual Luke informs us about is Rhoda, the maid of the house-church that held an all-night prayer meeting for an imprisoned Peter, and whose joyous reaction was to hearing the voice of a released Peter at the gate when she responded to the knock; in her case, taking responsibility for her feelings meant informing the prayers that he was there, overlooking at that moment letting him in. Last but not least, it is said of the Philippian jailer that "he and his entire household rejoiced that he had become a believer in God" (16:34b) after receiving the gospel from Paul and Silas, washing their wounds, being baptized by them, and then hosting the prisoners in his home; from this affectively full moment, the jailer stands in solidarity with Paul and Silas mediating their eventual release from the magistrates and police (16:35–39). In each of these cases, joy is surely a responsive aspect of the reception of the gospel. In that respect, it is a sign of conversion, an affective indicator, while also being an affective comportment accompanying if not also generating further converting commitments and actions.

There is one final reference to joy that I believe is significant for purposes, which is found at the end of the message Paul and Barnabas are

---

32. Consistent with the joyousness of Jesus and the seventy upon the latter's return from their mission to the countryside in Luke 10:17–21; see also Voorwinde, *Jesus' Emotions in the Gospels*, 128–32.

recorded to have given at the city gates of Lystra.[33] Upon healing the lame man in the city, the Lystrans instinctively reacted to Paul and Barnabas as if they were deities, at least in terms of how they were wielding divine healing power associated with Zeus and Hermes, and thus sought to offer up sacrifices to them (14:8–14). Luke's summary of the apostolic horror-filled reply—"they tore their clothes and rushed out into the crowd" (14:14)[34]—reads thus:

> Friends, why are you doing this? We are mortals just like you, and we bring you good news, that you should turn from these worthless things to the living God, who made the heaven and the earth and the sea and all that is in them. In past generations he allowed all the nations to follow their own ways; yet he has not left himself without a witness in doing good—giving you rains from heaven and fruitful seasons, and filling you with food and your hearts with joy. (14:15–17)

Today, we might consider this as a natural theological response: the apostles stay at a general theological level of how God nourishes (provides rain), feeds (ensures fruitful seasons), and makes life worthwhile (more precisely: enjoyable), not touching on the specifics of the gospel witness to and about Jesus Christ.

But staying at this level of *what* Paul says easily overlooks the affective *how* of what is communicated. Whereas in its broader context, this narrative extends the Pauline mission to the gentiles embarked upon more formally and recently in this first journey from Antioch in Pisidia and Iconium (13:46–51), what unfolds provides Paul with the opportunity to engage with the pagan cultures of "Lystra and Derby, cities of Lycaonia, and . . . the surrounding country[side]" (14:6), and to highlight to the profoundly religious Lycaonian speakers (14:11a)—which deep piety was exemplified in their readiness to offer sacrifices to Paul and Barnabas—the nature of the deity that had now drawn near to them.[35] In other words, touching on the heart religiosity, so to speak, manifest by these inhabitants of Lycaonian cities and their surrounding rural regions, apostolic witness

---

33. See Fournier, *Episode at Lystra*.

34. This description gives us a window into Paul's (and Barnabas's) serious emotional reaction, one indicative of their being horrified at the developing desperate situation; see Voorwinde, "Paul's Emotions in Acts," 78–79.

35. I am greatly helped in this rendition by Bechard, *Paul Outside the Walls*, whose study contrasts the mission to gentiles in rural spaces here at Lystra with the mission to gentiles in urban spaces later at Athens and the Areopagus.

both corrected misguided trust in and ritualistic service to mere idols and redirected pietistic instincts and populistic sensibilities affectively, toward a transcendent and yet recognizable monotheistic and creator God who is yet no less concerned about the mundane needs and enjoyments of their lives at the outskirts (the countryside) of the Pax Romana.[36]

Put otherwise, the mundane joys of life derive from God. When human creatures are satisfied via a good meal, when they work the land to produce crops for consumption, when they welcome rain from heaven or as that water flows down the rivers upon which human beings depend, these are the mere but no less real joys felt in their hearts. Our very sense of these joyous occasions and moments are divine gifts. On top of all these are other human joys, of holding a baby, embracing a loved one, spending time with friends, standing before a beautiful mountain or a vast ocean and hearing the waves, etc. While these words "scarcely restrained the crowds from offering sacrifice" (14:18b) to Paul and Barnabas, they are important reminders that we share the world and its provisions with fellow human (and other) creatures. These are mutual benefits and enjoyments that in turn can prompt gratitude and more general human solidarity. Taking responsibility for these joyous gifts of life is thereby a lifelong endeavor, precisely because these are gifts that never stop giving, and in that respect, joys that can continue to nurture enjoyment, for those of us who might be more open to be fully converted affectively.

Eating with Others: Fellowship and Affective Conversion in Luke-Acts

Having in this part of the chapter looked at the emotions of and in response to Jesus and the embodied joys of the apostolic experience, I now want to consider what Luke-Acts tells us about eating with others. How do the meals in the Lukan narrative illuminate affective conversion? Earlier in our discussion of Peter's intellectual conversion we passed briefly over the visions he received about eating "all kinds of four-footed creatures and reptiles and birds of the air" (Acts 10:12) that he refused to because they were "profane and unclean" (10:14b). Peter's disgust with these impure, polluting, and contaminating animals needed to be overcome in order for him to entertain the possibility of eating with, much less enjoying the fellowship

---

36. Keener, *Between History and Spirit*, ch. 10: "Turning from Idols in Acts 14:15–17."

of, gentiles like Cornelius.[37] Eating is thereby not only a physical endeavor but has an affective component, which is multiplied when we eat not by ourselves but with others.

Much can be gleaned from consideration of Jesus's meals with others, including with sinners. In the Gospel of Luke, there are over a dozen references to either Jesus eating with people—whether with his smaller or larger groups of his disciples, Pharisees, tax collectors, large groups (e.g., of five thousand!), or various individuals or pairs (Mary and Martha or the two on the Emmaus Road)—or Jesus talking about eating.[38] Pause then to also think about all of the emotions that are taking place in these various meal situations, for instance "burning hearts" in the presence of Jesus after his arising from the dead (Luke 24:32). Yet the affective dimension of eating together goes beyond what kind of emotions are present in any meal event. In the parable of the prodigal son, for instance, Jesus tells the story of the father who throws a celebratory party at the return of the lost son that includes eating, music, and dancing (15:23–25), although the older brother is unable to join in easily because of his indignation and anger. Each table needs to be approached with the relevantly appropriate affective composure for the meal to be enjoyable.

In chapter 2, we briefly commented on Jesus's teaching about the great dinner in the context of the coming divine reign's acceptance and inclusion of the most socially marginalized of the world. Note that those more well off, the ones usually invited to wedding banquets, would have felt most comfortable dining with friends, siblings, relatives, or "rich neighbors" including other land owners or business acquaintances (14:12a, 18–19), precisely the groups that Jesus says should be secondary on the guest list but are prioritized because these are in the best position to reciprocate hospitality (14:12b). Re-read according to our affective hermeneutic, however, we might also say that we eat most contentedly among those we know, trust, and are relaxed with. Others, especially strangers but also even those we know but yet are different from us culturally, ethnically, or socioeconomically, are more challenging. Class differences are even more unnerving, especially for the more affluent to interact with "the poor, the crippled, the lame, and the blind" (14:13b, also 14:21b). If back then there were already chasms separating rich folks eating sumptuously from poor folks at their gates eating out of the leftovers (e.g., 16:19–21), our current structures have

---

37. See also Beck, "Spiritual Pollution," 62–63.
38. For an overview, see Hell, *Meal Scenes in Luke-Acts*, ch. 17.

not changed much as our customs and conventions still do not facilitate eating together across social classes. Even in church potlucks, for instance, like-minded and, more relevantly, like-membered smaller cliques flock together. Our implicit biases make it extremely challenging for us to eat comfortably with "others," which is why Jesus eating with sinners might read well from an idealist christological perspective but is more challenging for us to implement, embody, and live out.[39]

The earliest apostolic community was as much a house-based movement as a mass movement: "Day by day, as they spent much time together in the temple, they broke bread at home and ate their food with glad and generous hearts," and "every day in the temple *and at home* they did not cease to teach and proclaim Jesus as the Messiah" (Acts 2:46, 5:42, emphasis added). Elsewhere in Jerusalem or perhaps in the wider Judean region, the house of "Mary, the mother of John whose other name was Mark" (Acts 12:12) had become an ecclesial site, at least one at which all night prayer meetings were held. Beyond Judea, we know already about Peter not only entering but staying over at Cornelius's house in Caesarea "for several days" (11:48), and this would have been after his ministry in Tabitha or Dorcas's home in Joppa (9:36–41).

Paul's apostolic ministries operated across a number of household sites. At Philippi, he and his compatriots stay with and cultivated the ecclesial community of that city at Lydia's house (16:15, 40), even if another site then also emerges at the home of the jailer (16:31–34); at Thessalonica, the first church was established at Jason's house (17:5–7); at Corinth, Titus Justus initially (18:7–8) and also Priscilla and Aquila later (18:26) opened their homes; at Troas, the nascent messianic community met on the third floor of an otherwise unidentified building, perhaps a home (20:8–11); and at Ephesus, Paul reminded the elders there in his farewell message to them that "I did not shrink from doing anything helpful, proclaiming the message to you and teaching you publicly and from house to house" (20:20).[40] Alongside the routine practice of breaking bread together on the first day of the week, mentioned specifically at Troas (20:7), it is safe to assume that in all of these cases, the earliest description, "they broke bread at home and ate their food with glad and generous hearts," remained applicable: that from day to day, members of the new messianic community in these various regions and cities of the Mediterranean world found ways to get to know each

---

39. See Croasmun and Volf, *Hunger for Home*, chs. 3–4.
40. Matson, *Household Conversion Narratives*, 154–68.

other, to overcome their ethnic, cultural, and linguistic prejudices, and to have meal fellowship in the Spirit.[41]

None of these would have been easy. We already noted, in our discussion of Peter's intellectual conversion in the preceding chapter, that he was inconsistent in transitioning from his practice of eating only with fellow Jews according to pre-established conventions to dining with gentiles. And even in the early Jerusalem community, we know that Greek-speaking and Hebrew-speaking widows found it difficult to sustain eating with each other, in this context divided by linguistic differences and challenges (6:1). The point here is that even the very basic act of eating, if not in our solitude, is shaped by presuppositions about who we sit with and share meals. It is easier to sit and eat my lunch in the cafeteria by myself surrounded by many others than it is for me to enjoy my lunch *together* with relative strangers. Observing this difference is being attentive to the affective dimension of our eating habits and practices.

Apostolic meal times therefore also provided occasions and spaces for reimaging common life outside of the predetermined conventions of our family, tribe, or clan, however those might be defined, to include others we had been warned to avoid, been alerted to be suspicious about, or been primed to engage only on our own clearly demarcated conditions. Early Christian practices reflected in the apostolic narrative and beyond suggest that meals were eaten with others in mind, including widows and other needy persons in the neighborhood or community.[42] Our guard is up in these circumstances of navigating life with others different from us. Eating with these "alien" others is the first step to reshaping our affections vis-à-vis these others. Beginning with the prayer of blessing that is also a moment for the deepening of gratitude, and continuing through with the conversation that re-socializes our hearts toward others, and culminating, over time, with ever widening circles of new friends from other clans, tribes, and also nations—now brothers and sisters: a new "family" dynamic under their creator God (cf. Acts 17:26a)—emerges out of such dining fellowship.[43]

Such affective transformation operates at two levels, that of hosts and that of guests. The former's homes need to be opened to welcome others,

---

41. See Smith, "House Church as Social Environment," 15–16.

42. Osiek and Balch, *Families in the New Testament*, 212–14.

43. Meal occasions for the early messianists were thus liminal moments and spaces when they forged new associations across ethnic-cultural lines and socioeconomic classes, relating to others in the neighborhood or the wider community; see Taussig, *In the Beginning*, 88–103 and 163–70.

while the latter's hearts need to be opened to enter strange spaces out of their control.[44] Both need affective reorientation by the Spirit poured out upon all flesh so that our bodies, instead of stiffening up in the presence of others, enable the appropriate vulnerability to mutual meal enjoyment. Early Christian evangelism operated in these home spaces, and were enacted in and through mealtimes. Evangelistic bodies in these places and moments interacted with those being evangelized, and the gospel resounded in and through the affective tones of such meal fellowship. Taking responsibility for enlarging our hearts toward others is perhaps most speedily enacted by making friends and eating with others who are different from ourselves.

Christian Evangelism and Affective Conversion Today: Feeling Spirit-ed Witness and Praxis

How might we summarize the foregoing about human feeling, emotions, and affections? What important takeaways about affection conversion emerge from our considerations above of Jesus's and apostolic emotions, including meal eating? What are the implications for our own Spirit-led conversion and evangelism today?

First, we might say that *the contemporary turn to the subject was anticipated two thousand years ago by the apostolic conversion of the heart*. Late modernity's "turn-to-the-subject" is in part a reaction to the modern emphasis on reason, a rationalism that was disembodied, that minimized the role of the emotions, and that marginalized human subjectivity. The apostolic narratives invite us to return to a Spirit-ed subjectivity, one attentive to the embodied and affective level of who we are. Intellectual conversion, in this respect, follows affective and emotional conversion. It is not that God is uninterested in our heads, but that if our hearts are not so converted, our cognitive commitments will continue to be affectively modulated. Where are we hurting, affectively, emotionally, at this deeper level? How might our feelings, emotions, and affections be more fully, joyously, and wholly reoriented by the Spirit?

Second, *adequate Christian witness involves ongoing conversion at least to the embodied and affective experience of others*. Evangelistically, then, the Spirit's turn to the heart invites our own focus: to what others are feeling, desiring, hoping for. This is the pathic dimension of who we are. Evangelism therefore is affectively charged, having to do not with bribing others with

---

44. Which I discuss especially in ch. 4 of my *Hospitality and the Other*.

AFFECTIVE CONVERSION

promises of material rewards for their bodies, but with being relationally authentic in our witness.[45] Recognition of our own embodied way of being in the world, including its fragmented and broken expressions, provides us with perspective on the embodied thriving experienced by and diseases afflicting others. Rather than taking advantage of such affective pain, we prepare ourselves to be accompaniers for the longer haul, to be in solidarity with the felt oppression. In fact, our attentiveness to the affective is not so we can be master manipulators of others,[46] but in order to be transformed in our feeling of others so we can feel our way forward with them. The first bridge, then, is not the intellectual or linguistic but the affective racial/ethnic or cultural turning our hearts to the hearts of others.

Third, *the evangelistic practice of accompaniment opens up to the missional practice of eating with others and the communal practice of sharing life with others.* Again, accompaniment means being willing to operate at a deeper level than simply the technical one, that which attempts to bring solutions to others from the outside. Instead, accompaniment involves pledging our full selves to walk alongside others even while recognizing that vulnerability goes in both directions (we are after all not already perfected and having all things figured out). Accompaniment then begs for deeper mutuality, one nurtured by sharing of meals, not always in "my" place but, as possible, in each other's, and over time, in "our" spaces.[47] We may begin transactionally—I invite you over so next it is your turn to invite me—but authentic relationality eventually moves beyond this or any kind of patronage or agenda-driven reciprocity toward a genuine sharing, of time if not also of living spaces. Our dispositions have been reconfigured so that the us/other binary is overcome: others are us and we are more than who we used to be as we persist in a particular space for an extended period of time. In this renewed "us," "we" cease to bring answers and resolutions

---

45. Chester, *Meal with Jesus*, 9, writes: "I fell in love with my wife while she was making me cheese on toast"; this tongue-in-cheek comment highlights the relational potency of embodied and affective interaction: not only are we more likely to "love" others when sharing our meals but so also is it more likely that others will fall in love with and be more open to who we are and what we love when we share of our homes and lives.

46. The history of revivalism is interwoven with the use of emotional forms of evangelistic communication as a means of mass conversion—e.g., Kircher, "Selling Timeshares in Heaven"—even if we should be careful about reducing such complicated religious phenomena to this single register.

47. See also Geitz, *Fireweed Evangelism*, ch. 5, about what she calls "backward evangelism."

for "their" problems; rather, both diagnoses and prognoses are shared, and so navigated.

But now the important and hard question: How easy might it be—how willing are we—to convert affectively so that "we" and "they" are less oppositional and contrasting and more harmonious, even if not necessarily homogeneously manifest? What then are the missiological challenges of the foregoing consideration of apostolic affective conversion? For those of us who would be missionaries and evangelists, here are a few more questions at this stage of our own journey.

First, *are we committed to the lifelong renewing of our hearts—including our feelings, emotions, and affections—in following the Spirit of Jesus who leads us into all truth and bears witness to/from the ends of the earth?* The question here is less *what we should know* than *how we should feel* in light of all we are called to traverse and who we encounter and engage. The invitation of the preceding is to attend to our embodiment, and through that, to observe how it provides cues into where our heart is and what we desire, aspire to, and yearn for. If, as Jesus said, "where your treasure is, there your heart will be also" (Luke 12:34), then how do we become more honest about and appraise our true selves, so far, and what are the implications for redirecting our own lives along the vocational and missional trajectory to which we are called? If the prophet Jeremiah is right in asking, "The heart is devious above all else; it is perverse—who can understand it?" (Jer 17:9), how then can we probe ourselves more deeply? Will we be content telling sanitized versions of our stories to us and others, or will we allow ourselves to be converted along the missiological road, and to begin to take responsibility at this depth dimension of who we are? We cannot be effective conduits for the affective and emotional conversion of others unless we understand our own affective and emotional pains and brokenness. Are we committed to the lifelong healing of our own hearts in the spirit of Jesus, who helps us to be more deeply connected?

Second, *is it OK that, often, the conversion of our hearts is facilitated through our affective encounter with and embodied experiences of others?*[48] We already know that in order to be good evangelists, we ought to know who we are evangelizing, feel deeply with and for these we are called to evangelize. I am asking a deeper and even prior question: Are we willing to feel deeply with these we are called to first and foremost for our own sake?

---

48. We are calling here for what might be termed a relational missiology; e.g., Reichard, "Mutually Transformative Missions."

Are we going to be vulnerable in the presence of those we believe we are called to evangelize? How can we have compassion on others if we do not on ourselves? Can we learn from others, including others we are called to bear witness to, about such self-compassion? Are we courageous enough to follow the Spirit into all truth if that includes shining a greater light on our hearts through the mirror of others God has placed in our lives, including those who we may be called to care for (as pastors, missionaries, etc.) and to evangelize? How willing are we to allow the Spirit's illumination of our dis-ease, brokenness, and traumas through the lives of such others? It is not just that God wants to continue to so heal and transform us but that often God chooses to do so through the persons we are called to be ambassadors of health and healing to![49]

Finally, for now, *are we willing to listen and open our hearts to be touched by those we are called to evangelize?* If the traumas of others will trigger our traumas, will we be continuously reactive and defensive? If our neuroses and psychoses inhibit our openness to others, will our hearts remain guarded against those the Spirit is calling us to? I am not here urging that victims of trauma or other injurious behaviors consider evangelizing their victimizers, since even if there is some degree of healing and forgiveness that has been attained we may need to leave such evangelism to others. Yet, if we are implicitly biased against people with different skin colors, phenotypes, and accents than us, can these be rooted out for us to approach them as equals? It is not just that we may be inhibited from bearing adequate witness if we objectify those we are evangelizing, but that the Spirit's means of bringing about our own joy from despair, and healing from brokenness, is also impeded. If others are or should not be mere objects of our evangelization activities, then our approach is as subjects to subjects, which involves the possibility of real give-and-take, interactivity, mutuality, and, finally, reconciliation, renewal, and redemption. This heart openness will be near to impossible unless we are already committed, affectively, to the lifelong journey of conversion of our feelings and emotions.

---

49. I take up some of these matters of witness in interfaith or interreligious contexts in my "Hospitality and Religious Others."

Chapter 5

Moral Conversion

Apostolic Interactions Then and Now

SO FAR IN THIS part of the book we have discussed intellectual and affective conversion, in effect explorations of what happens at the level of consciousness and in our subconscious. In this chapter, we turn to the moral dimension of conversion: how conversion is lived out in our choices, behaviors, actions, and deeds. On the one hand, we may say that the moral domain makes clear how our thoughts and words and feelings are being transformed; on the other hand, we might also say that, given the recursivity of these converting domains, our practices and performances also impinge upon if not also lead to changes of mind and heart. As has been repeatedly invoked, we are treating these disparately and in an order that is heuristic at best, although they operate often together and not even in the sequence of our discussion.

Here, as in the last two chapters, there are three parts. We begin with laying out the overarching missiological, theological, and christological terrain for our discussion of moral conversion and then turn to the apostolic witness in the book of Acts for deeper insight into the transformation that happens, or could happen, at this level. The shorter concluding section reviews our findings and probes into our capaciousness for embracing the kind of moral transformation that is needed for missional and evangelistic witness.

We must make one more point about moral conversion. The moral domain, as Gelpi helps to clarify,[1] involves both taking personal ownership of the conventional morality that we have been socialized into—whether in our families, education, or even churches—and then reasoning prudentially (not only logically or affectively) based on ethical principles and guidelines about what we ought to do in any circumstance (not, or not only what we *can* do if we have various options). Some might, in this sense, suggest that moral transformation is not about salvation, per se, but about sanctification, the fruits of redemption, so to speak. We are saved, after all, not by works (our efforts or deeds) but by grace, and in that sense, moral transformation emerges from intellectual and affective conversion. A careful reader of this volume to this point will realize that our overall understanding resists framings that too quickly separate out theologically weighty concepts, in this case for instance, salvation and sanctification. Rather, the horizon of argumentation assumes a dynamic theological journey that nevertheless is phenomenologically and existentially rich. The former provides perspective of God's saving lives, not just heads or emotions or deeds, but not excluding any of this, while the latter can be explored more piecemeal with various anthropological and related tools at our disposal.[2] Hence, again, we treat this aspect of conversion distinctly, but only because the moral is, as shall be even clearer at the end of this chapter, intertwined and interdependent with the intellectual and the affective but also considerable from its own perspective.

Moral Conversion: Some Missiological, Theoretical, and Normative Perspectives

If moral conversion involves a taking of personal responsibility for one's actions based on owning for oneself the moral and ethical principles guiding our lives and behaviors, then we ought first also to name and comprehend, at least in broad contours, the conventional moral frameworks that we mostly navigate, and even in the lifelong process of moral conversion, never completely leave behind. In this first section, we elaborate at a high level, then introduce the neo-Thomist framework of morality and the virtues within

---

1. Gelpi, *Conversion Experience*, 29–30.
2. My prior theological anthropological musings that reflect these approaches can be found in *Theology and Down Syndrome*, ch. 6; see also *Renewing Christian Theology*, ch. 8.

which Gelpi's proposal is developed, and then sketch in broad strokes a christological ethic, especially from Luke. None of the following is exhaustive since our parameters are missiological and evangelistic, with a more immediate goal of opening up to closer readings of moral conversion in the book of Acts in the second section of this chapter.

Missiological and Historical Developments

A bit of perspective from the history of Christian mission allows us to see how moral conversion is interrelated with Christian initiation and discipleship. In the patristic period, for instance, and then extending into the medieval centuries, Christian initiation was often an extended process, one that included a period, sometimes lasting over years, of catechetical instruction (indoctrination, in the descriptive, not pejorative sense), spiritual and devotional practices, and moral formation, culminating in rites of renunciation of the devil, baptism in water accompanied by Charismatic manifestations, and breaking bread with the community of faith (Eucharist or Lord's Supper, depending on tradition).[3] There would be catechetical variations in terms of order and length depending on regional location, and yet the moral dimension was always included with the instructional/intellectual and spiritual/affective aspects. Moral transformation was particularly assessed in monastic communal contexts. The Benedictine "Rule of Life," for instance, formed catechumens to self-modulate their affections in correlation with their practices for both spiritual and mundane realms of engagement. So moral conversion and formation has a deep and long history in the Christian tradition, regularly lodged on the front end of Christian initiation. In these respects, moral transformation was embedded within the Christian missional endeavor, always part and parcel of what Christian conversion accounted for.

The colonial mission enterprise, after the founding of the "new world," took European (then into the nineteenth century) and North American around the world. Christian initiation in these now global missiological contexts did not neglect the moral dimension but operationalized such endeavors within a racialized Eurocentric framework,[4] one that involved cultural conversion to Western moral standards. The task of "civilizing" the

---

3. For further discussion, see Yong, *Spirit Poured Out*, 99–100, and *Renewing Christian Theology*, 135–39.

4. E.g., Sechrest et al., *Can "White" People Be Saved?*

indigenous peoples of Asia, Africa, and Latin America, then, imposed such Western conventions. Therefore, distinctions now emerged from a normative perspective: in what ways were such moral conversions only cultural, e.g., from an Asian, African, or Latin American one to a European or North American one, or how else were moral and ethical norms to be discerned amid these interactions? What are the normative implications for moral transformation within a Christian framework, and how did the latter relate to the morality and ethics of Western and other cultures?

Natural law ethicists might urge that there are normative moral and ethical principles to be gleaned that are cross-cultural, under which, they might urge, cultural or religious moralities might be identified. Particularists of various sorts might urge instead that the more foundational are divinely or transcendently revealed moral and ethical laws, from which then we can generalize toward a universal morality and ethic. This argument might be made across religious traditions, for instance, whether that be Reconstructionists or Theonomists on the Christian side or advocates and defenders of Sharia law on the Muslim side, just to name two possibilities. This is not to suggest that these are equivalent to other moral positions, only that the public squares that we inhabit will continue to grapple with more universalist and more particularist—and everything in between—visions of the common good.[5]

We are beginning to bleed from moral conversion to sociopolitical conversion, which is our next chapter. However, for now, it is still important to insist that our own positionality respects the arguments made from each direction in the never-ending spiral of dialogue and debate. Even though there is no "resolution" on this side of the eschaton, that does not mean that moral and ethical progress is not made. Rather, new moral insights are imperative as new ethical questions and contexts emerge. Thus, from a missiological perspective, moral conversion will remain part and parcel of our journey. Ongoing moral evolution and development, at least, if not also transformation, are needed to enable adequate engagement with and taking of responsibility within new sociohistorical moments and their accompanying ethical questions and quandaries. If moral conversion has long been part of Christian initiation and discipleship, then the invitation to moral transformation will persist.

---

5. This is the point I have made in my work over two decades on theologies of religions and theologies of interreligious dialogue and encounter, e.g., *Hospitality and the Other*.

PART II: APOSTOLIC EVANGELISM AND CONVERSION IN THE 2020S

Moral Conversion: An Emerging (New-Thomist) Paradigm

As we press into the question of moral norms, I think it will be helpful for us to better situate Gelpi's theology of conversion that has guided our efforts. There are three streams flowing through Gelpi's Roman Catholic theological formation: the affective one carried by his initiation into the Society of Jesus and his then decades-long participation in the Jesuit tradition, the intellectual one shaped by what happened at the Second Vatican Council (1960–65), and the ensuing Charismatic renewal within the Roman Catholic Church, of which he partook.[6] His Jesuit education and formation, in part at St. Louis University and in part at Fordham University, introduced and then baptized Gelpi into the neo-Thomist tradition that dominated Roman Catholic theology and philosophy in the first half of the twentieth century. Within this framework, moral formation worked with evangelical or affective conversion and contemplative practice and intellectual studies to constitute the warp and woof of religious transformation.

In the background were theologians like Bernard Lonergan (1904–84). One of the leading lights of Vatican II, in lectures given in the wake of the council on transcendental religious philosophy, Lonergan urged that moral conversion "changes the criterion of one's decisions and choices from satisfactions to values."[7] Within the broader scope of Lonergan's transcendental method, including his theological method, such conversion happens via a recursive process of attending/experiencing, understanding/comprehending, judging/deciding, and acting/communicating, and in that respect, moral transformation happens when we observe how our choices are often driven by pursuit of satisfactions, to clarifying how these motivations work morally, discerning what values instead ought to be factored in, and then deciding to live as axiologically as possible. Now to the degree that our values are ultimately shaped religiously, then moral conversion is interwoven with religious or spiritual conversion as well.[8] Within the Jesuit tradition, then, religious life, including ritual/sacramental and habitual/devotional practices, absorbs theological and ethical values together to nurture virtuosity in disposition, behavior, and character.[9]

---

6. From the theological autobiography and memoir of Gelpi, *Closer Walk*.

7. From Lonergan's Boston College Lectures given in 1968; see Doran and Croken, *Early Works on Theological Method 1*, 564.

8. For a helpful discussion, see Kinberger, *Lonergan on Conversion*.

9. Spitzer, *Escape from Darkness*, part 2.

Returning back to Gelpi now, we are in a better position to appreciate why moral conversion, like other transformational domains, is dynamic and recursive. Later moments of taking responsibility build off prior ones, even as earlier experiences are deepened or even left behind as we go. Further, there is always a social/ecclesial context within which we are attending to our experiences, so life's journey will introduce other, new, social (and ecclesial) perspectives into our horizon that will propel another round of attentiveness, reasonableness, commitments, and decisions. If virtuous formation, within this framework, takes practice, the latter now unfolds within expanded communal horizons and may lead to new observations and their accompanying moments of ongoing moral transformation.

In that respect, moral conversion is not only about instances of taking moral responsibility but on setting out on a spiritually and religiously formative path, one that includes attentiveness to the moral dimension of dynamically contextualized experiences. More precisely, if moral conversion includes taking personal responsibility for one's moral commitments beyond what we have inherited from the conventions bequeathed by our families, churches, and communities, then the journey of habitual reformation must be carefully cultivated. Why and how might I be able to appropriately identify, question, engage, and revise, as needed, the moral "norms" I have presumed is itself a complicated consideration requiring multiple communities of moral inquiry. We do not often have the luxury of affiliating with any one of these for an extended period of time just to sort out our moral convictions. On the other hand, if we understand this moral domain as interwoven with other aspects of our lives, then we can be more alert to the occasions when moral transformation might be in order when experience, and life's feedback in the differing contexts we find ourselves, so warrant.

As Gelpi defines it, moral conversion "deals exclusively with interpersonal social dealings, while sociopolitical conversion seeks to influence the decisions of those who control the larger, more impersonal, social institutions" in which we live.[10] As we will turn in the next chapter to the latter, for now then, note that our attending to the necessity of moral conversion appropriately interfaces at the primary level of our relationship to and interactions with others. We might begin to take appropriate ownership of our moral commitments by taking stock of our relationships and communal networks. How do the communities to which I am devoted or within which

---

10. Gelpi, *Conversion Experience*, 31.

I participate as a member nurture my moral compass? Moral conversion itself emerges from out of the give-and-take of human life and relationships. If our initial moral sensibilities were formed out of growing up with this family, attending that church, and being schooled in the other community, then our ongoing moral transformation can be shaped by the (new) company we keep. This does not mean we do need to resituate ourselves (only we can answer such questions) but that the first step of taking moral responsibility allows for that question to surface.

Toward a Normative Account: Starting with Jesus

From a Christian theological perspective, any normative account is christological in some or other respect. In this book, missiological and evangelistic normativity is measured across the Lukan register: according to the two books in the New Testament from this evangelist. In this chapter, however, our apostolic forays in the next section will be derived primarily from the second, sequel volume of the book of Acts. Yet it is important here to briefly peek at the christological underpinnings in the Third Gospel.

Much has been published on the morality and ethics of Jesus.[11] When read within the Gelpian framework we have been working with in this book, we can understand that Jesus himself underwent at least one major moral conversion. It is not just that his teaching invites us to think about the ways in which our lives are oriented toward others, or that he insisted that setting out on the path of loving our neighbor and of acting justly toward our neighbor is the most fundamental moral expression of loving God with all our heart. Rather, what Jesus did was take this greatest of ancient Israel's commandments and enflesh that in ways that saw him take greater personal responsibility for such moral dictums that he then also handed on to his listeners and disciples. We thereby hear him regularly contrast his own beliefs and practices with the extant Mosaic law. This is most evident in the Sermon on the Mount in Matthew's Gospel when, after asserting his authority to insist that human righteousness should exceed that of the Law (Matt 5:20), his laying out of what the Law says in at least six moral areas is followed with a definitive, "But I say to you . . ." (5:22, 28, 32, 34, 39, 44). This basic trajectory is preserved in the Sermon on the Plain although, given the Lukan audience being broader than Matthew's Jewish one, the contrast is a bit less stark, with the former's "But I say to you" (Luke

11. Stassen and Gushee, *Kingdom Ethics*.

6:27) following quotations from the Law and the Prophets. The point here is that even as Jesus was raised on the Law, Prophets, and Writings (cf. Luke 24:44b), he had come to his own moral insight, one that compelled him to exceed the legal requirements he had inherited. Jesus's moral teachings, then, invite others to consider what they had presumed, with the tradition, the Law required, and then to take ownership of their own moral lives.

So, the cue is that Jesus taught across a full range of moral topics, e.g., loving one's neighbors and enemies, murder, adultery, caring for the needy, judging others, being peacemakers, self-giving service, etc.[12] Moral conversion denotes not just receiving these teachings from our elders but taking personal responsibility for them in our lives, our habits, and our character. How do we live into those norms in ways that are consistent with and also transformative of our own journey in our moral lives? The grand exemplar here, besides Jesus himself, is Zacchaeus. We briefly mentioned him in chapter 2 above in our discussion of Jesus's ministry of delivering those in oppressed situations and circumstances. Here was a rich chief tax collector, one who was perceived within the Jericho community to be a sinner, and hence in his own pursuit of Jesus seems also to have acknowledged his own having fallen short (pun intended). Despite the social conventions that would have inhibited interactions with Jesus,[13] Zacchaeus's repentance nevertheless makes possible the unexpected hospitality, which is then made explicit first and foremost morally: "Look, half of my possessions, Lord, I will give to the poor; and if I have defrauded anyone of anything, I will pay back four times as much" (Luke 19:8b). On the one hand, we might think that Zacchaeus's conversion did not go far enough, at least not to the point of giving up not just half but all that he had for the sake of the poor, as Jesus had earlier told the rich ruler (18:18–23); on the other hand, as has been noted by others, "Fourfold restitution is by almost any reckoning excessive; cf. Exod 22:1; Lev 6:5; Num 5:6–7; 2 Sam 12:6."[14] In this respect, Zacchaeus had internalized Jesus's own call to conversion and had begun taking the first major moral steps in this direction.

Religious conversion here is evidenced by moral transformation, one through which Zacchaeus takes personal responsibility for how he acts toward, treats, and repents in relationship with others. The latter, however, also shines a light on how moral conversion responds also to not just others

---

12. Wiebe, *Messianic Ethics*.
13. As signaled in the main title of Lourdusamy, *Barrier-Breaking Banquet*.
14. Green, *Gospel of Luke*, 671n208.

in general but the rights of others more particularly. Others now have a claim on us, effectively. Zacchaeus realized that he was now indebted to those who he had defrauded, and part of his encounter with Jesus allowed this realization to surface.[15] Moral responsibility always, then, has this relational horizon, emerging out of our give and take with others in our various communities of habitation, some overlapping, others distinct. In that respect, evangelism also always involves us and others unfolding across this moral trajectory.[16] Effective mission and evangelism requires recognition of and attentiveness to the moral register through which human relationality and indebtedness transpire.

Moral Transformation in Acts: Considering Moral Conversion Apostolically

How then might moral conversion emanate from and then also inform Christian witness and evangelism? In part 2 of this chapter, we look more substantially at the book of Acts. Three windows will be peered into: the initial apostolic community coming of the Day of Pentecost, that afforded by the conversion of the Philippian jailer, and then a comparative (dual-paned, to continue our window metaphor?) interface of Cornelius and Julius, two centurions. What kind of taking of moral responsibility is evidenced in the apostolic community, and how might these moral transformations inform our own theology of evangelism and conversion today?

Selling, Distributing, and Having All Things in Common: Apostolic Moral Conversion I

We have already (our first chapter above) unpacked part of the communalism of the early apostolic community. Whereas there our focus was on the Jerusalem chapter of the Lukan narrative (anticipating Judea, Samaria, and the ends of the earth), here we look more intentionally at the mutual sharing as part of our analysis of moral conversion in response to the gospel. Behind the telling of the rich ruler to sell all he had that we just referenced in our discussion of Zacchaeus was Jesus's repeated warnings about the

---

15. Developmentally, this is about the emergence of what my colleague Pam King calls the "reciprocating self"; see Balswick et al., *Reciprocating Self*.
16. See also Webber, *Ancient-Future Evangelism*, esp. part 1.

MORAL CONVERSION

seductions of wealth and its impediments to true discipleship (like the rich fool and ruler, and the parabolic rich man),[17] as well as other teachings like that urging against anxiousness since God will make provision for human creatures as he does the birds of the air and the lilies of the field (12:22–31). So, "Do not be afraid, little flock, for it is your Father's good pleasure to give you the kingdom. Sell your possessions, and give alms. Make purses for yourselves that do not wear out, an unfailing treasure in heaven, where no thief comes near and no moth destroys. For where your treasure is, there your heart will be also" (12:32–34). We can see the reception of these teachings by the Spirit-inspired apostolic community. Luke's description is worth reconsidering:

> So those who welcomed his message were baptized, and that day about three thousand persons were added. They devoted themselves to the apostles' teaching and fellowship, to the breaking of bread and the prayers. Awe came upon everyone, because many wonders and signs were being done by the apostles. All who believed were together and had all things in common; they would sell their possessions and goods and distribute the proceeds to all, as any had need. Day by day, as they spent much time together in the temple, they broke bread at home and ate their food with glad and generous hearts, praising God and having the goodwill of all the people. And day by day the Lord added to their number those who were being saved. (Acts 2:41–47)

Three sets of comments related to moral conversion commend themselves from this passage.[18]

First, this passage summarizes what happened in the wake of the crowd's response to Peter's Day of Pentecost message, "what should we do?" (2:37b). Repentance, baptism in water, and reception of forgiveness and the Holy Spirit ensued, resulting in a mass evangelistic ingathering. What's next? What are the implications of such a newfound sense of identity and community? There were practical considerations such as gathering together, continuing in prayer, worship, gratitude, and other spiritual activities. In retrospect, these were part of the resocialization processes through which the early messianists, as new believers in Jesus, reoriented themselves intellectually, affectively, and morally to Jesus's teachings and way of life. Yet the

---

17. E.g., Luke 12:18–19, 18:18–25, and 16:19–21, respectively vis-à-vis the order mentioned in my text above (cf. 14:33); see also Bennema, "Rich Are the Bad Guys."

18. See also Lindemann, "Beginnings of Christian Life."

socioeconomic context of these activities raised logistical questions, even as they begged relational considerations. Some, if not most, activities might have been possible in the temple, but at least eating, in smaller groups or with whoever was together at meal times, meant that the traffic between temple and homes was heavy, for thousands upon thousands as indicated.

More concretely, second, the moral sphere could not be compartmentalized or cordoned off from the spiritual or communal one. How to provide for and feed this large number of persons, some of whom, perhaps a good or even majority of the group, may have been Hellenized Jews from the diaspora around the Mediterranean as marginal residents of, partial residents within, or migrants coming and going in and out of Jerusalem for various personal, family, or other reasons? The community had to arrive quickly at a workable, and working and improvisational, solution, which Luke summarizes thusly: "All who believed were together and had all things in common; they would sell their possessions and goods and distribute the proceeds to all, as any had need" (2:44–45). There are at least two sides here, one reflecting the generosity of those who had disposable possessions and the other reflecting the precarity of those who benefited from the proceeds, yet these combined into one experience: of these believers in Jesus now also trusting one another in Jesus's Spirit to have all things together and in common.[19]

Luke elaborates on this situation not too much later on in this way:

> Now the whole group of those who believed were of one heart and soul, and no one claimed private ownership of any possessions, but everything they owned was held in common. With great power the apostles gave their testimony to the resurrection of the Lord Jesus, and great grace was upon them all. There was not a needy person among them, for as many as owned lands or houses sold them and brought the proceeds of what was sold. They laid it at the apostles' feet, and it was distributed to each as any had need. (4:32–35)

The theme of spiritual and communal togetherness has persisted, even as the economic practices of members giving up on private ownership of possessions, land, and houses for the common good has been sustained. The nascent apostolic community seemed to have taken seriously the messianic

---

19. This way of putting it is influenced by Hume, *Early Christian Community*, whose assessment foregrounds the friendship and trust between messianists in relationship to the God of Jesus Christ in their midst.

witness to the poor, although the result at least in part during these early days was that "the poor" were neither those outside of the community nor separated within it.

From the perspective of Jesus's invitation to sell possessions to give to the poor, Barnabas is named as a unique exemplar.[20] "There was a Levite, a native of Cyprus, Joseph, to whom the apostles gave the name Barnabas (which means 'son of encouragement'). He sold a field that belonged to him, then brought the money, and laid it at the apostles' feet" (4:36–37). Here was one of those diaspora Jews also resident in Jerusalem who sold his plot of land for the purposes of supporting needy members of the apostolic community. More pointedly, here was at least an observant Jew, of the Levitical order, by all indicators already on the faith-filled path as charted by the Law and the Prophets. Yet upon committing himself to the messianic way, or perhaps even as a sign of such commitment, he takes moral action, attending here to the needs of that community to which he wished to be a part. And beyond that, the new name Barnabas "may mean 'son' (*bar*) of 'prophet' (*nabi*), prophecy referring to exhortation,"[21] and that anticipates his prophetic activity, emanating from a multilevel conversion and manifest in a significant moral act of generosity. Submission of his moral deeds, expressed in his gift at the feet of the apostles, was consistent with his underlying compliance with the messianic call and way.

There is one final point to be made related to the moral generosity of the earliest messianists. Their mutuality and sharing were part and parcel of their evangelistic witness, so much so that Luke is careful to note, "day by day the Lord added to their number those who were being saved" (2:47). In fact, in apparently short order, we are told, by the time the lame man at the Beautiful Gate was healed with all of the ruckus caused to the apostolic witness thereafter, that the fledgling group had grown from three to five thousand believers (4:4). Believers would continue to be added (5:14), drawn also by signs and wonders, and healings and exorcisms, occurring at the temple gates or in homes—which continued (e.g., 5:42)—and on the streets in between (5:12–16). The point is that the generosity and mutuality of the early apostolic community was an effective aspect of the messianists' evangelistic witness.

---

20. See Kollmann, *Joseph Barnabas*.
21. Keener, *Acts*, 2:1180.

PART II: APOSTOLIC EVANGELISM AND CONVERSION IN THE 2020S

The Philippian Jailer: Apostolic Moral Conversion II

In the rest of this chapter, we will look at individuals, specifically the Philippian jailer and Cornelius. Whereas our consideration of Barnabas was against the backdrop of what transpired economically in the early messianic community, in these other cases, their moral agency is assessed along more individualized routes. Nevertheless, we will see clearly, even if differently, how each takes moral responsibility as a result of religious conversion.

If in the preceding chapter we mentioned the Philippian jailer's rejoicing with the apostolic message, lifting up thus the affective aspect of his conversion experience, here our focus will be on his moral transformation. The story is a notable one for those familiar with the book of Acts. Paul and Silas were apprehended by the owners of the slave girl and charged before the authorities of both disorderly conduct and of attacking Jewish customs. The magistrates' response was to strip them down and flog them severely, upon which "they threw them into prison and ordered the jailer to keep them securely. Following these instructions, he put them in the innermost cell and fastened their feet in the stocks" (16:23b–24). Was he just the jailer who was on rotation that day and that hour, or was he called in specifically because of his reputation for renowned methods of ensuring prisoner detention, a status perhaps also extending to the staff he kept (implied by his calling for lights mentioned in 16:29)?

Sleeping through both the singing of Paul and Silas and the earthquake's shaking of the prison's foundations, the jailer was awakened at the sound of the jail doors flying open and of chains rattling loose. At this realization, he "drew his sword and was about to kill himself, since he supposed that the prisoners had escaped" (16:27b). Here is an initial window into the affective underpinnings of the jailer's moral character. On the one hand, he clearly fears for his life, thinking that the escape of the convicts would have to be accounted for and this accounting would involve his loss of life instead (as is recorded to have happened earlier to those guarding Peter after he escaped also by means of an earthquake; see 12:19). On the other hand, there is also an underlying moral sense: these inmates are fleeing under my watch, and I had them securely fastened, although it appears insufficiently fortified, so I would be deserving of the relevant legal and related punishments in the circumstances. The former might have been more fundamentally activated by the quickly unfolding events, although we should not overlook the sense of responsibility with which he felt for these prisoners either, to the point that even with his family in mind, his felt sense of disgrace about failing to do his job led to the drastic step of being willing to suffer ultimately and swiftly the anticipated consequences. Giving the jailer the benefit of the doubt, suicide was the courageous option in this case, rather than the dishonor faced by not only him but also his family members should he have been found negligent and then executed.[22] The jailer was ready to take ultimate responsibility for his perceived moral lapse.

What happens next spares him (and his family) from this rash act, but opens him up, in hindsight, to another occasion of moral transformation. Paul's voice admonishing against taking his own life and reassuring him that none of the prisoners had absconded (16:28)—perhaps the apostolic singing made it possible for any other detainees that might have found themselves freed to imagine that staying with these witnesses would result in at least as good if not a better longer-term outcome than fleeing!—leads to an exchange that results in the jailer's believing in the Lord Jesus. Luke describes what unfolds after: "At the same hour of the night he took them and washed their wounds; then he and his entire family were baptized without delay. He brought them up into the house and set food before them; and he and his entire household rejoiced that he had become a believer in God" (16:33–34). There is surely a cognitional component of acknowledging Jesus as Lord, even as there are immediate moral decisions, which are carried out in washing the wounds of Paul and Silas (remember, they were scourged before being confined), welcoming them into their home, and feeding them. In this regard, the jailer was also exposing his family members as accomplices in his management and handling of a situation in which his detainees were no longer conventionally secured. His actions were thus jeopardizing not just himself but his closest kin. Brian Rapske's summary illuminates the depth of the moral conversion manifest in his choices:

> The jailer's actions are illegal, or grossly improper at the very least. However, seen within the context of . . . Christian risk-taking to help the prisoner, they take on a new light. The jailer before his conversion shows an overweened sense of responsibility in being prepared to take his own life because of the apparent escape of his prisoners; as a Christian, he casts caution and concern for legal

---

22. I am aided here by Keener, *Acts*, 3:2497–506.

niceties aside in his zeal to help the prisoners who have converted him.[23]

Might we consider what Rapske names as the jailer's "sense of responsibility" also in relation to his own conscience being pricked regarding his prior actions as a jailer, that, in terms of his treatment of prisoners, perhaps was also morally questionable? In other words, if in the prior chapter we were observing how the sinner woman's own affective conversion had to navigate being the victim at the hands of others, might this jailer narrative now invite consideration of how the moral conversion of victimizers—or at least those in the position of dealing legally, administratively, or practically with others in ways that bypass the moral register—involves efforts at making reparation? If victims are not usually counseled to approach their victimizers, at least not without adequate preparation and accompaniment, the latter might also consider what it means to be motivated by a moral change of heart to re-engage those they have injured or otherwise lorded over in injurious ways.

The ending of the story can be understood in ways not inconsistent also with this point. When morning arrived, the jailer was further confronted with if and how to follow through on what had happened. Luke's description is of the warden functioning mostly as a messenger between the magistrates and their police officers and Paul and his friends (old and new, perhaps). The unfolding sequence of events (16:35–39) shows that the jailer does not cease to function in his role. However, his actions extend the moral transformation experienced over the course of the night, and he carries out his responsibilities in a more politically nuanced and multidirectional manner. Hospitable washing of wounds and caring for inmates initially led now to being a mediator between the authorities and the prisoners, who were now not only unshackled from their chains but also, it appears, had been formally dismissed by the magistrates.[24] While the jailer would have been relieved since the discharge orders also suggest that he would have been alleviated from any liability for what had happened, he did not act on any obvious temptation to simply have Paul and Silas move on once informed they were free to go. Instead, he was willing to represent his new friends' position accurately and even persist firmly enough on their

23. Rapske, *Book of Acts*, 392.

24. Luke is silent about the reasons for the discharge, although commentators speculate that perhaps the earthquake and its effects were taken as an ominous sign; see Kurz, *Acts of the Apostles*, 259.

behalf until a formal apology had been secured from the authorities, effectively also the power brokers of the system within which he worked and in at least that respect with some clout over his ongoing occupation and deployment and therefore also in this way with access to the keys to his well being (read in contemporary parlance: paycheck for him and his family!). Before, he represented the "state" in relation to the prisoners, but now he also represented the latter to the former. In other words, the jailer's ongoing deeds and communicative actions were indicative of the moral upheaval that had taken place, sufficiently powerful and galvanizing so that he who was ready to end his life just a few hours ago was now willing to stand firm with his new colleagues in the face of uncertain headwinds.

Herein is a window into taking moral responsibility over significant moments in yet a brief period of time. The moral instincts manifest in the readiness to end his life reflected a certain kind of formation that was reoriented through encounter with Paul and the gospel. This redirection then brought with it other forms of responsible action that were nevertheless consistent with the character he had developed as a reputable jailer.

Moral Character in the Case of Two Centurions: Apostolic Moral Conversion III

The two centurions we will consider now are Cornelius and Julius. In each case, we explore what we have already touched on with the Philippian jailer: moral character. Whereas the above attempted to follow out the moral transformation that ensued with the jailer's crisis moment of losing his charge, our focus here is on how such moral formation precedes and informs intellectual and even religious conversion.

Our earlier mentions of Cornelius were in the context of Peter's intellectual conversion (ch. 3 above). The discussion now focused on how the Spirit's transformative work in Cornelius preceded and enabled dialogical interaction that illuminated Peter's transformation.[25] What does Luke tell us about Cornelius himself that helps us observe the moral aspects of his own conversion experience? Initially, we are told, "He was a devout man who feared God with all his household; he gave alms generously to the people and prayed constantly to God" (Acts 10:2). Here was a gentile God-fearer,

25. Thus effectively going behind and thereby supplementing what Richie, *Toward a Pentecostal Theology of Religions*, 50–51, accentuates about the Cornelius–Peter dialogical encounter.

not yet a formal convert to Judaism (who would be a proselyte),[26] with an impeccable reputation from pietistic (note his devoutness), moral (note his benevolence and generosity already acknowledged to be manifestations of the Spirit's enabling witness), and spiritual (note his unceasing posture and practice of prayerful communion with God) perspectives. As if anticipating readers' skepticism about the validity of Cornelius's character, the angel that appears to him during his time of regular prayer confirms: "Your prayers and your alms have ascended as a memorial before God" (10:4b). God has been personally attentive, and is now responding, to Cornelius's pleas. Upon being further instructed by the angel, the centurion sends to Peter "two of his slaves and a devout soldier from the ranks of those who served him" (10:7b).

At Peter's doorstep these three introduce themselves by speaking thus of Cornelius as "an upright and God-fearing man, who is well spoken of by the whole Jewish nation" (10:22a). Three more comments here are relevant to lifting up Cornelius's moral character. First, these are the direct witnesses borne by his servants and a leading member of his Italian cohort. Of course, whoever he might have sent would have been expected to represent him attractively to the intended audience (in this case Peter), yet truthful attestations, while not necessarily to be presumed, are here presented non-exaggeratedly in one voice by those serving effectively under (as his servants) and beside (as part of his troop) him. Second, then, "upright" is an understated translation of *dikaios*, when it is also rendered "righteous" in other theological contexts. For instance, Paul in Romans quotes from Habakkuk that "the one who is righteous [*dikaios*] will live by faith" (Rom 1:17). Hence, Cornelius is effectively exhibiting the kind of faithfulness that has been touched by the salvific power of God, here before he is cognitively evangelized.[27] Put otherwise, Cornelius's devoutness, benevolence, and prayerfulness are manifestations of moral virtues inculcated over time that have come to shape his life of righteousness as a God-fearer prior to his hearing, understanding, and receiving the gospel. Finally, then, consistent with all we have observed so far, the "whole Jewish nation" bears witness to Cornelius's moral character. More crucial here is that their "well spoken

26. Proselytes are mentioned in Acts 2:10 and 6:5; for discussion of Cornelius as God-fearer, see Keener, *Acts*, 2:1750–53.

27. Without needing to decide one way or another about Cornelius's religious conversion, biblical exegetes in the Roman Catholic tradition here appropriately cite Vatican II's consideration that there are those outside the church, not yet evangelized, initiated, or baptized, who might be saved; see Kurz, *Acts of the Apostles*, 177.

of," μαρτυρούμενός, comes from the same root as that which in the book of Acts derives from the Spirit's gift (1:8). In short, Jews are bearing confirming witness (to that provided by his men), Spirit-inspired it appears, about this gentile.

The goal here is not to minimize what happens with Peter's evangelistic visit and the subsequent gift of the Spirit to these gentiles, followed with glossolalia and baptism in water. If religious conversion includes these various christological, pneumatological, and intellectual elements, then these would have needed to be part of the narrative. Our emphasis, instead, is on the moral register that has been overlooked in these discussions of Cornelius. As a centurion he had already been virtuously formed and shaped. At some point in his carrying out his governmental duties in Caesarea, he took moral responsibility for engaging those he was serving benevolently, made possible by the virtue of generosity that had been cultivated over time. Along the way, he had nurtured a life of piety devoted to seeking after the God of Israel, and carried himself according to the recognized moral attributes, sensibilities, and behaviors, borne witness to by the community that he worked with and even sought to emulate. Cornelius's moral conversion was palpable, resulting in his being embraced as a God-fearer, a model one at that.

There are another handful of centurions in Acts, but only the last one Luke introduces is named: Julius, the commanding officer in charge of getting a number of prisoners (27:1), including Paul, to Rome.[28] Julius is referenced another handful of times on this journey, including when, at the first stop on the second day, he "treated Paul kindly, and allowed him to go to his friends to be cared for" (27:3). *Kindly*, from the Greek *philanthrōpos*, is also *considerately* or *humanely*. While he is mentioned next as agreeing with the captain and ship owner about departing from Fair Havens next to Lasea despite Paul's forewarning about a brooding storm and loss of lives (27:10–11), upon realizing that the latter was correct, he then heeded the apostle's next admonition about staying on the ship being the surest way to preserve lives, and had his soldiers, who were prepared to abandon the ship and its remaining inhabitants to save themselves, release and lose the almost deployed lifeboats instead (27:30–32). In the waning moments of the storm, with land in sight, the soldiers thought to kill the prisoners rather than allowing their possible escape and risking being charged with

---

28. On the centurions in Acts, see Brink, *Soldiers in Luke-Acts*, ch. 4; Julius is discussed on 119–25.

dereliction of duty. For the second time in relationship to the soldiers under his command,[29] Julius, now "wishing to save Paul," intervened; wielding the kind of emergency authority powers he had in his position under the circumstances,[30] he inserted himself in arranging for the vacating of the ship and the swimming ashore: "He ordered those who could swim to jump overboard first and make for the land, and the rest to follow, some on planks and others on pieces of the ship" (27:43–44a).

We do not hear again about Julius amid the developments on Malta where they found themselves, although of course Acts 28 clearly suggests that while experiencing the hospitality of the islanders alongside, and even perhaps chiefly because of the apostolic group, he fulfilled his responsibility of delivering Paul to Rome in custody. What we observe, however, is a person with moral character and virtue, including the kindness and humaneness specifically mentioned, which by the time of the shipwreck had motivated Julius to be not only in solidarity with Paul but also an advocate on his behalf. Does Julius experience a religious conversion? Not in so many words, but like Cornelius, he exhibited moral virtues and that opened him up to welcoming Jesus's emissaries.[31] And if at one point, "all hope of our being saved was at last abandoned" by Julius and others aboard alike (27:20b), in the end, by now heeding and working with the evangelistic mouthpiece, he and "all [on the ship] were brought safely to land" (27:44b).

Christian Evangelism and Moral Conversion Today: Transforming Spirit-ed Witness

What important takeaways about moral conversion emerge from our discussion of apostolic moral transformation and moral character? What are the implications for Spirit-led evangelism today? The following at least three considerations are suggestive.

First, *moral agency should be attended to in the lives of those being engaged evangelistically.* Whether it's the moral character of individuals as known within their communities or their observable virtuous deeds,

---

29. I was helped with this recognition by Cassidy, *Paul in Chains*, 221.

30. Keener, *Acts*, 4:4657.

31. And that is at least also Luke's point about Julius, about whom we have meaning in relationship to Paul, the protagonist of this part of the apostolic story; yet, in this case, I suggest, adopting partly the lens provided by Wilson, "Sight and Spectacle," we see Paul at least in part through Julius's eyes.

such persons may already be en route, so to speak, on the path of religious conversion. Such "saints in the making," Cornelius as the prime instance, have consistently manifested their moral commitments in their actions and dispositions and sensibilities, and this aspect of the Spirit's already present work will also be witnessed to by others. Who are those who may be ready to welcome further instruction in the gospel, we might wish to inquire at the front end of any evangelistic endeavor. Identification of those with the requisite moral behavior, therefore, can be anticipated as evidence of and also as possibly catalytic for ongoing conversion.

This means, second, that assuming the work of evangelism includes sustained interaction over time (rather than only one encounter, one evangelistic service, etc., which while not to be disregarded should not be the sole modality of evangelistic interface), *how we might observe the ongoing evolution of moral character and agency in the lives of those being evangelized*? Paul had been able to observe Julius for a few weeks, including during intensely turbulent times, and felt he could speak about salvation at an opportune moment: "Unless these men stay in the ship, you cannot be saved" (Acts 27:31). What ongoing moral development would be indicative of people ready to take the next step in their journey? How might the evangelistic message be tailored to address the hearts and lives of people who have made moral progress in the direction of the virtues heralding the coming divine reign?

Last but not least, for the moment, *how might we encourage ongoing conversion in its moral aspects*? Paul (and Silas) did not necessarily need to tell the Philippian jailer what to do next, but they welcomed and received the care given, the hospitality granted, and the representation provided. Without denying that these benevolent deeds might just as well be categorized under sanctification rather than justification, our own theology of conversion can include moral agency and transformation as part of the salvific and redemptive divine work in Christ by the Spirit. There is no need to limit the work of evangelism to when only certain cognitional understandings are reached; instead, we can appreciate, encourage, and foster ongoing moral conversion so that those on the Christian way can continue to take responsibility for their actions and lives in accordance with their growing messianic commitments.

Yet, as we have concluded each of the chapters in this part of the book already, we now want to turn also to the moral conversion not of those being evangelized but of any who might believe they are called to be evangelists.

What are the missiological challenges of the foregoing consideration of apostolic moral conversion? How is our own moral conversion to be continually facilitated? For us who would be missionaries and evangelists, here are a few more questions at this stage of our own journey.

First, *are we open to the Spirit of Jesus convicting us of how our own behaviors and actions are in need of continued conversion, and are we motivated to welcome moral transformation in our own lives?* Evangelists are not entirely sanctified, even for those in Holiness traditions that might embrace the possibility of such forms of consecration. Rather, each of us have moral compasses that may be more or less formed, and yet can be even more deeply aligned with the coming divine reign. Further, each of us can be further shaped in the virtues so that we can, when confronted with moral choices, opt more than less consistently for the right (or righteous) response, all in anticipation of being fully formed in the image of Jesus when we finally (eschatologically) see him as he is.

Second, *is it OK that, often, the conversion of our hands is facilitated through what circumstantial encounters with others demand of our choices?* Will we respond like Cornelius did to the arrival of Peter, or like the jailer did to the arrival of Paul? Alternatively, how will we respond to the centurions and jailers whose paths interact with our lives? How might the people we meet invite a deeper moral attunement and, possibly, hard moral choices and actions on our part? What roles do these have to play for our own ongoing faithfulness on the messianic way, discipleship on the Christian path, and conversion to the coming divine reign? What is the Holy Spirit attempting to accomplish in us through the people that are brought into our lives?

Finally, for the moment, *are we willing to link arms, lock hands, and act with those we are called to evangelize?* Recalling the parable of the sheep and the goats (Matt 25:31–46), the focus there was not on the salvation of the hungry, thirsty, naked, immigrant, or incarcerated, but on how Jesus's disciples, both evangelists and would-be evangelists, could find themselves on the "saved" or sheep side of the ledger at the final judgment, and the answer is by attending to Jesus in the midst of those we meet in the mundaneness of daily life. So, if at the end of the preceding chapter the invitation was to open our hearts to be in solidarity with others, here we are summoned to take the next step and accompany others on the next leg of their—now our—journey: in mutual service and in moral reciprocity. Evangelism, in this scheme of things, is what happens when we work with others, as neighbors, office mates, or community acquaintances, in Spirit-enabled ways that impact our behaviors. In so doing, we develop greater, more expansive capacities to respond in different circumstances in relationship, thus prompting mutual witness. This is what the moral conversion of us evangelists can engender.

Chapter 6

Sociopolitical Conversion
Apostolic Engagements Then and Now

THIS VOLUME HAS DEPLOYED a restorationist, that-is-this hermeneutic and therefore consistently looked at the apostolic witness for perspective on renewing Christian mission and evangelism today. Whereas in the first part of the book we looked in broad strokes at St. Luke's overarching theology of witness and mission as displayed in his two volumes, beginning with the book of Acts and then turning to the Gospel of Luke, in this second part we have looked more intently at the goals of evangelism, specifically that of conversion, and explored the multiple dimensions of such transformation, including that which occurs at the intellectual, affective, and moral domains, also in these two Lukan texts. Now we are arriving at what we are calling, following Jesuit theologian Donald L. Gelpi, sociopolitical conversion.

For Gelpi, sociopolitical conversion is an extension of moral conversion from the private and interpersonal realm to the societal and public sphere.[1] Conversion in this more extended direction encourages, enables, and inspires taking of responsibility for influencing and impacting public policy issues/crises, discussions, and initiatives. In that respect, sociopolitical conversion is accompanied also by intellectual conversion that provides the ideological (gospel-informed, for our purposes) content for such policies, and by affective conversion that enables us to overcome our

---

1. The following summarizes Gelpi, *Conversion Experience*, 51–56.

tribalist biases and prejudices that shore up the status quo of the systems and structures that privilege some and marginalize minority groups in any context. Given the recursivity of how conversion in any one domain also returns to deepen conversion in other domains, sociopolitical conversion, which is itself a multi-leveled and layered process having to do with specific policy arenas, returns to continually de-privatize our ongoing intellectual, affective, and moral transformation, even radicalizing our overall religious conversion for the common good of not only human but all creatures.

Yet our goal is not to politicize evangelism but to establish evangelism in relationship to the public square upon a more sure theological and gospel foundation.[2] This chapter therefore first sketches an overarching theology of evangelism for the common good before turning particularly to the book of Acts to peer through three disparate sets of windows into sociopolitical conversion found therein. We conclude this chapter, as the others in this part of the book, with some summary considerations for evangelism and implications particularly for any of us would-be or active evangelists.

Sociopolitical Conversion: Taking Evangelistic Responsibility for the Common Good

The sociopolitical foregrounds the wider societal and more systemic and structural realities within which we live, move, and have our being. What then does it mean for us to take responsibility for the sociopolitical dimensions of our lives? As the sociopolitical is an extension of the moral, we remain concerned here with the praxis aspects of Christian life, faithfulness, and witness. Orthopraxy, in this chapter, thereby concerns how we act vis-à-vis the broader public square for the common good. The following triangulates toward a theology of the common good from pneumatological, Lukan, and eschatological perspectives, in spiraling order.

The Spirit and the Social: Toward Sociopolitical Conversion

If the modern-day Pentecostal churches, of which I have been a part all my life, began in sectarian fashion in the early twentieth century and in that respect generally did not seek direct sociopolitical engagement with

---

2. We build on a long line of precedent works—e.g., Sider, *Evangelism, Salvation and Social Justice*; and Kirk, *Good News of the Kingdom Coming*—albeit prioritizing what happens in conversion and its implications for evangelization and evangelists both.

society, its parental generation, the nineteenth-century Holiness movement, especially in North America, was otherwise inclined to "spread scriptural holiness over the land," as John Wesley, the eighteenth-century founder of preceding generation of British Methodist-holiness preachers, put it.[3] Sanctification, the theological term, required holiness, a phenomenological description of a blameless way of life before God and others, and for the Methodists and Holiness adherents since Wesley, the latter had both private or personal and more public or social manifestations. In the northern states before the American Civil War, for instance, Holiness churches and members advocated for abolitionism in a context within which there was a national debate about the ownership of slaves as one dimension of how they considered holiness to be not just about personal rectitude.[4] Instead, commitments to scriptural holiness urged these toward abolitionism, to reordering society itself so that all people would be beneficiaries of, if not also participants in, holiness as a way of (social) life. Thus, biblical and "kingdom" principles should be enacted across political, economic, and social domains of our common existence. In this Wesleyan framework, Christian discipleship was irreducible to our personal lives, but had societal and political implications.[5]

As our own Luke-Acts approach has prioritized a Pentecost framework for reconsidering witness, evangelism, and conversion, we also celebrate recent voices that have lifted up the Pentecost theme for thinking about the sociopolitical and the common good. Daniela Augustine, a fellow Pentecostal colleague from Eastern Europe, has focused much of her own constructive theological efforts in the direction of articulating what we might call a pneumatology of the common good.[6] She also foregrounds the communal economics of the Day of Pentecost narrative yet develops such especially in dialogue with Eastern Orthodox theologians and other resources from this tradition that inform her own Eastern European horizon. The result is to reconsider Pentecostal communalism eucharistically, so that the contemporary market and its pressures and demands is reconfigured in light of the church's shared and sacramental praxis, albeit one always imbued by the life-giving Holy Spirit. Pentecostal mission and witness, then, fill up not just

---

3. See Wood, "John Wesley's Mission."
4. E.g., Strong, "Real Christian Is an Abolitionist."
5. See also Yong, "Sanctification, Science, and the Spirit."
6. E.g., Augustine, *Pentecost, Hospitality, and Transfiguration*, and *Spirit and the Common Good*.

human bodies but saturate the economic, political, and other public spaces wherein we navigate. Where violence reigns, forgiveness and mutuality arrive by the Spirit's power, resetting relationships between human beings as well as resituating human creatures also in relationship to other creatures in the world and our common terrestrial habitation. The common good of nineteenth-century social holiness becomes the creational flourishing of Augustine's twenty-first-century Orthodox-Pentecostal life in the Spirit.[7]

Missiologically, the inclusion of the social arena has been debated within the evangelical world for the last two generations now, but few will argue today that mission and evangelism exclude social witness altogether. Some might still wish to insist that the priority ought to be verbal proclamation and the planting and establishing of new churches, with social engagement being a secondary, if also necessary and complementary activity. Others might call for a more integrated and holistic approach, one that sees evangelism (here understood as verbal witness) and social endeavors to be fully mutual, one or the other side taking the lead in any particular time and space depending on contextual factors, but the other always following closely behind, if not the two mutually informing each other in an irreducible manner. Particularly in global evangelical and Pentecostal contexts, *misión integral* or integral/holistic mission is not only compatible with but includes evangelism and vice-versa, rather than being binarily contrasted.[8]

From this perspective, then, Christian mission and evangelism, as witnessing endeavors or activities, will include engaging the sociopolitical arena. Our focus, however, is squarely on how to approach Christian evangelism and witness with that as part of the objective. Considering only what evangelists and witnesses do is only half of what needs to be accounted for since by doing so, we are already taking active responsibility for engaging in this more public domain. Instead, what if we also asked about implications for engaging with those evangelized or witnessed to, if sociopolitical conversion were part of the desired outcomes? Does that mean our goal is to mobilize sociopolitical activists and advocates? Even if yes, this is too quick. How might we think through sociopolitical interfaces in Scripture for our questions and tasks?

---

7. See also the chapters in, and my "Afterword" to, Augustine and Green, *Politics of the Spirit*, 211–15.

8. At least since Samuel and Hauser, *Proclaiming Christ in Christ's Way*.

PART II: APOSTOLIC EVANGELISM AND CONVERSION IN THE 2020S

Luke as Sociopolitical Theologian?

In chapter 2 above, our discussion of Luke's Gospel already highlighted his situating of the Jesus story within the imperial Roman world of Palestine in the first century, one ruled by Caesar Augustus (at the birth of the messiah) and then by Caesar Tiberius (when the messiah came of age and was about to embark on his public ministry). We also explored how Jesus's own ministerial and missional self-understanding included various sociopolitical aspects, drawn from and in that respect consistent with how the Isaianic suffering servant—ancient Israel and its messiah—was going to herald and "proclaim the year of the Lord's favor" (Isa 61:2a; cf. Luke 4:18–19). Let us be clear: Jesus did not inaugurate a form of ministry or mission that involved sociopolitical advocacy and activism as we understand those notions in the twenty-first-century contexts of liberal democracies.[9] On the other hand, as we read these ancient Scriptures with our contemporary questions at hand, it is appropriate to reimagine Jesus and the apostles thinking, feeling, doing, and engaging their world. From that perspective, an old, but also new, radicality appears when we observe that Jesus came, and also commissioned his disciples, to preach good news *to the poor*! Whereas those of us blessed and privileged enough to live in "first world" conditions may not have to worry about where our next meal is coming from, what happens if we not only prioritized mission and evangelism in impoverished contexts but sought to bear witness specifically to those who were hungry? Such reprioritization, it can be seen, will immediately impact evangelistic strategy. How much and how far depends on how we traverse all of the other considerations coming up in this chapter.

Our re-reckoning also includes how we read St. Luke's sequel volume, the book of Acts. In the opening chapter of our book, we had already noted that the apostolic experience in this second book was also set against their expectations of what Jesus's messianic mission would ultimately accomplish, which was to free Palestine from Roman rule. Perhaps their question, "Lord, is this the time when you will restore the kingdom to Israel?" (Acts 1:6), understandably was motivated by their belief that Jesus's prior promise to them—"I confer on you, just as my Father has conferred on me, a kingdom, so that you may eat and drink at my table in my kingdom, and you will sit on thrones judging the twelve tribes of Israel" (Luke 22:29–30)—would be imminently fulfilled in relationship to the overthrow of the

---

9. As rightly argued by Twelftree, *People of the Spirit*, esp. ch. 13.

Roman regime.[10] Jesus's immediate reply was to forestall their eschatological speculation across a partially realized horizon—renewal and restoration of Israel in part now, but to be more fully accomplished later—even as his more extended response was to invite their living as the new people of the Spirit (1:7–8) into an alternative sociopolitical reality amid, rather than having rebelled or revolted against, imperial Rome.

If we have read this book so far as a narrative of apostolic mission and evangelism apart from sociopolitical engagement, however, this is to miss out on a good deal of Luke's account, which is precisely that of apostolic traversals of imperial Roman highways and waterways (across the Mediterranean) from and to Rome, the heart of the Pax Romana. Jesus's response to the disciples' question, then, does not necessarily or only mean that the restoration of Israel would not be accomplished but that the timing and modality of such achievements exceeded their apostolic comprehension at that time. Put alternatively, the gift of the Spirit can be understood also as part of what enables Israel's restoration, although this did not include Rome's immediate expulsion from Palestine then but rather enabled the apostolic community to live within the imperial state, however long it perdured, albeit according to the norms and values promoted by the year of the Lord's favor. If Roman expulsion was understood as a once-for-all undertaking led by a messianic revolution, then no! "It is not for you to know the times or periods that the Father has set by his own authority" (1:7). However, if the restoration of Israel as the new people of God that will include those from every people, tribe, and ethnicity living according to the mutuality and koinonia of the Lord's Jubilee provisions, then, even more importantly, "you will receive power when the Holy Spirit has come upon you; and you will be my witnesses in Jerusalem, in all Judea and Samaria, and to the ends of the earth" (1:8). The entirety of the apostolic narrative is, from this perspective, about God bringing about the divine rule across the world by the power of his Spirit.[11]

---

10. Horsley, "Kingdom of God," esp. 422–26, helpfully foregrounds this text in relationship to the disciples' question about the restoration and renewal of Israel; my reading does nothing to undermine his insistence that Jesus's Basileiac language was designed to enable the people to envision a different social order than they one under which they were trampled by the Romans, even as I do not think the rebellion of which he then believes Jesus's message promotes is any less radical if it did not specifically endorse an actual political revolution (which Horsley's rhetoric comes right up to but does not necessitate in the end).

11. As presented by Salmeier, *Restoring the Kingdom*.

From this perspective, while Luke did not write with our understanding of sociopolitical conversion in mind, his narrative of the apostolic community's sojourn under the power of the Spirit amid the Pax Romana has implications for our reconsideration of evangelism and its goals in the third millennium. In promising the Spirit to carry out the restoration of Israel, for instance, Jesus's teachings in that context focused not only on the scriptural anticipations of his rising from the dead but on "the kingdom of God" (1:3b), *tes basileias tou Theou*. While this coming Basileia or divine reign—my preferred nomenclature due to the patriarchal connotations of the older language of "kingdom"—is not then mentioned as frequently in the rest of the apostolic narrative as it appears in the Third Gospel, here are some important aspects of when it appears. First, the apostolic message follows Jesus's focus and stays on the divine Basileia, at least in three summary instances at important junctures of Luke's story: (1) Philip "proclaiming the good news about the kingdom of God and the name of Jesus Christ" in Samaria (8:12); (2) Paul, arguing boldly and "persuasively about the kingdom of God" in Ephesus (19:8); and (3) Paul, again, "testifying to the kingdom of God and trying to convince them about Jesus both from the law of Moses and from the prophets" in Rome (28:23). Apostolic evangelism, it is clear, is Basileiacally oriented and connected to the person of Jesus.[12]

Second, in a summary statement about how Paul's first missionary journey (so-called) concludes, Luke puts it this way: "After they had proclaimed the good news to that city and had made many disciples, they returned to Lystra, then on to Iconium and Antioch. There they strengthened the souls of the disciples and encouraged them to continue in the faith, saying, 'It is through many persecutions that we must enter the kingdom of God'" (14:21–22). Lystra and Iconium were, to be sure, locales where the apostles faced severe resistance, especially from Jews in the latter site who plotted and then carried out a stoning of Paul and Barnabas. Yet, intriguingly, suffering for the sake of the gospel was part of entry into the divine Basileia, or, put otherwise, the ongoing work of martyrological evangelization was part and parcel of the work of ushering in the divine reign, even in the imperial Roman world.

Luke concludes his writing career (we have no other record of his authorship) with this sentence: "He lived there for two whole years at his own expense and welcomed all who came to him, proclaiming the kingdom of God and teaching about the Lord Jesus Christ with all boldness and without

---

12. Ziccardi, *Relationship of Jesus*, 497–99.

hindrance" (28:30–31). Not coincidentally, I might add, he concludes this second volume exactly the way he began it: with the divine Basileia. In the first sentences, Jesus is speaking about *tes basileias tou Theou*, and here at the end, apostolic testimony continues to that same divine reign, ahead of them but also on its way, even for a witness in chains.[13] To be sure, Jesus tells Pilate, in the Fourth Gospel, "My kingdom is not from this world. If my kingdom were from this world, my followers would be fighting to keep me from being handed over to the Jews. But as it is, my kingdom is not from here" (John 18:36). Yet, there were Basileiac implications for Christian daily life, discipleship, and witness for messianists navigating the Pax Romana and its political, economic, and social spheres. The Spirit's witness in many tongues is uttered across these sociopolitical spaces, and there are implications throughout this apostolic testimony for Christian conversion and contribution to the common good.[14]

The Gospel Witness and the Divine Reign: Evangelism Toward Sociopolitical Conversion

Yet what exactly does heralding the divine Basileia mean? How might we redirect our evangelistic efforts toward the coming divine reign, one that is not quite yet, but also partially present? In preparing to discuss sociopolitical conversion in the book of Acts, then, I want to probe the Third Gospel's theology of the Basileia. Religious conversion in Luke-Acts, I suggest, is thoroughly christological but yet also Basileiac. To be converted to Jesus is also to be converted to the divine reign that he preached was in the future but that he also embodied as here presently. How can this be understood in Luke's story of Jesus, and what are the implications for considering conversion sociopolitically?

---

13. Cho, *Spirit and Kingdom*, rightly argues that Luke explicitly associates the Spirit with the kingdom in his discussions of Jesus and the apostolic proclamations regarding the latter, including both at the beginning and ending of the book of Acts, which is part of his argument that the Gospel authors' associations of life, righteousness, and ethics with the kingdom are associated instead with the Spirit by Paul in his letters (that predate Luke's writings). While Cho is on solid ground when focused on where the Spirit is explicitly mentioned in the Lukan corpus, his thesis is less impactful if the entirety of the Third Evangelist's two volumes are read as expressions of the Spirit's work, as I have done in this book, beginning in the first part above.

14. See also my "Spirit, the Common Good."

To be sure, in Luke's Gospel, the kingdom is never just here now, but it is also not only reserved to the future. On the one hand, earlier in his ministry, on one occasion he said to his followers, "truly I tell you, there are some standing here who will not taste death before they see the kingdom of God" (Luke 9:27). While enigmatic in many ways, in Jesus's own self-understanding, the arrival of the divine reign is clearly associated with the rest of his ministry, so that faithful discipleship would mean, in part, participation in that coming Basileia that includes viewing his glory as in the Transfiguration scene shortly following (9:28–36).[15] Further confirmation is received in the final year of his ministry when this exchange between Jesus and his disciples is recorded: "Once Jesus was asked by the Pharisees when the kingdom of God was coming, and he answered, 'The kingdom of God is not coming with things that can be observed; nor will they say, "Look, here it is!" or "There it is!" For, in fact, the kingdom of God is among you'" (Luke 17:20–21). Herein Jesus clearly indicates the divine Basileia is present, for those able to realize such, for instance, children: "Let the little children come to me, and do not stop them; for it is to such as these that the kingdom of God belongs. Truly I tell you, whoever does not receive the kingdom of God as a little child will never enter it" (18:16). All of this is consistent with the prophecies surrounding Jesus's coming, including that of Simeon's who, in taking up Mary's infant, glorified God, "for my eyes have seen your salvation" (2:30), and then also Anna's proclamation shortly thereafter celebrating that the arrival of this child was intended for and addressed "to all who were looking for the redemption of Jerusalem" (2:38b).

On the other hand, there is also no doubt the Basileia is coming in the sense of remaining ahead in some respects. For instance, after his meeting with Zacchaeus, Jesus tells the parable of the nobleman who is faithfully awaiting the Basileia explicitly "because he was near Jerusalem, and because they supposed that the kingdom of God was to appear immediately" (19:11). Then, Luke includes Jesus's teachings about the end of the age and, in this context, suggests that the appearance of certain future signs would be indicators "that the kingdom of God is near" (21:31b). Jesus also insisted at the Last Supper before his death that he would neither eat the meal again with them "until it is fulfilled in the kingdom of God" nor drink the cup with them "until the kingdom of God comes" (22:16, 18).[16] The not-yet

---

15. As interpreted by, for instance, Green, *Gospel of Luke*, 376.

16. That Christian meals were occasions for heralding the divine reign is further indication of how they functioned also to both subvert (explicitly) and resist (implicitly) the

aspect of this eschatological expectation of fellowshiping, among other activities, with the disciples seems unavoidable: "I confer on you, just as my Father has conferred on me, a kingdom, so that you may eat and drink at my table in my kingdom . . ." (22:29–30a). His passing meant that those "waiting expectantly for the kingdom of God," like Joseph of Arimathea (23:51b), would have to continue patiently in anticipation.

Having said all of this, what is clear is that the book of Acts' insistence that Jesus proclaimed the coming Basileia was but an extension of his preaching in the prequel volume. In fact, it is not an overstatement to say that "Jesus' entire mission was determined by his message about God's sovereign rule."[17] Soon after his initial Nazareth sermon was a harbinger of the year of Jubilee (4:19) and some preaching at Capernaum, Jesus forecasted his itinerary: "I must proclaim the good news of the kingdom of God to the other cities also" (4:43). Luke's periodic summary statements about Jesus's public ministry confirm that "he went on through cities and villages, proclaiming and bringing the good news of the kingdom of God" (8:1; cf. 9:11), even as the disciples were commissioned "to proclaim the kingdom of God and to heal" (9:2b; also 9:60 and 10:9–11). We are well aware that Jesus also taught his disciples to pray, "Your kingdom come" (11:2b), even as he urged them to "strive for his kingdom" (12:31), while reassuring, "it is your Father's good pleasure to give you the kingdom" (12:32). To be sure, welcoming, much less entering, the Basileia will not be easy: "How hard it is for those who have wealth to enter the kingdom of God! Indeed, it is easier for a camel to go through the eye of a needle than for someone who is rich to enter the kingdom of God" (18:24b–25). And yet, it is also not impossible: "Truly I tell you, there is no one who has left house or wife or brothers or parents or children, for the sake of the kingdom of God, who will not get back very much more in this age, and in the age to come eternal life" (18:29–30). With his ministry, then, the law and the prophets were giving way to "the good news of the kingdom of God" (16:16). In all of this, Jesus introduced and pointed to the Basileia in both eschatological aspects: temporally present and future and geographically for Israel and for all people everywhere who "will come from east and west, from north and south, and will eat in the kingdom of God" (13:29).[18]

Roman imperial order; see Taussig, *In the Beginning*, 125–30 and 176–78.

17. De Jonge, "Christological Significance," 10.

18. Jesus inaugurates the divine reign on behalf of Israel as the Son of David (18:38–39) and on behalf of the rest of humankind as the Son of God (1:35, 3:38, and passim);

Jesus is, and should be, the personal object of messianic piety, and yet, the messianic message was how he proclaimed and heralded the divine Basileia, succinctly identified at his first sermon at Nazareth (see chapter 2 above) and then elaborated on throughout the rest of his public ministry. Christian mission and evangelism, then, preaches no less than Jesus Christ as the representative and embodiment of the coming reign of God. In this respect, Christian witness has an irreducible sociopolitical dimension to it, not one that seeks to replace any present government (even one as violent as was imperial Rome),[19] but that nevertheless manifests the values of the Basileia Jesus preached and lived to promote the thriving of as many as possible and to work for the full flourishing of the common good. Conversion to Jesus, then, involves alignment toward the divine reign that he inaugurated. How else can we comprehend such and so orient ourselves in light of the apostolic narrative?

Sociopolitical Transformation in Acts: Considering Sociopolitical Conversion Apostolically

In the rest of this chapter, our focus will be on the book of Acts. We will unpack, in order, apostolic policies developed to address socioethnic challenges to common life, apostolic strategies for engaging cultural-religious pluralism, and apostolic interfaces with the earth and our geophysical environment. In each case, our goals are quite limited, less aiming to claim that Luke provides a coherent agenda for sociopolitical conversion than that there are apostolic resources within the narrative of early messianic witness to inspire our attending to and taking sociopolitical responsibility in ways consistent with welcoming the divine Basileia in our contemporary global context. Put another way, the giving of the Spirit empowering apostolic witness in Acts is part of the unfolding of the heralding of the coming divine Basileia in Luke.[20]

---

see here Hahn, "Kingdom and Church"; and also Ziccardi, *Relationship of Jesus*, 500–503.

19. I am thinking here, for instance, of contemporary Christian nationalism, particularly (although not only prevalent in) the United States, supported by Reconstructionist, Dominionist, and Seven-Mountain mandates that problematically seek to establish nations and countries today on divine law and rule, precisely what Jesus's response to the disciples in Acts 1 discouraged; see also Lemons and Yong, *Trump and the Politics of Prayer*.

20. Intriguingly, this parallels the argument made regarding especially Protestant missiology across the twentieth century by Kim, "Edinburgh 1910 to 2010," even if we

The Jerusalem Council: Apostolic Sociocultural Interventions

In chapter 3, we took an initial look at the Jerusalem Council in the context of discussing Peter's intellectual conversion, focused particularly on how he came to understand gentiles were no longer impure as previously defined by the law, even as he was then needing to follow this up morally by taking responsibility for eating with gentiles especially when Jews were present. Here, our focus is on the Council's deliberations and solidifying of such an understanding for the community, including for how to guide the divergent factions of this community into a more than less coherent whole. How, in other words, do individuals come to take sociopolitical responsibility? How might Luke's discussion of the Jerusalem Council illuminate such sociopolitical conversion in the early church?

Let us set the scene. Since Peter's visit to Cornelius's home, Jews were questioning fellowship with gentiles, those of the uncircumcision (Acts 11:2–3), and these gathered steam during Paul's first missionary journey, sparking resistance from Jewish leaders in especially Pisidian Antioch (13:45, 50) and Iconium (14:2, 5, 19). As word of Paul's interactions with the uncircumcised continued to spread, Judean Jews came to Antioch (in Syria) insisting, further, "Unless you are circumcised according to the custom of Moses, you cannot be saved" (15:1b), prompting Paul and Barnabas to trek to Jerusalem to hash out the issue with the apostles there. At Jerusalem, the members of the Pharisees reiterated, "It is necessary for [gentiles] to be circumcised and ordered to keep the law of Moses" (15:5).

Peter re-emerges here, and his speech, as recorded by Luke, besides the autobiographical introduction that we have already discussed above, charts a path forward for the messianic community's embrace of gentiles in at least the following respects. First, Peter recognizes that the time has come for leadership to make a more formal pronouncement in this situation, since otherwise, retention of the status quo, even by being silent about any other way forward, would amount to "placing on the neck of the disciples a yoke that neither our ancestors nor we have been able to bear" (15:10b). If Jewish and gentile hearts are purified equally by faith and both are "saved through the grace of the Lord Jesus" (15:9, 11), then this would become the new standard and norm for the messianic community.

---

don't have to say that Edinburgh 1910 was more christological and Edinburgh 2010 was more pneumatological.

Second, James the son of Alphaeus, another leading apostle (1:13, 12:17), now draws on Peter's testimony to retrieve Scripture for these developments, with one of the prophets noted as writing, "After this I will return, and I will rebuild the dwelling of David, which has fallen; from its ruins I will rebuild it, and I will set it up, so that all other peoples may seek the Lord—even all the Gentiles over whom my name has been called. Thus says the Lord, who has been making these things known from long ago" (15:16–18a; cf. Amos 9:11–12).[21] Here, the new relationship between Jew and gentile that is being discerned through Spirit-ed fellowship is now understood as anticipated in ancient Israel's scriptural writings.

Finally, then, continuing to draw on scriptural authority, now particularly Moses (15:21), the apostolic elders and leaders sought to formalize this view, "that we should not trouble those Gentiles who are turning to God, but we should write to them to abstain only from things polluted by idols and from fornication and from whatever has been strangled and from blood" (15:19–20). Those gathered agreed and said as much to the Christians in Antioch through a letter sent back by duly authorized members that read, in large part:

> . . . we have decided unanimously to choose representatives and send them to you, along with our beloved Barnabas and Paul, who have risked their lives for the sake of our Lord Jesus Christ. We have therefore sent Judas and Silas, who themselves will tell you the same things by word of mouth. For it has seemed good to the Holy Spirit and to us to impose on you no further burden than these essentials: that you abstain from what has been sacrificed to idols and from blood and from what is strangled and from fornication. If you keep yourselves from these, you will do well. (15:25–29)

Notice here that the apostolic elders have been traversing backward from Jesus to David and Moses, but in formulating the elemental encumbrances, went to retrieve and reappropriate an even earlier tradition of Noahide laws in ways that now sought to bind all human community together regardless of ethnic identity under a common (quadratic) set of creational abstentions.[22]

---

21. This is a very loose rendition of the Septuagint; see Park, *Book of Amos*, 96–97.

22. Hilary, *Intercultural Theology*, 253–54 and 265; see also Butova, *Four Prohibitions*, 15.

This decision meant that Peter, who had struggled with taking moral responsibility for his newfound theological insights, was now leading the apostolic community to take sociopolitical responsibility on behalf of multiethnic messianic congregations in the diaspora in accordance to what was primordially basic to human intercourse before Jews were separated out from the descendants of the sons of Noah. When the Christians at Antioch were informed about the Council's decision, "they rejoiced at the exhortation" (15:31b), and later, Paul reaffirms this Petrine proposal (21:25), thus presenting a united apostolic front across the Acts narrative.[23]

The issues were cultural, ethnic, and sociostructural. They had to do with long-standing religious law that had organized Jewish life as distinct from the gentiles, which fed ethnic and cultural sentiments—including biases and prejudices against outsiders—forged over centuries if not millennia. The bearing of messianic witness en route to the ends of the earth, however, was enlarging the previously more often segregated Jewish and Yahweh-fearing community. So long as the apostolic leadership did not formally act, the dynamic community would continue to be wracked by divergent and contrary voices and practices. To be sure, the Council's establishing of these new "rules" for communal fellowship did not resolve the dispute but widened the chasm between Jewish leadership perspectives and those of the growing number of gentiles who had come to recognize Jesus the Jew as messiah. Yet sociopolitical conversion does not mean that everyone agrees, but that we have to commit ourselves to the messianic path for the betterment (and common good) of the people of God, to the degree that we can discern that this involves embrace and enactment of the coming divine Basileia's values. Membership within and relationships forged out of this community, now, would be open to navigating a "new normal," one that not only allowed for but encouraged Jewish and gentile fellowship across heretofore largely uncrossed socioethnic and cultural lines.

Pagans in the Public and Political Domains: Apostolic Cultural-Religious Strategies

In previous chapters we have already commented on the gospel witness extending beyond Judea to Samarian territory (Acts 8), long cordoned off from Jewish life, and beyond that, arriving to the ends of the earth, even to the point of receiving the witness of island barbarians (of Malta in Acts 28).

23. See Dawson, *Message of the Jerusalem Council*, ch. 5.

Picking up on this line of inquiry moves us from the socioethnic issues impinging on fellowship to the sociocultural and religious realities that have implications for initial evangelistic contact to begin with. The question here involves how to posture ourselves toward not just ethnic and cultural others but to those who are also religious others in some or other respects. Pressing the question specifically in this direction brings to mind earlier comments also about the Pauline witness at Lystra, drawing on natural theological themes, and at the Areopagus at Athens, here appealing to the thinkers, philosophers, and poets of the Greco-Roman religious canon. If interactions with Samarians and barbarians were initiated or reinforced by signs and wonders, including exorcisms and healings (cp. 8:6–7, 13, and 28:8–9), then, as we have also seen already, witness to rural pagans involved both healings and agricultural references (14:8–10, 15–17) and to urban pagans included establishing points of contact with their immediate religious and philosophical realities (17:16–23). Intellectual and other layers of conversion presume prior contextually sensitive connections. These invite a level of sociopolitical intelligence, so to speak, one that presumes some willingness of evangelists to inhabit these spaces at some level.

Against this backdrop, I want to turn to Ephesus, to observe how Paul engaged this cultural-religious milieu in a sociopolitically savvy manner.[24] Luke reports that there is a lot going on apostolically in this city, e.g., a group of disciples familiar only with John's baptism of repentance (19:1–7); two years of Paul's lecturing—with all of the debate and persuasive argumentation that accompanies such discourse—at the Hall of Tyrannus (19:8–10);[25] and extraordinary miracles, healings, exorcisms, and public denouncement and destruction of libraries of magic texts in a publicly felt revivalist atmosphere (19:11–20), among other developments. What happens along the way, however, concerns the rousing up of devotees of the goddess Artemis. Demetrius, "a silversmith who made silver shrines of Artemis" (19:24a), was sensing that as "the word of the Lord grew mightily and prevailed" (19:20), Artemis devotion was being negatively impacted:

> in Ephesus but in almost the whole of Asia this Paul has persuaded and drawn away a considerable number of people by saying that gods made with hands are not gods. And there is danger not only

---

24. I have discussed Paul's mission to Ephesus elsewhere, e.g., Yong, *Hermeneutical Spirit II*, ch. 5.

25. See Keener, *Between History and Spirit*, ch. 21: "A Spirit-Filled Teaching Ministry in Acts 19:9."

that this trade of ours may come into disrepute but also that the temple of the great goddess Artemis will be scorned, and she will be deprived of her majesty that brought all Asia and the world to worship her. (19:26-27)

As a result, the crowd he gathered was "enraged and shouted, 'Great is Artemis of the Ephesians!'" (19:28) and, in reaction to an attempted intervention by a Jew named Alexander (19:33)—in hindsight a bad choice since Jews were the precursors of any messianist downplay of idols as worthless![26]—Luke documents: "for about two hours all of them shouted in unison, 'Great is Artemis of the Ephesians!'" (19:34).

If Demetrius was correct that Paul had indeed disdained Artemisian practice by ridiculing and belittling their silver shrines as mere idolatry,[27] then the ferocity of the people's response is not only comprehensible but justifiable. On the other hand, the silversmith's rhetorical effectiveness in aggravating and fomenting a mob is questionably related to the truth of what might have been actually said. Christian readers no doubt approach the apostolic experiences charitably while they consider the apostolic opposition with greater suspicion. Indeed, we would default to reducing Demetrius to his business interests and being a mere charlatan at that. And yet, when we consider things from his perspective, perhaps he named the economic register since it was a way to galvanize response to the even greater threat of Artemis being deprived of due honor. The point is that in the sociopolitical public square, there are often many motivations at work—sometimes ideologically driven and hence sinister from other perspectives, and on other occasions perhaps honestly forged but perceived as menacing by those impacted, even as usually there is a combination of well-intentions coupled by burdened histories and injustices[28]—and they are almost always intertwined with life's religious and moral realms.

It is in this politicized context of mass confusion that the town clerk, "the highest official in the Roman provincial administration,"[29] emerges, manages to quiet the mob, and bears witness (consciously or not) to the

26. See Brinks, "Great Is Artemis," esp. 789-90.

27. Perhaps Paul had argued as much at Athens (17:24, 29), although careful reading of that message reveals his approach to the altars, inscriptions, and idols was not contemptuous but focused more in emphasizing the living character of the God of Jesus Christ; see Klauck, *Magic and Paganism*, 84-91.

28. E.g., as unfolded with great analytical perspicacity regarding the religiously pluralistic context of postcolonial South Asia by Kim, *In Search of Identity*.

29. Klauck, *Magic and Paganism*, 108.

apostolic sociopolitical and socioreligious awareness manifest over the last few years in this city. The first part of what Luke depicts of his words is most pertinent for our purposes: "Citizens of Ephesus, who is there that does not know that the city of the Ephesians is the temple keeper of the great Artemis and of the statue that fell from heaven? Since these things cannot be denied, you ought to be quiet and do nothing rash. You have brought these men here who are neither temple robbers nor blasphemers of our goddess" (19:35–37). Two points are worth mentioning.

First, to Demetrius's indictment that the apostles were belittling Artemis saying that her silver shrines "made with hands are not gods," the town clerk corrects the record, insisting that Artemis's heavenly origins are uncontested. On this front, if indeed apostolic evangelism in Ephesus had impugned Artemis in this way, then, according to the town clerk, "the missionaries were mistaken."[30] Second, however, whereas in the rest of his recorded speech the town clerk redirects Demetrius's complaints to the courts, I suggest that the crowd is finally pacified and then dispersed (19:41) because of his testifying to the less-than-aggressive apostolic witness.[31] In contrast with the approach taken among the rural inhabitants of Lycaonia when rituals to the Greco-Roman pantheon of deities was specifically diminished as "worthless" (14:15; see ch. 4 above), the evangelistic endeavor over the extended period of Paul's stay in this urban metropolis seems much more tempered. The town clerk specifically alleviates apostolic evangelism from charges of being hostile either economically/culturally to the city or religiously to its deity. Rather than subverting local cultic practices or demonizing Artemisian religiosity, Pauline proclamation about the Basileia and the word of God (19:8, 10, 20) was cleared from either disrespect to Artemis or derisiveness to Ephesian piety.

Contemporary Christian interreligious apologetics has often been more polemical, perhaps doing what Demetrius claimed Paul did and even more since such diatribes are found in ancient Israelite prophetic literature vis-à-vis the idolatrous practices of her surrounding nations. Yet even if justifiable on such scriptural grounds,[32] Luke's portrait of apostolic witness

30. Trebilco, *Early Christians*, 162.

31. While I would not deny that Christian claims are variously exclusive of those related to Artemis, or magic practices, or sectarian Jewish exorcists, etc.—which are the "evils" taken up by Steve Walton, "Evil in Ephesus"—the narrative here reflects a greater sense of sociocultural and interreligious sensitivity than many contemporary exclusivist missionaries and evangelists might display.

32. Elsewhere I explore specifically a more binary us-versus-them approach when

in the Ephesian context belies any efforts to canonize only practices that are confrontational with the religious sensibilities of those being evangelized. In each of the cases we have considered in the book of Acts, from Lystra through Athens to Malta, and here in between, the prevalent religious commitments are engaged but not scornfully.

In this episode sociopolitical conversion is evidenced not at the level of policy that we saw coming of the Jerusalem Council, but in the day-to-day sociopolitically aware practices of witnessing that is sensitive to the generally contextual and specifically religio-cultural dynamics of those being evangelized. Evangelical conversion in Ephesus no doubt prompted affective reorientation away from Artemis to "the Way" (19:23b) and generated moral transformation in turning citizens and inhabitants of this Asian city from idolatry to the living deity. Further, socioeconomically, it may even have been that some of the new messianists ceased investing in Artemisian trinkets while others committed much more radical acts like confiscating their libraries to the tune of fifty thousand silver coins (19:19b)! And yet, the town clerk observed, all of this transpired without any bellicosity and antagonism toward the dominant religiosity of the citizens. Perhaps having observed the Pauline evangelistic practice unfolding at the Hall of Tyrannus, he could argue that apostolic evangelism had proceeded, contrary to Demetrius's claims, blamelessly. At the very least, we can, in reading this Ephesian mission as part of Luke's theology of mission,[33] conclude that Pauline Spirit-empowered and thus divinely authorized evangelism in a religiously pluralistic environment had proceeded in full awareness of, and appropriate sensitivity to, the existing religio-cultural and sociopolitical milieu.

Apocalyptic and the Earth: Apostolic Eco-Political Horizons

If engaging with religio-cultural diversity, as in the preceding brief discussion, represents the personal dimension of evangelistic witness in the sociopolitical arena, navigating ecological issues, as we now also seek to traverse, brings to the fore the common environmental domain of evangelism in the public square. Might focusing on the earth as our habitat provide a way for us to explore sociopolitical conversion in the apostolic experience and for

---

read off the surface of the Fourth Gospel in order to discern a more dialogical path; e.g., Yong, "Light Shines in the Darkness."

33. Which is the main point argued by Shauf, *Theology as History*.

us now?[34] Luke was not an ecological theologian by today's definition, and yet, I believe that he can be read ecologically in ways that retain the integrity of his account while also inviting our taking sociopolitical responsibility as part of Spirit-filled discipleship and evangelism. My point of entry for this topic continues to be that at the center of Luke's apostolic narrative: the Day of Pentecost.

We know that Peter's Pentecost Day sermon draws from the prophet Joel. In Luke's retelling, the outpouring of the Spirit, prophesying sons and daughters, visioning slaves and freed-persons, all of these were part of "the coming of the Lord's great and glorious day" that would also be heralded by "portents in the heaven above and signs on the earth below, blood, and fire, and smoky mist. The sun shall be turned to darkness and the moon to blood" (Acts 2:19–20).[35] The apocalypticism of this message was even more pronounced in the ancient prophecy, preceding "the great and terrible day of the Lord" (Joel 2:31). In short, the gift of the Spirit was no mere anthropocentric phenomenon, but one that registered itself cosmically so that the heavens and earth, all of which is by the hands of the sovereign creator God (4:24, 14:15b, 17:24), also reverberated with the manifestation of the divine wind. On the Day of Pentecost, as had happened repeatedly with the earlier prophets, apocalyptic manifestations were moments in which the Earth resounded the judgments of God, and in those instances, heralded also new opportunities for God's creatures to respond.[36]

We might think at this point that the apostles did not then attend explicitly to the environmental elements of their lives and witness. Yet, an argument has been made that the apostolic community that ensued, which moral transformation we considered in the prior chapter, can also be read in what we are calling a sociopolitically informed manner, and, more to the point, as manifesting a kind of ecologically renewed household,

---

34. What Pope Francis calls "ecological conversion"; see *Laudato Si'* §§216–21. For more on "ecological conversion," see also Arcamone, *Conversion as Transformation*, chs. 12–13.

35. My first environmentally conscious reading of Acts 2 goes back almost two decades (by now) to *Spirit Poured Out*, ch. 7; most recently, see my essay, "Spirit Poured Out in the Last Days."

36. Biblical apocalyptic texts have thus taken on new, creational significance in our era of the Anthropocene. For an exemplary rereading, see Davis and Grey, "Apocalyptic Destruction." My own reading of the Apocalypse includes segments read specifically from an environmentalist and eco-theological perspective: *Revelation*, 146–52. A broader review of apocalyptic in the Christian Scriptures from an environmental perspective is found in Adams, *Stars Will Fall*, 257–59.

or community, within which the early messianists not only converged but committed to. In this reading, apostolic selling and sharing are ecologically sustainable practices that contrast with the consumerism which only hoards (like the rich fool who was only self-concerned; Luke 12:16–21) or altogether ignores how we steward our environmental resources. The mutuality and generosity of the messianists thus reflects a collective ecology that provides a basis for both communal flourishing and the broader common good (as evidenced by the drawing of those in the Judean countryside into the messianic network).[37] In addition, this locally renewed household is a harbinger of the "universal restoration" (3:21) when the promise to Abraham, "in your descendants all the families of the earth shall be blessed" (3:25b; see Gen 12:3), will come to cosmic fruition: earth's families will prosper and thrive only to the degree that earth also blossoms. Insofar as "From one ancestor [creator God] made all nations to inhabit the whole earth, and he allotted the times of their existence and the boundaries of the places where they would live" (17:26), to that same degree, then, the redemptive work of Pentecost would stretch out to and renew the ends of the times and spaces of this same earth and its creatures.

Thus, the story of the apostles is not only also about the Spirit, but is also an Earth-story. From the mundane references to Simon the tanner (10:6) to Paul being a tentmaker—both hence as those who worked with animal skins and hair, etc.[38]—to the more cosmically impactful reactions like destructive widespread famines on the one side (11:28) to tremors that result in the shattering of prison shackles (16:26) and tempests that wreck ship (27:14–44) on the other, Earth not only holds together the messianists and individuals and the apostolic community within the wider human and creaturely families but also reacts with and to human actors and actions (groans and travails, as Paul elsewhere put it; Rom 8:22). Earth bears its own witness, in this regard, as also pronounced by Peter's kerygmatic exposition of Joel.

If Luke's second book can thereby be read at least in part as an Earth-story, then his first volume could also be approached as a chronicle of Earth's child.[39] Jesus arrives in a manger with his fellow creatures, is wrapped in Earth's cloths, is heralded by Earth's angelic hosts (Luke omits mention of

37. See Trainor, *Acts*, chs. 3–4.

38. Trainor, *Acts*, ch. 11.

39. Trainor, *About Earth's Child*. A less exegetical and more christologically driven effort is Edwards, *Jesus the Wisdom of God*.

magi who follow these heavenly signs as is found in the First Gospel), and is welcomed by shepherds who tend to Earth and carefully domesticate its creatures. He prefers to live on the road, in the rural peasant world, on the one hand being just as comfortable on shorelines, at the water's edges, or crossing lakes, and other the hand being drawn repeatedly to the wilderness and mountainsides, always abiding in, nourished by (not just himself but also with his followers, miraculously, with mere loaves and fishes), thus able to observe and to envision, even across open plains, a *basileia-ecotopia*, the "year of the Lord's favor." Indeed, as we saw in chapter 2 above, such heralding was exactly the heart of Jesus's proclamation—wherein the heavenly Father cares for human creatures like the birds of the air and the lilies of the field, where fig trees and mustard seeds enable anticipation of the divine reign, and where sabbath rest and sustainable contentment rather than accumulation of resources characterize creational flourishing—and what his entire ministry sought tireless to inaugurate.[40] And while Earth's child embraces his fate with the help of a colt and along a roadway paved by the cured skins of other creatures, he also realizes that even when the Son of Man is rejected by the world, the heavens will resound, the stones will sing out, and Earth's wood will hold up the Son of God in his waning moments even as Earth's hollows will receive and preserve his limp body. From this perspective, we can appreciate that Jesus lives out of and acts with ecological and environmental awareness, attentive to Earth's witness and its many voices even as his followers are reflected as "ecologically meditative and contemplative."[41]

If in its original context, the prophecy of Joel signaled the divine and heavenly response to the Earth's plague of destructive locusts, then, the Pentecost outpouring is similarly apocalyptic, albeit now signaling realignment of Earth's creatures with the heavens above and the earth below as an extension of the Spirited/messianic ushering in of the Basileia-ecotopia in the life and ministry of the carpenter from Nazareth. None of this lays out the details of a contemporary policy to address environmental degradation and climate change, but perhaps such a Basileiac vision might prompt sociopolitical awareness, motivate sociopolitical transformation, and empower sociopolitical engagement. The beginnings and next steps of our sociopolitical conversions in this arena may be practicing recycling, living "green" in our city planning, planting trees, etc., and living sustainably in

---

40. On this point, see Harris, "Synoptic Gospels," 224.
41. Trainor, *About Earth's Child*, 304.

sync with creation and its resources (rather than consumeristically). The many tongues of Pentecost open up to, in the biblical imagination, the many tribes and languages of the New Jerusalem and the New Creation where the leaves of the trees of the New Earth will provide for the healing of Earth's peoples.[42] We cannot undo overnight what modernity has wrought over centuries, but the opportunity for sociopolitical conversion nevertheless invites an evangelistic message that calls for the caring of our fellow creatures and environmental commons within which we all live, move, and have our being.[43]

Sociopolitical Conversion and Apostolic Evangelism: Extending Spirit-ed Public Witness

What takeaways about sociopolitical conversion emerge from our discussion of apostolic interfaces with the public square? What are the implications for Spirit-led evangelism today? The following are suggestive from the preceding.

First, *we should do more to recognize and lift up the public square within which apostolic witness is borne*. Luke's multi-part Spirit-ed story is recognizably so situated in the widest of all possible publics, one extending to the edges of the known world, even as Jesus the Spirit-filled, anointed, and inspired one announces the arrival of good news that reverberates for all creation. We live amid very different public times and circumstances and yet oftentimes do not consider our evangelistic mandate to address the opportunities and challenges that exist in the common environment we share with those we evangelize and with other creatures. Any initial sociopolitical engagement for the next evangelism, so to speak, ought to begin with the first steps of our own sociopolitical conversion.

Second, then, *wherever we find ourselves presents the question and invitation: How can and should we be in solidarity with both the least of these and alien others as we see from the apostolic narrative?* In this frame, Barnabas becomes the second most important apostolic exemplar—after the Nazarite himself—insofar as he takes up habitation with those in greater need and with fewer resources than he. This is not to say that the gospel should not be proclaimed to the middle and upper middle classes, even to the affluent;

---

42. See my chapter, "Many Tongues, Many Biocultural Niches."

43. What some call "eco-evangelism"; see Heath, *Mystic Way*, 100–101; see also ch. 6, "Redeeming the Earth."

it is to say that engagements at these socioeconomic class levels need to be undertaken with the full awareness that the messianic and apostolic witness resounds first and foremost "underneath," as it were. Perhaps this is liberation theology's preferential option for the poor, although the claim here is that such a hermeneutical privileging is fundamentally apostolic and only secondarily, if at all, Marxist or otherwise ideologically freighted.[44]

Finally, for now, *what kinds of programmatic and structural interventions might we envision supporting in our sociopolitical witness?* Keeping in mind how the Jerusalem Council decided to act, and pulling forward Pauline engagement with the principalities and powers against the backdrop of Jesus's Basileiac-ecotopian message, how do we act on behalf of others, resisting or subverting the oppressive status quo on the one hand, and advocating for social transformation on the other hand? Informed by lives in solidarity with the marginalized, what are concrete next steps in heralding the coming Basileia amid the imperial constraints of this world? What collective steps present themselves in our vocational endeavors for the common good? Who are the shepherds, town clerks, soldiers, sailors, and even gardeners the Spirit could lead us to work collaboratively with for our common salvation and for our common prosperity?[45]

As we bring this chapter to a close, like the others in this part of the book, I now want to turn also to the sociopolitical conversion not of those being evangelized but of any of us who believe we are called to an evangelist's vocation. How is our own sociopolitical conversion to be continually facilitated, and how are these sociopolitical transformations important for our missional and evangelistic witness? For our kerygmatic and Basileiac proclamation, here are a few more questions at this stage of our own journey.

First, *are we open to the possibility that others who are sociopolitically different from ourselves we are called to evangelize might also reform and transform how we relate to them and engage with the systems and structures of society?* How open are we evangelists, then, to be guests and hosts of such persons not just from different walks of life but from diverse socioeconomic strata of society? If we were going to be hosts of those from whom Jesus urged we should not expect reciprocity or repayment, then we would want

---

44. See Yong, "Jubilee, Liberation, and Pentecost."

45. I mention gardeners here in light of a recent Easter (2024) message preached by my pastor Rev. Marcos Canales about Jesus being mistaken for one (John 10:15), wherein he also powerfully explored the implications of that (mis)recognition for creation care and renewal; see also Suggit, "Jesus the Gardener"; and Denton-Daly, *John*.

to have less lavish or elegant accommodations where these less-to-do can more comfortably enjoy, and that itself suggests we may need to simplify and live more sustainably with resources more evenly distributed within our communities; if we were open to being guests of these more marginalized others, then how we comport ourselves will dictate whether we get invited into less extravagant or fashionable spaces. Either way, this is not about being guilty about being more socioeconomically upwardly mobile, but it is about how to hold whatever resources we may have access to in ways to enable our solidarity with the less fortunate. The latter is a tall order since that means setting aside privileges that most who have them have worked hard to attain. Perhaps a few of us will be called to be evangelists to the well-to-do; for most of the rest of us, the call is to open up our moral compass to begin asking if and how we can be more intentional about finding ourselves at home in these other sociopolitical spaces of our world.

Second, *beyond entering in and leaving these spaces, to what degree are we willing to abide more evangelically amid and be in solidarity with those more sociopolitically different than us?* Rather than coming in and out of socioeconomically depressed spaces, are we willing to welcome a new Pentecost, one that involves our locking hands around, linking arms with, and being in solidarity with those in these places? Isn't this evangelism: to partner mutually and dialogically with those otherwise different than us not only because of culture, language, and religion but also because of divergent race/ethnicity, politics, and economics? Is this not good news for the world that God so loves, to accompany those who are sick and to commiserate with our fellow human creatures?

Finally, *beyond being in solidarity with others, are we willing to seek the peace and shalom of the commons wherein we find ourselves?* These are the next steps, to work curatively with and for those who are sick, to collaborate for the social uplift of the entire community, to prophetically partner with the God-fearing social agents to turn the world upside down so that socioeconomic centers and margins are no longer stratified but reconciled and renewed. This was also Yahweh's invitation to the people of Israel carried and exiled off to Babylon: to "seek the welfare of the city where I have sent you into exile, and pray to the Lord on its behalf, for in its welfare you will find your welfare" (Jer 29:7). This remains the call to the people of God wherever we may find ourselves: to work for the shalom of the social and wider environmental spaces that we inhabit so that all creatures, fellow human and other animals, and our common ecosphere will experience the redemptive and renewing work of the divine wind.

Conclusion
Toward a New Evangelization in the Footsteps of the Apostles

How then might we summarize what our journey with the apostles has revealed about Christian witness, evangelism, and conversion, and what that means and entails for us today? The good news is that the gospel of Jesus remains relevant today. It is relevant for individuals, for what they believe and know, but even more importantly for who they are and for their lives and relationships, to God and to others. The gospel is thereby also relevant for us and our communities, how we live interpersonally with others. Last but not least, the gospel is relevant for our world, not just in terms of all the people that live in it but also for how we structure our lives and how we live with other non-human creatures and with the environment that nurtures us altogether. In short, the ongoing relevance of the gospel means that evangelism—the sharing of this good news—remains essential and needed.

And yes, as we have seen, evangelism and conversion lay comprehensive claim on us: on ourselves including the depths of our hearts, on our relationships, on our social systems and structures, and on our environmental situatedness also. Thus, the call to conversion is one that persists across each of these dimensions—effectively each a realm, sphere, and even world of its own, yet all interrelated. Precisely also for this reason, the evangelistic invitation requires our own ongoing conversion in each of these domains—the depths of our hearts, the world of relationships, our social world, and our environmental habitat—effectively, our continual transformation in anticipation of the coming divine reign.

The call for us as evangelists then is twofold. On the one hand, the invitation is for us to love God and others.[1] Loving God, the transcendent creator of all things is mediated by our loving Jesus. Yet loving Jesus is no mere sentimentality but embracing who he is in relationship to the divine Basileia that he welcomed us to. In the latter respect, loving Jesus includes loving his brothers and sisters, especially (even if not only) the poor, the naked, the hungry and thirsty, and the incarcerated of the world. Further, loving Jesus can be extended also to the other non-human creatures that he walked with and the Earth that he walked (and sailed) on. To love Jesus is to love God and neighbor and to participate with them in mutually transformative witness.[2]

On the other hand, then, the invitation is for us to continue to be converted as evangelists or witness bearers. Christian life, discipleship, and witness is a journey, one that involves ongoing formation and transformation. We have elaborated on these vis-à-vis our intellectual, affective, moral, and sociopolitical spheres, urging that they all contribute variously and in different moments of our lives to our ultimate conversion to the image and likeness of Jesus Christ. What are the broader missiological implications of our conversion in these arenas?

In summary, our openness to ongoing intellectual conversion invites our repudiation of any anti-intellectualism that may be part of our religious or ecclesial tradition, especially that motivated by a rigid exclusivism that would insulate us from considering the views, experiences, and perspectives of others outside of our immediate social (and ecclesial) circles. Unfortunately, those who are inclined to be the first to speak are also less ready to listen and absorb. We have confused the Spirit's empowering of witness with the ability to speak louder and longer, not realizing that this "gift of gab" may well be uninformed, and may be spreading misinformation as much as shedding the light of the gospel in any circumstance. This is not to say that any and all learning is devoid of ideology or bias, since all human knowing emerges from out of context and situation. Yet it is to say that the Spirit leads us to all truth oftentimes through the witnesses born of others, including of the media, in the fields of education, via scientific inquiry, through medical expertise, and etc.[3] Thus, a Christian missiology

---

1. See also Peyton, *Second Commandment*.
2. Also, Stephenson and Wienk, *Redemptive Service*.
3. See Coulter and Yong, *Holy Spirit and Higher Education*, including ch. 5 on the disciplines of human knowledge; also, my *Spirit of Creation*, esp. ch. 2, on scientific inquiry

CONCLUSION

for the third millennium ought to be informed, and continuously so, as part of the Spirit-led journey through and "in a mirror, dimly" (1 Cor 13:12a). Similarly, our theology of evangelism should be propelled by our own ongoing intellectual conversion, always testing knowledge claims in light of the gospel but also understanding the good news of Jesus Christ and the coming divine Basileia deeper in light of our growing understanding of the creation and ourselves as creatures in it.

As we now have seen, however, the conversion of our intellects impacts not only our heads but is intimately linked with our hearts, so ongoing affective conversion has missiological and evangelistic implications for how we see ourselves in relationship with others, not least those we intend on evangelizing. Unfortunately, the most enthusiastic missionaries and evangelists among us confused the Spirit's empowering witness as boldness in pressing forward amid challenges, intensity of evangelistic speech, and/or aggressiveness toward the "targets" of our evangelizing activity, not realizing that these more often than not are alienating or inhibit others from hearing or experiencing the good news of the divine Basileia. And the point is not that we must reach some mystical point of being entirely sanctified since that itself is an ideal construct in light of our historically understood condition. After all, as the ancient prophet insightfully understood, "The heart is devious above all else; it is perverse—who can understand it?" (Jer 17:9). Thus, our affective transformation will be an ongoing endeavor, always plumbing the depths of our hearts while anticipating that, "when he is revealed, we will be like him, for we will see him as he is [for] all who have this hope in him purify themselves, just as he is pure" (1 John 3:2b–3). And, as we continue to understand ourselves, and by extension others, better and deeper, we are empowered to take responsibility for what we feel and how we continue to become in ways that embody the good news of the coming divine reign. Witness to the gospel is now less impeded by our grandiosity or self-absorption, becoming more inviting, and opening up the hearts of others to Jesus (not just to us). Our own affective maturation, in short, empowers deeper missional and evangelistic levels of loving response to others, by which "everyone will know that [we] are [Jesus's] disciples, if [we] have love for one another" (John 13:35).[4]

Such love of our neighbors opens up to our ongoing moral conversion, which achieves full missiological potential in our continual sociopolitical

and interdisciplinarity.

4. Yong, *Spirit of Love*.

conversion for the common good. This is because we are now committed not just to sharing interpersonally with others in need but in repairing whatever structural, systemic, and societal dysfunctions that may hinder the full flourishing of all creatures and the environmental commons within which we all live, more, and have our being. Again, this is not to minimize religious conversions to Jesus as Lord nor the establishing or planting of churches for the purpose of nurturing believers in the faith. It is to say that these are essential but not exhaustive expressions of Spirit-inspired witness. And we are not hereby also embracing what is widely embraced by Pentecostal and Charismatic churches as the Seven-Mountain mandate that not just seeks Christian influence but actively pursues Christian sociopolitical authority in the realms of family, religion, education, media, arts/entertainment, business, and even government. Rather, our thesis of Christian witness not just to but with others means that sociopolitical conversion generates a *soft power* dynamic that invites messianists today to partner with any and all who might be invested—whether other believers, fellow religionists, pagans, thought leaders, scientists, educators, politicians, economists, environmentalists, or anyone else sociopolitically motivated—to seek the common good. The issues are many, and there will be no end to opportunities for further and ongoing sociopolitical conversion for any one of us, that will open us up to the many other communities that are addressing these various and complex matters for creational sustainability and thriving.[5]

The good news is both that these conversions happen through our walking with Jesus and the others he brings onto our path even as their deepening enables more powerful witness of the good news to those we are accompanying. I was once saved, I am being saved, and I will be saved. You and I were once evangelized, you and I are being evangelized, and you and I will be evangelized. We were once converted, we are being converted, and we will be converted. This means I do not yet know everything but will continue to grow in truth as the Spirit leads; it means I am not yet fully mature emotionally and will continue to be shaped in the image of Jesus as the Spirit purifies; it means I am not yet fully loving in our actions and behaviors to others or living for the common good but remain willing to follow the divine winds wherever they come from or blow. If part of the problem of late modern persons is the lack of capacity for self-transcendence and encountering transcendence, then part of the answer involves facilitating

---

5. E.g., Baron and Yong, *Pentecostal Missiology and Environmental Degradation*.

CONCLUSION

encounter of and integration with God.[6] Divine encounters, as Luke tells us, happens in our being open by the Holy Spirit to others different from ourselves. The solution to moribund Christian mission after colonization is conversion once again to the gospel.

I am writing to missionaries and evangelists both those already active in these vocations and who sense a calling in these directions. However else we might prepare for these tasks, my claim is that in the 2020s and for the foreseeable future, the effectiveness of our witness hinges on our willingness to be honest with the depth and authenticity of our own spiritual and religious journeys, on how honest we will be with ourselves in the presence of others to whom we are called to share our lives and faith. If we do not attend to our own conversions and transformations, we might obtain conversions, but others will be turning to us rather than being turned by and toward the gospel; if we continue to die daily to ourselves in the presence of others, that witness will accomplish the purposes of the coming divine Basileia better than whatever programmatic interventions our missiological and evangelistic strategies might concoct.

In sum: We have reconsidered Christian evangelism, mission, and witness *after Pentecost* for the 2020s, as involving orthodoxic (right beliefs), orthopathic (right feelings), and orthopraxis (right actions) dimensions, particularly as related to our Christian life, before expectations of how they would unfold among those who are being witnessed to (the evangelized). Our testimony, evangelism, and proclamation are most authentic and persuasive when emergent from out of a fully converted way of life. Others are drawn into the mission of God when they experience the presence of the living Christ through the power of the Spirit. Come Holy Spirit, continue to transform us and our lives and witness.

---

6. As Edward Rommen, an Orthodox theologian, argues; see Rommen, *Get Real*, 193–96 and 214–22.

Bibliography

Abraham, William J. *The Art of Evangelism: Evangelism Carefully Crafted into the Life of the Local Church.* Eugene, OR: Wipf & Stock, 1988.
———. *The Logic of Evangelism.* Grand Rapids: Eerdmans, 1989.
Adams, Edward. *The Stars Will Fall from Heaven: Cosmic Catastrophe in the New Testament and Its World.* Library of New Testament Studies 347. New York: T. & T. Clark, 2007.
Arcamone, Dominic. *Conversion as Transformation: Lonergan, Mentors, and Cinema.* Eugene, OR: Pickwick, 2020.
Augustine, Daniela C. *Pentecost, Hospitality, and Transfiguration: Toward a Spirit-Inspired Vision of Social Transformation.* Cleveland, OH: CPT, 2012.
———. *The Spirit and the Common Good: Shared Flourishing in the Image of God.* Grand Rapids: Eerdmans, 2019.
Augustine, Daniela C., and Chris E. W. Green, eds. *The Politics of the Spirit: Pentecostal Reflections on Public Responsibility and the Common Good.* Lanham, MD: Seymour, 2023.
Bahmann, Manfred K. *A Preference for the Poor: Latin American Liberation Theology from a Protestant Perspective.* Lanham, MD: University Press of America, 2005.
Balch, David L. *Contested Ethnicities and Images: Studies in Art and Acts.* Wissenschaft Untersuchungen zum Neuen Testament 345. Tübingen: Mohr Siebeck, 2015.
Balswick, Jack O., et al. *The Reciprocating Self: Human Development in Theological Perspective.* Downers Grove, IL: InterVarsity, 2005.
Baron, Eugene, and Amos Yong, eds. *Pentecostal Missiology and Environmental Degradation.* London: Langham Global, 2025.
Barram, Michael. *Missional Economics: Biblical Justice and Christian Formation.* Grand Rapids: Eerdmans, 2018.
Barreto, Eric D. "Crafting Colonial Identities: Hybridity and the Roman Empire in Luke-Acts." In *An Introduction to Empire in the New Testament*, edited by Adam Winn, 107–21. Resources for Biblical Study 84. Atlanta: SBL, 2016.
Bechard, Dean Philip. *Paul Outside the Walls: A Study of Luke's Socio-Geographical Universalism in Acts 14:8–20.* Analecta Biblica: Investigationes Scientificae in res Biblicas 143. Rome: Editrice Pontificio Instituto Biblico, 2000.
Beck, Richard. "Spiritual Pollution: The Dilemma of Sociomoral Disgust and the Ethic of Love." *Journal of Psychology and Theology* 34 (2006) 53–65.
Beers, Holly. *The Followers of Jesus as the "Servant": Luke's Model from Isaiah for the Disciples in Luke-Acts.* The Library of New Testament Studies 535. New York: T. & T. Clark, 2016.

BIBLIOGRAPHY

Bennema, Cornelis. "The Rich Are the Bad Guys: Lukan Characters and Wealth Ethics." In *Characters and Characterization in Luke-Acts*, edited by Frank E. Dicken and Julia A. Snyder, 94–108. Library of New Testament Studies 548. London: Bloomsbury, 2016.

Björkander, Martina. *Worship, Ritual, and Pentecostal Spirituality-as-Theology: A Rhythm That Connects Our Hearts with God.* Global Pentecostal and Charismatic Studies 48. Leiden: Brill, 2024.

Boer, Harry R. *Pentecost and Missions.* Grand Rapids: Eerdmans, 1961.

Bonk, Jonathan J., et al, eds. *Speaking About What We Have Seen and Heard: Evangelism in Global Perspective.* New Haven, CT: OSMC, 2007.

Bradley, Susan J. *Affect Regulation and the Development of Psychopathology.* New York: Guilford, 2000.

Bridge, Edward. "Christians and Jews in Antioch." In *Into All the World: Emergent Christianity in Its Jewish and Greco-Roman Context*, edited by Mark Harding and Alanna Nobbs, 208–36. Grand Rapids: Eerdmans, 2017.

Brink, Laurie. *Soldiers in Luke-Acts: Engaging, Contradicting, and Transcending the Stereotypes.* Wissenschaftliche Untersuchungen zum Neuen Testament 2:362. Tübingen: Mohr Siebeck, 2014.

Brinks, C. L. "'Great Is Artemis of the Ephesians': Acts 19:23–41 in Light of Goddess Worship in Ephesus." *Catholic Biblical Quarterly* 71 (2009) 776–94.

Budiselić, Ervin. *Uniqueness of the Concept of Witness in Lukan Writings Within the Biblical Canon.* Carlisle: Langham, 2024.

Butova, Elena. *The Four Prohibitions of Acts 15 and Their Common Background in Genesis 1–3.* Eugene, OR: Wipf & Stock, 2018.

Callan, Terrance. *Psychological Perspectives on the Life of Paul: An Application of the Methodology of Gerd Theissen.* Studies in the Bible and Early Christianity 22. Lewiston, NY: Edwin Mellen, 1990.

Cassidy, Richard J. *Paul in Chains: Roman Imprisonment and the Letters of St. Paul.* New York: Crossroad, 2001.

Cattermole, Giles N. "Global Health: A New Paradigm for Medical Mission?" *Missiology* 49 (2021) 189–206.

Chester, Tim. *A Meal with Jesus: Discovering Grace, Community, and Mission Around the Table.* Wheaton, IL: Crossway, 2011.

Cho, Youngmo. *Spirit and Kingdom in the Writings of Luke and Paul: An Attempt to Reconcile These Concepts.* Milton Keynes: Paternoster, 2005.

Christiansen, Ellen Juhl. "Sinner According to Words of the Law, Righteous by Works of Love: Boundary Challenges in Relation to the Woman Who Anoints Jesus (Luke 7:36–50)." In *Jesus and Paul: Global Perspectives in Honor of James D. G. Dunn for his 70th Birthday*, edited by B. J. Oropeza et al., 35–45. Library of New Testament Studies 414. London: T. & T. Clark, 2009.

Clapper, Gregory. "*Orthokardia*: John Wesley's Grammar of the Holy Spirit." In *The Spirit, the Affections, and the Christian Tradition*, edited by Amos Yong and Dale M. Coulter, 259–78. Notre Dame, IN: University of Notre Dame Press, 2016.

Clark, Andrew C. *Parallel Lives: The Relation of Paul to the Apostles in the Lucan Perspective.* Carlisle: Paternoster, 2001.

Coalter, Milton J., and Virgil Cruz, eds. *How Shall We Witness? Faithful Evangelism in the Reformed Tradition.* Louisville, KY: Westminster John Knox, 1995.

BIBLIOGRAPHY

Conn, Walter E. *Christian Conversion: A Developmental Interpretation on Autonomy and Surrender.* New York: Paulist, 1986.

Conway, Colleen M., and David M. Carr. *A Contemporary Introduction to the Bible: Sacred Texts and Imperial Contexts.* Hoboken, NJ: Wiley Blackwell, 2021.

Coulter, Dale M., and Amos Yong. *The Holy Spirit and Higher Education: Renewing the Christian University.* Waco, TX: Baylor University Press, 2023.

Couray, David J. *What Has Wittenberg to Do with Azusa? Luther's Theology of the Cross and Pentecostal Triumphalism.* New York: T. & T. Clark, 2015.

Croasmun, Matthew, and Miroslav Volf. *The Hunger for Home: Food and Meals in the Gospel of Luke.* Waco, TX: Baylor University Press, 2022.

Dahl, N. A. "Nations in the New Testament." In *New Testament Christianity for Africa and the World: Essays in Honour of Harry Sawyerr*, edited by Mark E. Glasswell and Edward W. Fasholé-Luke, 54–68. London: SPCK, 1974.

Damasio, Antonio. *Feeling and Knowing: Making Minds Conscious.* New York: Pantheon, 2021.

Davis, Anita, and Jacqueline N. Grey. "The Apocalyptic Destruction of the Earth in Isaiah 24 and Its Place in a Pentecostal Ecotheology." In *Pentecostal Missiology and Environmental Degradation*, edited by Eugene Baron and Amos Yong, 21–40. London: Langham Global, 2025.

Dawson, Zachary K. *The Message of the Jerusalem Council in the Acts of the Apostles: A Linguistic Stylistic Analysis.* Linguistic Biblical Studies 22. Leiden: Brill, 2022.

de Jonge, Marinus. "The Christological Significance of Jesus' Preaching of the Kingdom of God." In *The Future of Christology: Essays in Honor of Leander E. Keck*, edited by Abraham J. Malherbe and Wayne A. Meeks, 3–17. Minneapolis: Fortress, 1993.

Denton-Daly, Margaret. *John: Supposing Him to Be the Gardener.* An Earth Bible Commentary. New York: T. & T. Clark, 2017.

Descartes, René. "The Passions of the Soul." In *The Philosophical Writings of Descartes*, translated by John Cottingham et al., 1:325–404. Cambridge: Cambridge University Press, 1985.

Dillon, Carol. *Emotional Health: From Science to Whole Being.* Newcastle upon Tyne: Cambridge Scholars, 2021.

Dinkler, Michal Beth. "The Politics of Stephen's Storytelling: Narrative Rhetoric and Reflexivity in Acts 7:2–53." *Zeitschrift für die neutestamentliche Wissenschaft* 111 (2020) 33–64.

Donahue, John R. "Who Is My Enemy? The Parable of the Good Samaritan and the Love of Enemies." In *The Love of Enemy and Nonretaliation in the New Testament*, edited by Willard M. Swartley, 137–56. Louisville, KY: Westminster John Knox, 1992.

Doran, Robert M., and Robert C. Croken, eds. *Early Works on Theological Method 1.* The Collected Works of Bernard Lonergan 22. Toronto: University of Toronto Press, 2010.

Dowsett, Rose, et al., eds. *Evangelism and Diakonia in Context.* Regnum Edinburgh Centenary Series 32. Oxford: Regnum, 2016.

Dunn, James D. G. "The Incident at Antioch (Gal 2:11–18)." In *The Galatians Debate: Contemporary Issues in Rhetorical and Historical Interpretation*, edited by Mark D. Nanos, 199–234. Peabody, MA: Hendrickson, 2002.

Edwards, Denis. *Jesus the Wisdom of God: An Ecological Theology.* Maryknoll, NY: Orbis, 1995.

Edwards, Jonathan. "Sinners in the Hands of an Angry God." In *The Sermons of Jonathan Edwards: A Reader*, edited by Wilson H. Kimnach et al., 49–65. New Haven, CT: Yale University Press, 1999.

Elliott, Matthew A. *Faithful Feelings: Rethinking Emotion in the New Testament*. Grand Rapids: Kregel Academic, 2006.

Ferguson, John. *The Religions of the Roman Empire*. Ithaca, NY: Cornell University Press, 1970.

Fournier, Marianne. *The Episode at Lystra: A Rhetorical and Semiotic Analysis of Acts 14:7–20a*. American University Studies Series 7: Theology and Religion 197. New York: Peter Lang, 1997.

Fowler, James W. *Stages of Faith*. New York: HarperCollins, 1981.

Fox, Bethany McKinney. *Disability and the Way of Jesus: Holistic Healing in the Gospels and the Church*. Downers Grove, IL: IVP Academic, 2019.

Francis, Pope. *Laudato Si'*. Washington, DC: United States Conference of Catholic Bishops, 2015. https://www.vatican.va/content/francesco/en/encyclicals/documents/papa-francesco_20150524_enciclica-laudato-si.html.

Garrett, Susan R. *The Demise of the Devil: Magic and the Demonic in Luke's Writings*. Minneapolis: Fortress, 1989.

Geitz, Elizabeth R. *Fireweed Evangelism: Christian Hospitality in a Multi-Faith World*. New York: Church Publishing, 2004.

Gelpi, Donald L. *Charism and Sacrament: A Theology of Conversion*. New York: Paulist, 1976.

———. *Closer Walk: Confessions of a U.S. Jesuit Yat*. Lanham, MD: Hamilton, 2006.

———. *The Conversion Experience: A Reflective Process for RCIA Participants and Others*. New York: Paulist, 1998.

———. *The Firstborn of Many: A Christology for Converting Christians*. 3 vols. Milwaukee: Marquette University Press, 2001.

Girgis, Ragy. *On Satan, Demons, and Psychiatry: Exploring Mental Illness in the Bible*. Eugene, OR: Wipf & Stock, 2020.

Gosbell, Louise A. *"The Poor, the Crippled, the Blind, and the Lame": Physical and Sensory Disability in the Gospels of the New Testament*. Wissenschaftliche Untersuchungen zum Neuen Testament 2:469. Tübingen: Mohr Siebeck, 2018.

Gowler, David B. *Host, Guest, Enemy and Friend: Portraits of the Pharisees in Luke and Acts*. Repr., Eugene, OR: Wipf & Stock, 2007.

Green, Joel B. "A Cognitive Narratological Approach to the Characterization(s) of Zacchaeus." In *Characters and Characterization in Luke-Acts*, edited by Frank E. Dicken and Julia A. Snyder, 109–20. Library of New Testament Studies 548. London: Bloomsbury, 2016.

———. *Conversion in Luke-Acts: Divine Action, Human Cognition, and the People of God*. Grand Rapids: Baker Academic, 2015.

———. *The Gospel of Luke*. The New International Commentary on the New Testament. Grand Rapids: Eerdmans, 1997.

———. "'To Turn from Darkness into Light' (Acts 26:18): Conversion in the Narrative of Luke-Acts." In *Conversion in the Wesleyan Tradition*, edited by Kenneth J. Collins and John H. Tyson, 103–18. Nashville: Abingdon, 2001.

———. "'Witnesses of His Resurrection': Resurrection, Salvation, Discipleship, and Mission in the Acts of the Apostles." In *Life in the Face of Death: The Resurrection*

Message of the New Testament, edited by Richard N. Longenecker, 227–46. Grand Rapids: Eerdmans, 1998.

Gurtner, Daniel M. "Luke's Isaianic Jubilee." In *From Creation to New Creation: Essays in Honor of G. K. Beale*, edited by Daniel M. Gurtner and Benjamin L. Gladd, 123–46. Peabody, MA: Hendrickson, 2013.

Hahn, Scott W. "Kingdom and Church in Luke-Acts: From Davidic Christology to Kingdom Christology." In *Reading Luke: Interpretation, Reflection, Formation*, edited by Craig G. Bartholomew et al., 294–326. The Scripture and Hermeneutics Series 8. Grand Rapids: Zondervan, 2005.

Harris, Mark. "Synoptic Gospels." In *The Oxford Handbook of the Bible and Ecology*, edited by Hilary Marlow and Mark Harris, 211–27. Oxford: Oxford University Press, 2022.

Hartt, Julian N. *Toward a Theology of Evangelism*. New York: Abingdon, 1955.

Heath, Elaine A. *The Mystic Way of Evangelism: A Contemplative Vision for Christian Outreach*. 2nd ed. Grand Rapids: Baker Academic, 2017.

Hell, John Paul. *The Meal Scenes in Luke-Acts: An Audience Oriented Approach*. SBL Monograph Series 52. Atlanta: SBL, 1999.

Hengel, Martin. *Between Jesus and Paul: Studies in the Earliest History of Christianity*. Translated by John Bowden. Minneapolis: Fortress, 1983.

Hensman, C. R. *Agenda for the Poor, Claiming Their Inheritance: A Third World People's Reading of Luke*. Colombo: Centre for Society and Religion, 1990.

Hilary, Mbachu. *Intercultural Theology of the Jerusalem Council in Acts 15: An Inspiration for the Igbo Church Today*. European University Studies 22: Theology 520. Frankfurt: Peter Lang, 1995.

Hindmarsh, D. Bruce. *The Evangelical Conversion Narrative: Spiritual Autobiography in Early Modern England*. Oxford: Oxford University Press, 2005.

Horsley, Richard A. "The Kingdom of God and the Renewal of Israel." In *The Bible and Liberation: Political and Social Hermeneutics*, edited by Norman K. Gottwald and Richard A. Horsley, 408–27. Maryknoll, NY: Orbis, 1993.

Hume, Douglas A. *The Early Christian Community: A Narrative Analysis of Acts 2:41–47 and 4:32–35*. Wissenschaftliche Untersuchungen zum Neuen Testament 2:298. Tübingen: Mohr Siebeck, 2011.

Jennings, Willie James. *The Christian Imagination: Theology and the Origins of Race*. New Haven, CT: Yale University Press, 2011.

Jenson, Matt. *Gravity of Sin: Augustine, Luther, and Barth on* homo incurvatus in se. New York: T. & T. Clark, 2006.

Jipp, Joshua. *Divine Visitations and Hospitality to Strangers in Luke-Acts: An Interpretation of the Malta Episode in Acts 28:1–10*. Supplements to Novum Testamentum 153. Leiden: Brill, 2013.

———. *Reading Acts*. Eugene, OR: Cascade, 2018.

Johnson, Luke Timothy. *The Gospel of Luke*. Sacra Pagina 3. Collegeville, MN: Liturgical, 1991.

Jonker, Louis. "The Exile as Sabbath Rest: The Chronicler's Interpretation of the Exile." *Old Testament Essays* 20 (2007) 403–19.

Keener, Craig S. *Acts: An Exegetical Commentary*. 4 vols. Grand Rapids: Baker Academic, 2013–15.

———. *Between History and Spirit: The Apostolic Witness in the Book of Acts*. Eugene, OR: Cascade, 2020.

Kgatle, Mookgo S. "Missiology as Social Justice: A Contextual Reading of the Mission of Christ in Luke 4:16–19." *Missionalia: Southern African Journal of Mission Studies* 47 (2019) 58–71.

Kidman, Antony. *Staying Sane in the Fast Lane: Emotional Health in the 21st Century*. St. Leonard, NSW: Biochemical & General Services, 2011.

Kilgallen, John. *The Stephen Speech*. Analecta Biblica 67. Rome: Biblical Institute Press, 1976.

Kim, Kirsteen. "Edinburgh 1910 to 2010: From Kingdom to Spirit." *Journal of the European Pentecostal Theological Association* 30 (2010) 3–20.

———. "From/To the Ends of the Earth: Mission in the Spirit." In *African Pentecostalism and World Christianity: Essays in Honor of J. Kwabena Asamoah-Gyadu*, edited by Nimi Wariboko and Adeshina Afolayan, 45–56. African Christian Studies 18. Eugene, OR: Pickwick, 2020.

Kim, Sebastian C. H. *In Search of Identity: Debates on Religious Conversion in India*. New Delhi: Oxford University Press, 2003.

Kinberger, Mary Kay. *Lonergan on Conversion: Applications for Religious Formation*. New York: Peter Lang, 1992.

Kircher, Nena Leann. "Selling Timeshares in Heaven: A Psychological-Historical Analysis of Revival Preaching in the United States." MA thesis, Missouri State University, 2010.

Kirk, J. Andrew. *Good News of the Kingdom Coming: The Marriage of Evangelism and Social Responsibility*. Downers Grove, IL: InterVarsity, 1983.

Klauck, Hans-Josef. *Magic and Paganism in Early Christianity: The World of the Acts of the Apostles*. Translated by Brian McNeil. Repr., Minneapolis: Fortress, 2003.

Kling, David W. *A History of Christian Conversion*. Oxford: Oxford University Press, 2020.

Knight, Henry H. *Evangelism Renewed: The Theological Revisioning of Evangelism*. Eugene, OR: Cascade, 2025.

Kollmann, Bernd. *Joseph Barnabas: His Life and Legacy*. Translated by Miranda Henry. Collegeville, MN: Liturgical, 2004.

Kurz, William S. *Acts of the Apostles*. Grand Rapids: Baker Academic, 2013.

Lemons, J. Derrick, and Amos Yong. *Trump and the Politics of Prayer: Inside the Spiritual World of His Faith Advisory Team*. New York: Bloomsbury, 2026.

Leslie, Robert C. *Jesus and Logotherapy: The Ministry of Jesus as Interpreted Through the Psychotherapy of Victor Frankl*. New York: Abingdon, 1965.

Lindemann, Andreas. "The Beginnings of Christian Life in Jerusalem According to the Summaries in the Acts of the Apostles." In *Common Life in the Early Church: Essays Honoring Graydon F. Snyder*, edited by Julian V. Hills, 202–18. Harrisburg, PA: Trinity Press International, 1998.

Linton, Olof. "The List of Nations in Acts 2." In *New Testament Christianity for Africa and the World: Essays in Honour of Harry Sawyerr*, edited by Mark E. Glasswell and Edward W. Fasholé-Luke, 44–53. London: SPCK, 1974.

Lourdusamy, Joseph. *Barrier-Breaking Banquet: An Exegetical Study of Jesus' Meal with Zacchaeus (Luke 19:1–10) in the Background of the Hellenistic Banquet Traditions*. New Delhi: ISPCK, 2020.

Macnamara, Luke. *My Chosen Instrument: The Characterisation of Paul in Acts 7:58—15:41*. Rome: Gregorian & Biblical, 2016.

BIBLIOGRAPHY

Marguerat, Daniel. "The Resurrection and Its Witnesses in the Book of Acts." In *Reading Acts Today: Essays in Honour of Loveday C. A. Alexander*, edited by Steve Walton et al., 171–85. London: Bloomsbury, 2011.

Matson, David Lertis. *Household Conversion Narratives in Acts: Pattern and Interpretation*. Journal for the Study of the New Testament Supplement Series 123. Sheffield: Sheffield Academic, 1996.

McCabe, David R. *How to Kill Things with Words: Ananias and Sapphira Under the Prophetic Speech-Act of Divine Judgment (Acts 4.32—5.11)*. The Library of New Testament Studies 454. London: T. & T. Clark, 2011.

Méndes-Moratalla, Fernando. *The Paradigm of Conversion in Luke*. Journal for the Society of New Testament Studies 252. London: T. & T. Clark, 2004.

Menéndez-Antuña, Luis. "Of Social Death and Solitary Confinement: The Political Life of a Gerasene (Luke 8:26–39)." *Journal of Biblical Literature* 138 (2019) 643–64.

Metzger, James A. *Consumption and Wealth in Luke's Travel Narrative*. Biblical Interpretation 88. Leiden: Brill, 2007.

Miller, Amanda C. "Good Sinners and Exemplary Heretics: The Sociopolitical Implications of Love and Acceptance in the Gospel of Luke." *Review and Expositor* 112 (2015) 461–69.

Milton, Grace. *Shalom, the Spirit and Pentecostal Conversion: A Practical-Theological Study*. Global Pentecostal and Charismatic Studies 18. Boston: Brill, 2015.

Mittelstadt, Martin William. *The Spirit and Suffering in Luke-Acts: Implications for a Pentecostal Pneumatology*. Journal of Pentecostal Theology Supplement Series 26. London: T. & T. Clark, 2004.

Montero, Roman A. *All Things in Common: The Economic Practices of the Early Christians*. Eugene, OR: Resource, 2017.

Nadella, Raj. *Dialogue Not Dogma: Many Voices in the Gospel of Luke*. Library of New Testament Studies 431. New York: T. & T. Clark, 2011.

Olson, Mark J. "Freedmen, Synagogue of the." In *The Anchor Yale Bible Dictionary*, edited by David Noel Freedman et al., 2:855. London: Bloomsbury, 2022.

Olson, Mark K. *Wesley and Aldersgate: Interpreting Conversion Narratives*. New York: Routledge, 2019.

Osiek, Carolyn, and David L. Balch. *Families in the New Testament: Households and House Churches*. Louisville, KY: Westminster John Knox, 1997.

Painter, Dean. "The Gospel of Luke and the Roman Empire." In *Jesus Is Lord, Caesar Is Not: Evaluating Empire in New Testament Studies*, edited by Scot McKnight and Joseph B. Modica, 93–107. Downers Grove, IL: IVP Academic, 2013.

Park, Aaron W. *The Book of Amos as Composed and Read in Antiquity*. Studies in Biblical Literature 37. New York: Peter Lang, 2001.

Parkinson, Brian. *Heart to Heart: How Your Emotions Affect Other People*. Cambridge: Cambridge University Press, 2019.

Parsons, Mikeal C. *Body and Character in Luke and Acts: The Subversion of Physiognomy in Early Christianity*. Waco, TX: Baylor University Press, 2011.

———. *Luke: Storyteller, Interpreter, Evangelist*. Peabody, MA: Hendrickson, 2007.

Peyton, Joey R. *The Second Commandment: Loving Your Neighbor in Today's Changing World*. Eugene, OR: Wipf & Stock, 2024.

Phillips, Thomas E. *Paul, His Letters, and Acts*. Library of Pauline Studies. Peabody, MA: Hendrickson, 2009.

BIBLIOGRAPHY

———. *Reading Issues of Wealth and Poverty in Luke-Acts*. Lewiston, NY: Edwin Mellen, 2001.

Pilgrim, Walter E. *Good News to the Poor: Wealth and Poverty in Luke-Acts*. Minneapolis: Augsburg, 1981.

Pope-Levison, Priscilla. *Models of Evangelism*. Grand Rapids: Baker Academic, 2020.

Price, Robert M. *The Widow Traditions in Luke-Acts: A Feminist-Critical Scrutiny*. SBL Dissertation Series 155. Atlanta: Scholars, 1997.

Prior, Michael P. *Jesus the Liberator: Nazareth Liberation Theology (Luke 4.16–30)*. Sheffield: Sheffield Academic Press, 1995.

Rapske, Brian. *The Book of Acts in Its First Century Setting*. Vol. 3: *The Book of Acts and Paul in Roman Custody*. Grand Rapids: Eerdmans, 1994.

Reichard, Joshua D. "Mutually Transformative Missions: A Postcolonial, Process-Relational Pentecostal Missiology." *Missiology* 43 (2015) 245–57.

Reid, Barbara E. "'Do You See This Woman?': A Liberative Look at Luke 7.36–50 and Strategies for Reading Other Lukan Stories Against the Grain." In *A Feminist Companion to Luke*, edited by Amy-Jill Levine, 106–20. Repr., Cleveland, OH: Pilgrim, 2004.

Richie, Tony. *Toward a Pentecostal Theology of Religions: Encountering Cornelius Today*. Cleveland, OH: CPT, 2013.

Ringe, Sharon H. *Jesus, Liberation, and the Biblical Jubilee: Images for Ethics and Christology*. Minneapolis: Fortress, 1985.

Rommen, Edward. *Get Real: On Evangelism in the Late Modern World*. Pasadena: William Carey, 2010.

Rosenblatt, Marie-Eloise. *Paul the Accused: His Portrait in the Acts of the Apostles*. Collegeville, MN: Michael Glazier/Liturgical, 1995.

Rothschild, Clare K. *Paul in Athens: The Popular Religious Context of Acts 17*. Tübingen: Mohr Siebeck, 2014.

Saayman, Willem, and Klippies Kritzinger, eds. *Mission in Bold Humility: David Bosch's Work Considered*. Eugene, OR: Wipf & Stock, 2013.

Salmeier, Michael A. *Restoring the Kingdom: The Role of God as the "Ordainer of Times and Seasons" in the Acts of the Apostles*. Eugene, OR: Pickwick, 2011.

Samuel, Vinay, and Albrecht Hauser, eds. *Proclaiming Christ in Christ's Way: Studies in Integral Evangelism*. Oxford: Regnum, 1989.

Santos, Boaventura de Sousa. *The End of the Cognitive Empire: The Coming of Age of the Epistemologies of the South*. Durham, NC: Duke University Press, 2018.

Scazzero, Peter. *Emotionally Healthy Spirituality: Unleash a Revolution in Your Life in Christ*. Nashville: Thomas Nelson, 2006.

Scott, James M. "Luke's Geographical Horizon." In *The Book of Acts in Its Graeco-Roman Setting*, edited by David W. J. Gill and Conrad Gempf, 483–544. Vol. 2 of *The Book of Acts in Its First Century Setting*. Grand Rapids: Eerdmans, 1994.

Sechrest, Love L., et al., eds. *Can "White" People Be Saved? Triangulating Race, Theology, and Mission*. Missiological Engagements. Downers Grove, IL: IVP Academic, 2018.

Shauf, Scott. *Theology as History, History as Theology: Paul in Ephesus in Acts 19*. Beihefte zur Zeitschrift für die neutestamentliche Wissenschaft und die Kunde der älteren Kirche 133. Berlin: de Gruyter, 2005.

Shellberg, Pamela. *Cleansed Lepers, Cleansed Hearts: Purity and Healing in Luke-Acts*. Minneapolis: Fortress, 2015.

Sider, Ronald J. *Evangelism, Salvation and Social Justice*. Bramcote, UK: Grove, 1979.

BIBLIOGRAPHY

Siegel, Daniel J. *The Developing Mind: How Relationships and the Brain Interact to Shape Who We Are*. 3rd ed. New York: Guilford, 2020.

Smith, Dennis E. "The House Church as Social Environment." In *Text, Image, and Christians in the Greco-Roman World: A Festschrift in Honor of David Lee Balch*, edited by Aliou Cissé Niang and Carolyn Osiek, 3–21. Eugene, OR: Pickwick, 2012.

Smith, Gordon T. *Transforming Conversion: Rethinking the Language and Contours of Christian Initiation*. Grand Rapids: Baker Academic, 2010.

Smith, James K. A. *You Are What You Love: The Spiritual Power of Habit*. Grand Rapids: Brazos, 2016.

Smith, John E. *The Works of Jonathan Edwards*. Vol. 2: *Religious Affections*. New Haven, CT: Yale University Press, 1959.

Soggin, J. Alberto. *Israel in the Biblical Period: Institutions, Festivals, Ceremonies, Rituals*. Translated by John Bowden. Edinburgh: T. & T. Clark, 2001.

Spencer, F. Scott. *Passions of the Christ: The Emotional Life of Jesus in the Gospels*. Grand Rapids: Baker Academic, 2021.

———. "A Woman's Touch: Manual and Emotional Dynamics in Female Characters in Luke's Gospel." In *Characters and Characterization in Luke-Acts*, edited by Frank E. Dicken and Julia A. Snyder, 73–94. Library of New Testament Studies 548. London: Bloomsbury, 2016.

Spitzer, Robert. *Escape from Darkness: The Light of Christ in the Church, Spiritual Conversion, and Moral Conversion*. San Francisco: Ignatius, 2021.

Stassen, Glen H., and David P. Gushee. *Kingdom Ethics: Following Jesus in Contemporary Context*. Downers Grove, IL: InterVarsity, 2003.

Stendahl, Krister. *Paul Among Jews and Gentiles, and Other Essays*. London: SCM, 1977.

Stephenson, Lisa P., and Ruthie Wienk. *Redemptive Service: Loving Our Neighbors Well*. Grand Rapids: Baker Academic, 2024.

Stone, Bryan. *Evangelism After Christendom: The Theology and Practice of Christian Witness*. Grand Rapids: Brazos 2007.

Story, J. Lyle. *Joyous Encounters: Discovering the Happy Affections in Luke-Acts*. New York: Herder & Herder, 2018.

Strong, Douglas. "A Real Christian Is an Abolitionist: Conversion and Antislavery Activism in Early American Methodism." In *Conversion in the Wesleyan Tradition*, edited by Kenneth J. Collins and John H. Tyson, 69–82. Nashville: Abingdon, 2001.

Stroope, Michael. *Transcending Mission: The Eclipse of a Modern Tradition*. Downers Grove, IL: IVP Academic, 2017.

Stroup, Christopher. *The Christians Who Became Jews: Acts of the Apostles and Ethnicity in the Roman City*. New Haven, CT: Yale University Press, 2020.

Studebaker, Steven M., and Amos Yong, eds. *Pentecostal Theology and Jonathan Edwards*. T & T Clark's Systematic Pentecostal and Charismatic Theology series. New York: Bloomsbury, 2019.

Suggit, John. "Jesus the Gardener: The Atonement in the Fourth Gospel as Re-Creation." *Neotestamentica* 33 (1999) 161–68.

Szkredka, Swalomir. *Sinners and Sinfulness in Luke: A Study of Direct and Indirect References in the Initial Episodes of Jesus' Activity*. Tübingen: Mohr Siebeck, 2017.

Takatemjen. *Banquet Is Ready: Rich and Poor in the Parables of Luke*. Delhi: ISPCK, 2003.

Tan, Kim. *The Jubilee Gospel: The Jubilee, Spirit and the Church*. Milton Keynes: Authentic Media, 2008.

Taussig, Hal. *In the Beginning Was the Meal: Social Experimentation and Early Christianity.* Minneapolis: Fortress, 2009.

Thiessen, Elmer John. *The Ethics of Evangelism: A Philosophical Defense of Proselytizing and Persuasion.* Downers Grove, IL: IVP Academic, 2011.

Thiselton, Anthony C. *Thiselton on Hermeneutics: Collected Works with New Essays.* Grand Rapids: Eerdmans, 2005.

Trainor, Michael. *About Earth's Child: An Ecological Listening to the Gospel of Luke.* The Earth Bible Commentary 2. Repr., Sheffield: Sheffield Phoenix, 2017.

———. *Acts—About Earth's Children: An Ecological Listening to the Acts of the Apostles.* An Earth Bible Commentary. London: T. & T. Clark, 2020.

Trebilco, Paul. *The Early Christians in Ephesus from Paul to Ignatius.* Wissenschaftliche Untersuchungen zum Neuen Testament 166. Tübingen: Mohr Siebeck, 2004.

Trimingham, J. Spencer. *Christianity Among the Arabs in Pre-Islamic Times.* London: Longman Librairie du Liban, 1974.

Twelftree, Graham H. *Jesus the Exorcist: A Contribution to the Study of the Historical Jesus.* Repr., Tübingen: Mohr Siebeck, 2019.

———. *People of the Spirit: Exploring Luke's View of the Church.* Grand Rapids: Baker Academic, 2009.

Voorwinde, Stephen. *Jesus' Emotions in the Gospels.* New York: T. & T. Clark, 2011.

———. "Paul's Emotions in Acts." *The Reformed Theological Review* 73 (2014) 75–100.

Walaskay, Paul W. *"And So We Came to Rome": The Political Perspective of St. Luke.* Society for the Study of New Testament Monograph Series 49. Cambridge: Cambridge University Press, 1983.

Walton, Steve. "Evil in Ephesus: Acts 19:8–40." In *Evil in Second Temple Judaism and Early Christianity*, edited by Chris Keith and Loren T. Stuckenbruck, 224–34. Wissenschaftliche Untersuchungen zum Neuen Testament 2:417. Tübingen: Mohr Siebeck, 2016.

Warner, Laceye C. *Saving Women: Retrieving Evangelistic Theology and Practice.* Waco, TX: Baylor University Press, 2007.

Webber, Robert E. *Ancient-Future Evangelism: Making Your Church a Faith-Forming Community.* Grand Rapids: Baker, 2003.

Welker, Michael. *God the Spirit.* Translated by James F. Hoffmeyer. Minneapolis: Fortress, 1994.

Wells, David F. *God the Evangelist: How the Holy Spirit Works to Bring Men and Women to Faith.* Grand Rapids: Eerdmans, 1987.

Wenhem, David. "The Purpose of Luke-Acts: Israel's Story in the Context of the Roman Empire." In *Reading Luke: Interpretation, Reflection, Formation*, edited by Craig G. Bartholomew et al., 79–103. The Scripture and Hermeneutics Series 8. Grand Rapids: Zondervan, 2005.

Westhelle, Vitor. *Eschatology and Space: The Lost Dimension in Theology Past and Present.* New York: Palgrave Macmillan, 2012.

Whitenton, Michael R. "Rewriting Abraham and Joseph: Stephen's Speech (Acts 7:2–16) and Jewish Exegetical Traditions." *Novum Testamentum* 54 (2012) 149–67.

Wiebe, Ben. *Messianic Ethics: Jesus' Proclamation of the Kingdom of God and the Church in Response.* Scottdale, PA: Herald, 1992.

Wilson, Brittany E. "Sight and Spectacle: 'Seeing' Paul in the Book of Acts." In *Characters and Characterization in Luke-Acts*, edited by Frank E. Dicken and Julia A. Snyder, 140–53. Library of New Testament Studies 548. London: Bloomsbury, 2016.

BIBLIOGRAPHY

Witherup, Ronald D. *Conversion in the New Testament*. Collegeville, MN: Liturgical, 1994.

Wood, Laurence W. "John Wesley's Mission of Spreading Scriptural Holiness: A Case Study of World Missions and Evangelism." *The Asbury Journal* 73 (2018) 8–49.

Yeh, Allen. *Polycentric Missiology: 21st-Century Mission from Everyone to Everywhere*. Downers Grove, IL: IVP Academic, 2016.

Yong, Aizaiah G. *Multiracial Cosmotheandrism: A Practical Theology of Multiracial Experiences*. Maryknoll, NY: Orbis, 2023.

Yong, Amos. "Afterword." In *The Politics of the Spirit: Pentecostal Reflections on Public Responsibility and the Common Good*, edited by Daniela C. Augustine and Chris E. W. Green, 211–15. Lanham, MD: Seymour, 2023.

———. "Apostolic Evangelism in the Postcolony: Opportunities and Challenges." *Mission Studies* 34 (2017) 147–67.

———. *The Bible, Disability, and the Church: A New Vision of the People of God*. Grand Rapids: Eerdmans, 2011.

———. "Children and the Spirit in Luke and Acts." In *Child Theology: Diverse Methods and Global Perspectives*, edited by Marcia J. Bunge, 108–28. Maryknoll, NY: Orbis, 2021.

———. *The Hermeneutical Spirit: Theological Interpretation and the Scriptural Imagination for the 21st Century*. Eugene, OR: Cascade, 2017.

———. *The Hermeneutical Spirit II: Migrations, Diasporas, and Cultures After Pentecost*. Edited by Rudolfo Galvan Estrada III. Eugene, OR: Cascade, 2026.

———. "Hospitality and Religious Others: An Orthopathic Perspective." In *A Charitable Orthopathy: Christian Perspectives on Emotions in Multifaith Engagement*, edited by John W. Morehead and Brandon C. Benziger, 183–95. Eugene, OR: Pickwick, 2020.

———. *Hospitality and the Other: Pentecost, Christian Practices, and the Neighbor*. Maryknoll, NY: Orbis, 2008.

———. "In Search of Foundations: The *Oeuvre* of Donald L. Gelpi, S.J., and Its Significance for Pentecostal Theology and Philosophy." *Journal of Pentecostal Theology* 11 (2002) 3–26.

———. *In the Days of Caesar: Pentecostalism and Political Theology*. Grand Rapids: Eerdmans, 2010.

———. "Jubilee, Liberation, and Pentecost: The Preferential Option *of* the Poor on the Apostolic Way." In *Evangelical Theologies of Liberation*, edited by Elise Mae Cannon and Andrea Smith, 306–24. Downers Grove, IL: IVP Academic, 2019.

———. *The Kerygmatic Spirit: Apostolic Preaching in the 21st Century*. Edited by Josh Samuel, commentary and afterword by Tony Richie. Eugene, OR: Cascade, 2018.

———. *Learning Theology: Tracking the Spirit of Christian Faith*. Louisville, KY: Westminster John Knox, 2018.

———. "'The Light Shines in the Darkness': Johannine Dualism and the Challenge of Christian Theology of Religions Today." *Journal of Religion* 89 (2009) 31–56.

———. "Many Tongues, Many Biocultural Niches: A Pentecostal Missiological Response to Environmental Degradation." In *Pentecostal Missiology and Environmental Degradation*, edited by Eugene Baron and Amos Yong, 81–105. London: Langham Global, 2025.

———. *The Missiological Spirit: Christian Mission Theology for the Third Millennium Global Context*. Eugene, OR: Cascade, 2014.

———. "Mission After Colonialism and Whiteness: The Pentecost Witness of the 'Perpetual Foreigner' for the Third Millennium." In *Can "White" People Be Saved?*

Triangulating Race, Theology, and Mission, edited by Love L. Sechrest et al., 301–17. Downers Grove, IL: IVP Academic, 2018.

———. *Mission After Pentecost: The Witness of the Spirit from Genesis to Revelation*. Grand Rapids: Baker Academic, 2019.

———. "'Not Many of You Should Become Teachers . . .': Whose (Established) Professoriate? Which (Diasporic) Faculty?" In *Now to God Who Is Able—Vocation, Justice, and Ministry: Essays in Honor of Mark Labberton*, edited by Neal D. Presa and Anne E. Zaki, 139–54. Eugene, OR: Wipf & Stock, 2023.

———. "Proclamation and the Third Article: Toward a Pneumatology of Preaching." In *Third Article Theology: A Pneumatological Dogmatics*, edited by Myk Habets, 367–94. Minneapolis: Fortress, 2016.

———. *Renewing Christian Theology: Systematics for a Global Christianity*. Images and commentary by Jonathan A. Anderson. Waco, TX: Baylor University Press, 2014.

———. *Revelation*. Belief: A Theological Commentary on the Bible. Louisville, KY: Westminster John Knox, 2021.

———. "Sanctification, Science, and the Spirit: Salvaging Holiness in the Late Modern World." *Wesleyan Theological Journal* 47 (2012) 36–52.

———. *The Spirit of Creation: Modern Science and Divine Action in the Pentecostal-Charismatic Imagination*. Grand Rapids: Eerdmans, 2011.

———. *Spirit of Love: A Trinitarian Theology of Grace*. Waco, TX: Baylor University Press, 2012.

———. "The Spirit Poured Out in the Last Days: Toward a Pneumatology of Final Creation." In *The Spirit of Prophecy and Reconciliation: Essays in Honor of Rickie D. Moore*, edited by Robby Waddell and Chris E. W. Green, 151–66. Sheffield: Sheffield Phoenix, 2023.

———. *The Spirit Poured Out on All Flesh: Pentecostalism and the Possibility of Global Theology*. Grand Rapids: Baker Academic, 2005.

———. "The Spirit, the Common Good, and the Public Sphere: The 21st Century Public Intellectual in Apostolic Perspective." In *Public Intellectuals and the Common Good: Christian Thinking for Human Flourishing*, edited by Todd C. Ream et al., 21–41. Downers Grove, IL: IVP Academic, 2021.

———. *Theology and Down Syndrome: Reimagining Disability in Late Modernity*. Waco, TX: Baylor University Press, 2007.

———. *Who Is the Holy Spirit: A Walk with the Apostles*. Brewster, MA: Paraclete, 2011.

———. "Zacchaeus: Short and Un-Seen." In *Christian Reflection: A Series in Faith and Ethics—Disability*, 11–17. Waco, TX: The Center for Christian Ethics at Baylor University, 2012.

York, John O. *The Last Shall Be First: The Rhetoric of Reversal in Luke*. Sheffield: JSOT, 1991.

Zhang, Wenxi. *Paul Among Jews: A Study of the Meaning and Significance of Paul's Inaugural Sermon in the Synagogue of Antioch in Pisidia (Acts 13:16–41) for His Missionary Work Among the Jews*. Eugene, OR: Wipf & Stock, 2011.

Ziccardi, Costantino Antonio. *The Relationship of Jesus and the Kingdom of God According to Luke-Acts*. Tesi Gregoriana Serie Teologia 165. Rome: Editrice Pontificia Università Gregoriana, 2008.

Scripture Index

Genesis
12:3	145

Exodus
22:1	111

Leviticus
6:5	111
25	48n21

Numbers
5:6–7	111

1 Samuel
17:31–9	68
17:36–37	68

2 Samuel
1:20	68
3:18	68
12:6	111

1 Kings
17:23	44n21

2 Chronicles
36:20–21	48

Psalms
2:1–2	21
2:7	73
16:10	73

Isaiah
6:1–2	66
19:19–25	19
40–66	35
40:3–5	33
40:5	33n3
42:1	35
42:6	33n3, 35
43:9	35
49:6	33n3, 35
52:10	33n3
55:3	73
61	35
61:1	34
61:2	130

Jeremiah
17:9	102, 153
25:11	48
29:7	149
29:10	48

Joel
2:31	144

SCRIPTURE INDEX

Amos

9:11–12	138

Matthew

5:3	37
5:6	37
5:20	110
5:22	110
5:28	110
5:32	110
5:34	110
5:39	110
5:44	110
25:31–46	41, 124

Mark

5:1–20	40n15
14:7	38

Luke

1:1–2	32
1:3	32
1:3–4	32
1:19	58
1:35	135n18
1:49–53	50
2:1	33
2:8	58
2:10	58
2:29–32	33
2:30	134
2:38	134
2:44–45	114
3:1	33
3:3	57, 58
3:4–6	33
3:12	58
3:14	58
3:18	58
3:38	135n18
4:18	37–39, 39–41, 39–41, 42–44, 44–48
4:18–19	130
4:19	48–50, 135
4:21	36
4:31–37	40
4:32–35	114
4:38–39	42
4:40	42
4:43	134
5:12–15	45
5:13	45
5:17–26	42, 91n26
6:6–11	42
6:18	40
6:20–21	37
6:27	88, 110–111
6:32–35	88
7:1–10	42, 87
7:11–17	89n24
7:12	44
7:15	44n21
7:18–35	47n25
7:21	40
7:22	38, 42, 45
7:37	90
7:37–38	45
7:39	91
7:41–24	48
7:44	46–47
7:44–46	46
7:47	90, 91
7:47–48	46
7:48	90
7:49–50	90
8:1	135
8:5	58
8:6–7	140
8:13	140
8:26–39	40
8:35	40
8:39	57–58
8:43–48	42
9:2	58, 135
9:11	135
9:27	134
9:28–36	134
9:37–33	40
9:60	135
10: 8–9	42–43
10:9–11	135
10:29	88

10:30–37	24, 89	21:9	58
10:31–32	89	21:31	134
10:33	89	22:16	134
10:37	89	22:18	134
11:2	135	22:29–30	130–131, 134–135
11:4	48	23:51	135
12:4–5	84	24:32	97
12:12–34	102	24:44	111
12:16–21	145	24:46–47	33–34
12:18–19	113	24:48–49	34
12:18–25	113		
12:22–31	113		

John

12:32	135		
12:32–34	113	4:1	34
13:11	40	4:14–21	34–35
13:12	40–41	4:20	25
13:16	40	7:38–39	92
13:29	135	13:20	87
14:9	15	13:35	153
14:12	97	18:36	133
14:13	97, 113		
14:13–14	38		

Acts

14:14	42		
14:15	38	1	12–16, 136n19
14:18–19	97	1:1–2	32
14:21	38, 42, 97	1:6	9, 130
15:23–25	97	1:7–8	131
16:16	135	1:8	10–17, 24, 34, 36, 120–121
16:16–17	58	1:13	138
16:19–21	97, 113	1:22	74n37
16:21–22	38	2	13, 14, 15, 17–20, 35, 144n35
17:11	45	2–6	23
17:12	45	2:2–4	92
17:20–21	134	2:5	14
18:1–3	38	2:6–11	17–18
18:16	134	2:8	58
18:18–23	38, 111	2:9	15
18:24–25	135	2:12	15
18:29–30	135	2:17	16, 33, 58, 120n26
18:35–43	42	2:18	58
18:38–39	135n18	2:19–20	144
19:3	45	2:20–21	16
19:4	47	2:37	16, 63, 113
19:5–7	45	2:38	63
19:7	46	2:38–39	16
19:8	111	2:39	38
19:9	45–46	2:41–47	113
19:11	134	2:42–47	20

Acts (continued)

Reference	Page
2:46	98
2:47	115
2:50–53	120n26
3–6	20–23
3:1–10	21
3:21	145
3:25	145
4	21–22
4–6	13
4:1–3	41
4:4	115
4:19	67
4:20	21
4:23–31	22
4:24	144
4:36–37	115
5	22
5:12–15	21
5:12–16	115
5:14	115
5:16	21
5:34	72
5:41	94
5:42	98, 115
6	20, 23
6:1	65, 99
6:2	65
6:3	65
6:5	65
6:7	65
6:9	65
6:14	65, 66
7	12, 66
7:2	66
7:4	66
7:6	66
7:37	66
7:38	66
7:47–50	66
7:51–53	67
7:58	74
8	13, 23n35, 24–26
8:1	24
8:3	74
8:4	57
8:5	58
8:8	93
8:12	132
8:39	94
9	15
9–10	26
9–28	26–29
9:2	7n2, 74
9:4–5	72
9:15	72–73
9:15–16	73n34
9:16	74
9:17	72
9:20	58
9:23–24	74
9:36–41	98
10	27
10:2	119
10:4	120
10:7	120
10:12	96
10:14	96
10:17–21	94n32
10:22	120
10:27	67
10:28	27, 67
10:33	27, 68, 69
10:34–35	67
10:44	26
10:47–48	69
11:2–3	137
11:3	69, 71
11:12	69
11:14	69
11:19	70
11:20	70
11:20–21	58
11:22	70
11:26	70
11:27	70
11:28	145
11:48	98
12:1–4	41
12:12	15, 98
12:14	94
12:19	116
13:5	57, 58
13:7	26
13:9	72

SCRIPTURE INDEX

13:16–41	73	16:26	145
13:24	58	16:27	116
13:30–37	73	16:28	117
13:32	58	16:29	116
13:33–35	73	16:31–34	98
13:38	57, 58	16:33–34	117
13:45, 50	137	16:34	94
13:46–51	95	16:35–39	94, 118
13:47	15	16:40	98
13:48	58	17:6	49
13:52	93	17:13	57
14	12	17:16–34	73
14:2	137	17:18	73
14:5	137	17:22–29	73
14:6	95	17:24	141, 144
14:8–10	140	17:26	99, 145
14:8–14	95	17:28	19n28
14:11	95	17:29	141n27
14:14	95	17:31	19
14:15	142, 144	18:25–26	7n2
14:15–17	95	18:26	98
14:18	96	19:8	132, 142
14:19	74, 137	19:9	7n2
14:20–21	58	19:10	142
14:21–22	132	19:11–20	140
14:26–37	73n35	19:19	143
15	70n31	19:20	140, 142
15:1	71, 137	19:23	7n2, 143
15:3	93	19:24	140
15:5	71, 137	19:26–27	140–141
15:7	71	19:28	141
15:8–11	71	19:30–31	74
15:9	137	19:33	141
15:10	137	19:34	141
15:11	137	19:35	26
15:16–18	138	19:35–37	142
15:19–20	138	19:41	142
15:21	138	20:7	98
15:25–29	138	20:8–11	98
15:31	93–94, 139	20:20	98
15:35–36	57	20:25	58
15:21	58	21:9	58
16:10	58	21:16	26
16:14–15	26	21:25	139
16:15	98	22:2	72
16:16–17	58	22:3	72
16:22–24	41, 74	22:4	74
16:23–24	116	23:8	72, 73

Acts (continued)

24–26	73n34
24:14	7n2
24:15	73
24:21	73
25:19	74
26:5	72
26:8	73
26:9	72
26:11	74
27:1	26, 121
27:3	121
27:10–11	121
27:14–44	145
27:20	121
27:44	121
27:30–32	121
27:31	123
27:43–44	121
28	15, 26, 76, 139–140
28:1–10	27n41
28:2–3	26
28:8–9	140
28:23	132
28:30–31	132–133
28:31	41, 58

Romans

1:17	120
8:22	145
11:17–24	14
12:2	76

1 Corinthians

13:12	76
15:13–14	74
15:31	74–75

2 Corinthians

11:23–29	74

Galatians

1:17–18	74
2:1–10	70n31
2:11–13	70
4:21–31	19

Ephesians

4:11	65

2 Timothy

4:5	56

Titus

1:12	18

Hebrews

13:8	76

2 Peter

1:4	60

1 John

3:2	76
3:2–3	153

Revelation

5:5	12
5:6	12
12	12
13:8	12

www.ingramcontent.com/pod-product-compliance
Lightning Source LLC
Chambersburg PA
CBHW032152160426
43197CB00008B/885